Richard W. Johnson

A Soldier's Reminiscences in Peace and War

Richard W. Johnson

A Soldier's Reminiscences in Peace and War

ISBN/EAN: 9783337133597

Printed in Europe, USA, Canada, Australia, Japan

Cover: Foto ©ninafisch / pixelio.de

More available books at **www.hansebooks.com**

A

SOLDIER'S REMINISCENCES

IN

PEACE AND WAR.

BY

BRIG.-GEN. R. W. JOHNSON, RETIRED,
BREVET MAJ.-GEN. U. S. A.
AUTHOR OF "LIFE OF GEN. GEO. H. THOMAS."

PRESS OF
J. B. LIPPINCOTT COMPANY,
PHILADELPHIA.
1886.

Copyright, 1886, by R. W. Johnson.

TO HER

WHO HAS BEEN A TRUE HELPMEET, AND WHO HAS BORNE UP WITH NOBLE FORTITUDE UNDER THE MANY HARDSHIPS AND PRIVATIONS WHICH HAVE FALLEN TO HER LOT AS THE WIFE OF A SOLDIER IN

PEACE AND WAR,

AND WHO HAS CHEERFULLY ENDURED ALL WITHOUT COMPLAINTS OR MURMURINGS,

THIS VOLUME

IS AFFECTIONATELY DEDICATED BY HER HUSBAND,

THE AUTHOR.

St. Paul, Minn., July 1, 1886.

PREFACE.

ONCE, in familiar conversation with a friend, recalling incidents of our early and later lives, I was asked, "Why do you not employ your leisure hours in recording some of your experiences in the various and interesting vicissitudes through which you have passed?" It was added, "The occupation would be a pleasure for yourself, and your relatives and friends would preserve such reminiscences with an affectionate appreciation."

Almost involuntarily I drifted into the line of the suggestion, never thinking for a moment of publishing the sketches and reflections which have formed a panorama of my hours of recreation.

The accumulations, however, of these recitals and delineations came at last to equal a volume, and then came the urgent solicitations of friends to publish them in book form. I consented to do so, and this volume is now presented to the public.

R. W. J.

ACKNOWLEDGMENTS.

I DESIRE to acknowledge my indebtedness to General R. C. Drum, U.S.A., Colonel R. N. Scott, U.S.A., Thomas W. Teasdale, Esq., Lieutenant A. B. Johnson, U.S.A., and Lieutenant William C. Brown, adjutant U.S.M.A., for copies of official papers embodied within this volume.

R. W. JOHNSON.

A SOLDIER'S REMINISCENCES
IN PEACE AND WAR.

CHAPTER I.

My Fourth Great-grandfather—Date of Birth—The First Railroad Iron laid in the United States—My First School-house—Haley, the Teacher—A Dull Razor—Keeping the Sabbath—Catechism and Bible, and Bible and Catechism—Teaching the Negroes—Death of Parents—A Good Rifle Shot—'Possum and 'Coon Hunting—Cooking 'Possums—Corn Huskings—Old Conch Shell.

WHEN one has passed the meridian mile-post on his life's journey he lives in the past rather than in the present or future. He delights more in memories than in anticipations, and the recollections which come to him from the remotest past yield the greatest pleasure. We love to dwell upon the incidents of childhood, to recall the love and tenderness of fond and devoted parents, to think of Santa Claus, when we considered him the real, genuine giver of every good and of every perfect gift. But these early recollections, however pleasant, are of little interest to the public, and hence few will be referred to in these pages.

My fourth great-grandfather emigrated to this country in 1655 and settled in Virginia, and engaged in the cultivation of a large landed estate. My father removed from Virginia and first located at the Falls of the Ohio, now Louisville, but in a short time removed to Barren County, thence to Livingston County, near the mouth of the Cumberland River, where I was born, February 7, 1827.

The year of our Lord 1827, in which I came "into this breathing world," is a memorable one in the history of our country. It was in that year the first railroad iron was laid in the United States, and from that date to the present time there has been an average of about two thousand miles of road constructed annually. Then the distance separating the two oceans was so great that there was no intercourse between the people of the East and the sparse settlements in the West. Now a trip from the Atlantic to the Pacific is performed in less than six days.

When six years old my father placed me in school. The distance of this institution of learning from our house was about two and a half miles, and to reach it in time I had to rise and partake of an early breakfast. This school-house was a model in its way,— one story high, built up with unhewn logs, and covered by ordinary clapboards, held in place by logs or poles placed on their upper surfaces. The spaces between the logs were plastered with black mud. We are told that in the building of King Solomon's temple the sound of the hammer was not heard. Neither was it when my first school-house was erected, for there were no nails used in its construction. The only

KENTUCKY COUNTRY SCHOOL-HOUSE,
FIFTY YEARS AGO.

window in the building was made by leaving out the greater part of one log, about four feet above the floor. Into this opening a rude, rough frame was fitted, and over this was fastened oiled paper. The floor was made of puncheons,—logs split in half, the level surfaces of which were made as smooth as they could be with an axe. The seats were made of the same material, and were held up by four pins driven into auger-holes bored in the bark or round surface. These benches were simply instruments of torture. When seated the feet could not reach the floor, and in this position the children had to sit from " early morn till dewy eve," with only an intermission of one hour for dinner. Under the window was a sloping shelf, at which the writing scholars were permitted to sit. Well can I remember how envious I was of them, and how anxious I was to advance so that I could sit near that window. After passing through the primer, I was advanced to Noah Webster's spelling-book ; and when I could read the stories of the rude boy in the apple-tree and the foolish girl who counted her chickens before they were hatched, I was about as happy as education ever makes one. By the way, these two stories, embracing morality and philosophy, and which have been impressed on so many minds, should not be omitted from our present spelling-books.

. Our school-house was situated in a rough, ugly spot, around which there were no houses, neither was it enclosed. I suppose it was located just there to be convenient to a fine spring of pure, cold water, and to be so far removed from other habitations that the boys could not be troublesome to their neighbors. The teacher was an Irishman by the name of Haley, thoroughly educated and one of the best teachers I ever knew, although he had his faults. Sometimes it seemed necessary for him to take a spree, though he never indulged his desire for liquor while he was conducting his school. But sometimes he would feel a spree necessary, and would notify the scholars that there would be no more school until he sent them word. At the close of the day, coolly and dignifiedly he would dismiss the children and then deliberately go to work to get thoroughly drunk. He would continue this spree for a week or more, then send around word that on a certain day school would be resumed. During study hours no two boys could be out at the same time. This rule, which was never to be violated, however pressing the necessity, was enforced in this way: the door to the school-house was kept closed by a large wooden pin, which fitted into an auger-hole bored obliquely into one of the logs, against which the door closed. When one of the scholars passed out he had to take the pin with him, or her, and until the same was returned to its proper place no one else could think of crossing the threshold of that institution of learning. At that time there was not a public school at every cross-road, where an education could be obtained without money and without price; but we had to pay tuition and all other expenses.

For several years I was a student under Mr. Haley, and finally mastered enough of the arts and sciences to be promoted to the writing-class and transferred to a seat at the window. My cup of happiness was full when I began to make my "pot-hooks and hangers." Of all the children who were associated with me at that school, how few there are left! Nearly all passed away before they grew up to mature man- and womanhood. In fact, I cannot recall a single one at this time whose head is above the sod.

Saturday afternoon was always occupied in making the necessary preparations for the keeping of the Sabbath as a holy day. Every one about our home was taught to "remember the Sabbath day, to keep it holy. Six days thou shalt labour, and do all thy work; but the seventh day is the Sabbath of the Lord thy God: in it thou shalt not do any work, thou, nor thy son, nor thy daughter, thy manservant, nor thy maidservant, nor thy cattle, nor thy stranger that is within thy gates; for in six days the Lord made heaven and earth, the sea, and all that in them is, and rested the seventh day: wherefore the Lord blessed the Sabbath day and hallowed it."

The children were taught to lisp this commandment as soon after they left the cradle as possible, and to practise it at once. I do not remember ever to have seen any warm food, except coffee or tea, on my father's table on the Sabbath day, nor do I recall that I ever heard the sound of the axe, hammer, or saw. After rising on Sabbath morning, the first thing in order was the usual Scripture reading and prayers. Then a little time was devoted to the catechism, then breakfast, followed by catechism and Bible reading; more catechism and more Bible until church time. Dinner was served on our return from church, after which we had to teach the negroes what we had learned during the forenoon. Then we had tea, and closed up the day with a little more catechism, followed by evening prayers. I remember hearing my father say that "this preparation is necessary in order to fit us for the enjoyment of the eternal Sabbath of heaven." And I can well remember that the old Adam that was in me, even at that tender age, prompted me to think in my own heart, if heaven is like this, "I do not want any of it in mine."

Things have changed since then. We seem to have gone to the other extreme. Many parents leave all religious instruction of their children to the teachers in the Sabbath-schools, and the catechism is neglected. While we have made grand strides in almost all directions, in some we have retrograded, and in none so much as religious instruction to our children.

It is curious how customs have changed in fifty years. When a boy it was a very unusual thing to see a man with beard on his face. On one occasion a gentleman called at our house and was admitted by the servant-girl. When she returned to the kitchen I asked her who it was, and she said, "Dun know; some fellow with old dog mouf." I was very anxious to see a man with a mouth like a dog, and rushed into the house to find a man with a moustache, and he was the first one I had ever seen with beard on his face. My father was in the habit of shaving himself three times a week, and I always noticed that he was invariably cross after completing his tonsorial duties. I could not account for this idiosyncrasy; but when I grew to be a man the secret became known—his razor must have been dull.

Several years since I visited Kentucky and brought back with me an old conch shell, which has been in the family for more than fifty years. It was purchased in the South in the year 1832, by a brother, just before stepping on board of the "Helen McGregor," to engage passage to his home. Having made the purchase, he passed along the gang-plank and up the stairway to the office, where he registered his name, secured his berth, and then engaged in conversation with an acquaintance, who suddenly interrupted him with the remark, "Doctor, I smell burning steam, and I feel sure that there will be an explosion of the boiler very soon; let us go back to the ladies' cabin." The words were scarcely uttered before the explosion occurred, carrying the doctor up some distance and landing him in the river, surrounded by pieces of the wreck, the dead, and dying. My brother was soon picked up, burnt, bruised, and bleeding, holding the shell in his hand. His injuries proved to be but slight, and he was soon on his way home. The tip of the shell was cut off, and it was used as a horn to call the negroes from the field to their daily meals. On Saturdays there was no school, and the boys were required to do such light work about the farm as they could, and how well I can remember the welcome sound of that old conch when it called me, dusty and tired, from labor to refreshment.

I have heard the dulcet strains of Ole Bull's violin. I have heard some of the most highly cultivated human voices, which seemed for the time to lift me above the earth, and transport me to another world where all was harmony; yet none of these were near so sweet as the sound of that old shell when it called me to dinner and repose. When a boy I have often placed it to my ear to hear the roaring sound within, which the negroes said was the roar of the sea. The same sound is still heard in its innermost cells, but it is not the roar of the sea I hear now, but a solemn requiem in memory of the dear ones who have long since passed away, and upon some of whom rests the grave-dust of more than forty years.

In fact, nearly all of those who heard it a half-century ago have passed through the dark, dim waters of death, and now as I look upon the dear old shell how many memories it brings up from the fountains of the past. It was handled by my father and mother, played with by my brothers, and idolized by a long list and line of faithful slaves.

If it could speak in notes to be understood, how many tales it could tell of happy faces, occasionally saddened as one by one have fallen out of the ranks, leaving vacancies never to be filled. A few more years, at most, and the youngest member of that large family will necessarily fall by the wayside, and the grand old conch will descend to the members of another generation, who will prize it for the many pleasant and dear memories that cluster around it. It called the tired and careworn slave to his meals up to the very day upon which the emancipation proclamation was issued, and while its voice is as clear and distinct as ever, it has ceased to call slaves to dinner. The country is free, and this venerable old shell, having performed its duty long and faithfully, has been promoted to a place of honor in my household, and retired from active service to pass with me a life of quiet and repose.

My parents died in 1837. I lived with a brother until his death, and then with a brother-in-law. The latter required me to work on the farm during the summer months and go to school in the winter months.

While on the farm I became a fine shot with the rifle for one of my age, and could "bring down" a squirrel from the tallest tree, rarely ever missing my aim.

Often at night I would go out hunting with some of the negroes, and we never failed to bring in a 'coon or a 'possum. The latter we could always find in some of the persimmon-trees around the farm; then branching out into the adjacent timber, the dogs were sure to tree a 'coon. Often I have climbed up a tall tree and shaken one off some small limb where it felt secure, and when the "varmint" reached the ground the dogs and the negroes would secure it. I have never seen a Kentuckian who was not fond of 'possum, cooked just as our old cooks knew so well how to prepare them. There are some things that no white cook, male or female, can do, and one of these is to cook a 'possum properly. For this kind of culinary perfection we must ever look to the colored race.

Corn huskings or, as they are called in Kentucky, corn shuckings, were pleasant little episodes in the lives of boys and of negroes. Farmers would haul their corn in and store it against their corn-cribs, and then notice would be sent out that on a certain night there would be a "corn shucking." At an early hour there would be a large concourse of people on hand.

Whiskey would be passed around, and the negroes would begin their favorite corn songs. When well warmed up, two captains would be selected, the corn pile divided by a pole or rope, the captains would choose alternately until all the people were divided into two equal parts, then the contest would begin as to which party would get through first. The victorious side would then select some of their strongest men to hoist their captain upon their shoulders and bear him around as the hero of the hour. When the work was done, all hands were called to a good supper, and when all were supplied an adjournment was had to the yard, where dancing, speech-making, and singing were indulged in until the short hours. Then all hands would leave for their homes, and as they radiated from the place by the various neighborhood roads, each singing a different song and yet all apparently in harmony, one would naturally believe that they were the happiest people on the face of the earth.

This life did not suit me, and I left to reside with my brother, Dr. John M. Johnson, who secured for me an appointment as cadet at the United States Military Academy.

CHAPTER II.

Appointed Cadet—Arrival at West Point Hotel—General Scott—Cadet R. B. Ayers—Lieutenants Clarke and Reynolds—Monotonous Life of a Cadet—Speaking Disrespectfully of the President of the United States—In the Guard-House—Cadet W. L. Crittenden—Police Duties—Book-keepers, Clerks, and Salaried Men—Attachments between Classmates—Other Attachments—Marriages—Frontier Duties—Absent from Tattoo—Acting Sergeant-Major—Color-Bearer—Cadet Lieutenant S. V. Benét—Graduation—The Professors.

In the month of March, 1844, I received my appointment to West Point, through the kindness of Hon. Willis Green, at that time a member of Congress from the Second Congressional District of Kentucky, in which I resided.

I was instructed to report myself at the Academy between the 1st and 20th of June following.

I arrived on the 18th, and proceeded to the hotel, intending to remain there for a few days before reporting; but I was soon recognized as a candidate for admission, and hurried off to report to the adjutant of the Academy.

Timothy O'Maher, who had for more than fifty years filled the position of chief clerk, was charged with receiving the new cadets, and he thoroughly understood how "to hold a fellow up" and deprive him of all his loose change. He did this service for me speedily but very completely, and I was despatched to the cadet barracks to report to some one else.

Before night I had been furnished with a complete outfit for juvenile military house-keeping.

Having resided all my life in the interior of the country, I had never seen a soldier. On my way to the Point I learned that General Winfield Scott was on a visit to the Academy, and I longed to see the old war-worn veteran. As I ascended the hill from the steamboat landing, the band was playing on the plain. The drum-major, with his party-colored trousers, bearskin cap, and huge baton with a brass ball on one end, was the most conspicuous person I saw, and at once I supposed that my eyes rested upon the hero of Lundy's Lane.

Gazing, as I thought, upon the greatest living warrior, I was carried away with his gaudy uniform and equipments, and at that very moment I would have given all my earthly possessions for the rightful privilege of encasing myself within its gorgeous folds. However, it did not take long to learn that the great man I had taken for General Scott was Drum-Major Boussey, and that Scott would never permit himself to appear in public in the habiliments of a drum-major.

On the morning following my arrival in the cadet barracks, all of the plebes were turned out for drill and divided up into small squads, and turned over to instructors taken from the class just merging from plebeship. I fell to the lot of Cadet R. B. Ayers, subsequently the gallant and distinguished General Ayers, now colonel of the Second Regiment of Artillery. I was an awkward boy, and Ayers seemed to me to be unnecessarily cross and severe, so when the squad was dismissed I retired to my quarters considerably disgusted with my brief experience in the Art of War.

I suppose there never was a cadet who did not at some time during his course resolve on whipping some one when he graduated. I had three names on my black-list, and Ayers was the first one thereon because he was the first offender. Lieutenant F. N. Clarke and Lieutenant J. J. Reynolds were the second and third in the order named. I imagined that the two last were prejudiced against me, and that if there was the slightest cause for it either would have me declared deficient. Of course this state of things existed only in my own imagination, yet it tended to spur me up to unusual activity in their respective departments. But when I changed the "gray for the blue" I buried all of my West Point prejudices under the accumulated rubbish which I left behind me.

I never met Clarke after I left the Academy. He did good service during the war in the Army of the Potomac, and died August 13, 1866. I had the pleasure of serving in the same army with Reynolds, and I found him a good officer and a clever gentleman.

The life of a cadet is one of extreme monotony, and the history of one day is the history of every day in the year, and the history of one year is the history of all passed at the Academy.

As soon as the plebes had been examined an order was issued to go into camp. Trunks and all other personal property were stored away in the academic buildings, and the corps was placed upon a light war footing. The plebes were formed in line according to height and divided equally among the four companies; the tallest were assigned to A and D companies and the others to B and C companies. At first I was attached to Company A, but was subsequently assigned to Company D. While in Company A, on one hot afternoon, I was lying down in my tent and the sentinel with measured tread walked his post near me. Stopping for a moment, he said, "Plebe, what do you think of the President of the United States?"

Tyler was at that time in the executive chair, having succeeded to it by the death of Harrison, and had abandoned the Whig party, which had elected him Vice-President, and was held up as a traitor and turncoat by every Whig in the land. My family from the organization of that party had belonged to it, and so I was bitterly opposed to him. I replied, "I regard him as a rascal and traitor to his party." "What!" said the sentinel, "do you speak disrespectfully of the President of the United States, in open, flagrant violation of the Articles of War?" Before giving me any time to explain, he called for the corporal of the guard. The call was answered, my offence reported, and I was marched off to the guard-tent. The name of the sentinel was Harris, and he was from the State of Missouri. There was an inward feeling of gladness when I learned that he had been found deficient in his studies and was only awaiting the pleasure of the War Department in his case. Soon he was sent home, and I have never heard of him since.

Well, I was in the guard-house,—the jail, the culprit's abiding-place. Thoughts of home and dear friends who took a kindly interest in me, and whose good-will I desired to merit, flitted across my brain. Oh, if they should hear of my disgrace they will never be able to hold up their heads again. I was assigned a place in the guard-tent, and every time any one passed I imagined that they were anxious to see the criminal.

About sundown the cry was given, "Turn out the guard for the officer of the day!" Out went the guard; the prisoners were hastened into line. The officer of the day, Cadet Lieutenant W. L. Crittenden, a nephew of Hon. John J. Crittenden, of Kentucky, recognizing me among the prisoners, asked me why I was there. I told him all the circumstances, and he remarked, "Go back to your camp; your offence is not very great, and if it is I am chargeable with it also, for I believe there is not a more consummate rascal on earth than one who betrays his party and his friends." I felt better, but I was always on guard as to the expression of my opinions with reference to the Chief Magistrate of this great nation.

Crittenden was always my friend. Poor fellow, he was shot for his participation in the Lopez invasion of Cuba. When he was led out for execution he was told to kneel down. "No," replied the brave man; "an American kneels only to his God." The fatal shot was fired, and the spirit of a noble man ascended to his God.

The camp having been regularly established, a proper regard for cleanliness required the adoption of certain police regulations. The custom had been, previous to my admission, to require the plebes to do all such menial service; accordingly, in each company,

at certain hours of the day, they were paraded on
their company grounds, marched to the cadet quartermaster's tent, where spades, shovels, and wheelbarrows were provided, and with these they were
marched around the company grounds and required
to pick up pieces of paper, stumps of cigars, old tobacco quids, and such other filth, trash, and litter as
could be discovered by the keen eye of the corporal
of police. I can well remember the feeling of mortification and humiliation that came over me when this
distasteful duty was first imposed upon me. Looking
back now I can see the necessity of just such training.
It was to teach obedience to all orders, the first lesson
that all must learn before they can properly exercise
command. Another very important lesson was to
teach cleanliness in camp; the only means, at least the
most efficient, by which the health of troops is preserved. It was, however, terribly humiliating at the
time, and I felt that I had been misled in regard to the
high character of the Academy, and tried by all means
in my power to get my guardian's consent to allow
me to resign. He would not pay any attention to my
requests, and I reluctantly remained to endure the
mortification and shame which came to me when
called out on police duty. At the close of a year a
new class relieved us from scavenger duty, and when I
saw others engaged in the same occupation it did not
seem near so degrading. Young people are apt to
look upon all manual labor as degrading. This is a
sad mistake, and results in filling our cities with young
men who seek to live by other means by crowding
into the professions, for which they are not fitted, and

where they manage to make a bare living. These same men, if they would turn their attention to some honorable labor, would not only prosper, but live happy and contented lives. Commercial colleges throughout the land are flooding the country with book-keepers and clerks, few of whom ever rise above salaried positions.

Notwithstanding the general monotony of cadet life, there are many interesting circumstances and incidents which serve to relieve it, and in after-life one recalls the days passed at West Point as among the most pleasant of his life. Attachments between classmates are formed there which never fade and die; on the contrary, they grow with our growth and strengthen with our strength.

There are other attachments of quite a different nature formed in the many quiet and secluded nooks and corners adjacent to "Flirtation Walk." When flowers bud and bloom, and all nature seems to rejoice in its own loveliness, appears to be the time for love-making.

It is at this season of the year that the young delight to separate in pairs and walk out to hear the birds sing and to enjoy the cool and invigorating breezes which never fan the cheek in the presence of the "old folks." And when a man, filled with the new wine of youth, is thrown with a young, handsome, sprightly girl, what subject has more interest to them than that of love? Around that lovely walk many a young fellow has poured into the willing ears of beauty protestations of undying love. On that same walk many youthful maidens, with their breasts heaving with emotions they could not suppress, and with their voices tremulous with excitement, have said "yes," when "no" would have been far better for their future comfort and happiness. This little word yes has filled the heart of many a man with joy unspeakable, when it passed the ruby lips of her he loved. Time passes on and graduation day comes, when the marriage is to take place, for be it remembered that cadets are prohibited from having "dogs or wives," and so after graduation these promises are to be fulfilled. The expectant bride delays for a few months. In fact, how few women are ever ready! All want time, it matters not how long they have been engaged. About the time autumnal leaves begin to fall the wedding-day is settled upon, and if you would watch the couple you would see that they seem to think that their engagement is the only one ever entered into; that they are the only ones ever married; forgetting that in the days of Noah they did eat, they drank, they married wives, they were given in marriage. Engagements and marriages will be continued as long as the world is stocked with men and women. No two or more persons can get up a corner in this business. At last the appointed time arrives, friends are invited, the preacher takes his position, the bridal party enters the church or parlor, and then and there the young lieutenant proceeds to endow his youthful bride with all his worldly goods, which in many cases consists of a new trunk, hair-brush, and a few brass buttons, and nothing more. A bridal tour is dispensed with for the reason that the services of the lieutenant are required with his company, and he must needs join the regiment at some remote frontier station. By rail, river, stage, ambulance, or wagon the young wife is taken to some out-of-the-way place, and then she begins to realize some of the hardships and privations incident to army life on the frontier. Would it be strange if she should soon begin to yearn for the comforts of that pleasant home she left behind her? It is now too late to make a change; she must share the fortunes of the young man who won her affections somewhere on "Flirtation Walk."

During my entire cadetship I did not speak to a female,—something I suppose no other graduate can say, —and hence no woman has any cause to regret a hasty and inconsiderate promise made to me in any of the many love-making nooks in or about that historic place.

The ladies of a garrison, when agreeable, make frontier life endurable, and do much to restrain young men and keep them from falling into bad habits. There is something ennobling and elevating in the society of refined women which is seen and felt by all who come in contact with them. No garrison is complete without ladies, and there should be a number at every military post.

During my plebe encampment the duties imposed on me were so heavy and unusual that when darkness came on I was ready to retire for the night. On one occasion I fell asleep and did not hear tattoo, so I was reported absent. In making my excuse to Captain J. A. Thomas, who was then commandant of cadets, I found that he was not disposed to view my offence with much leniency. I promised him faithfully that if he would pardon me for that one offence I would never be guilty of it again. "What assurance have I that you will keep your promise?" queried he. I replied, "The honor of a gentleman, sir." "That, sir, is sufficient; I shall remove the report," replied Captain Thomas; and I can say truthfully that I complied with my promise. From that day to this I have never missed tattoo roll-call when duty required me to attend.

During my third-class year my military bearing and soldierly qualities were not recognized,—at least I was not appointed a corporal,—but on my entrance into the second class I was promoted to the grade of sergeant. As I did not go home on furlough, I was detailed to act as sergeant-major during the encampment; and when the class returned, and we struck camp and went into the barracks, I joined my proper company, D, and was designated color-bearer, which gave me some privileges and exempted me from certain duties. When I became a member of the first class I was appointed a lieutenant in Company A, and was subsequently promoted to be captain of the same company.

I have during my active service had some important commands, but these cadet appointments elevated me more in my own estimation than any rank I ever held or exercised. I really felt that a greater responsibility rested upon me than when, during the war, I commanded a division of veteran soldiers.

Scarcely a graduate ever escapes without having some nickname applied to him, and these names are gained, sometimes, by the most trivial circumstances. I was not an exception. When acting sergeant-major, Cadet E. B. Bryan was adjutant. I was of course subordinate to him, and he was in the habit of calling me subaltern, which was in time abbreviated and I was called Sub. Johnson, and better known by that cognomen among my classmates and friends than by my proper name. Even now, whenever I meet a classmate he is sure to greet me with "Hello, here's Sub. Johnson!"

Bryan was one of the handsomest men I ever saw. Soon after graduating he resigned and located in Charleston, South Carolina, as an architect and surveyor. Subsequently I heard of him as a planter on St. John's Island, where I believe he died.

On entering the first class I was greatly rejoiced, for it was nearing the end of the course, and in previous years any one reaching that class was reasonably certain of graduating. But unfortunately for the ease and comfort of some of the "Forty-Niners," Professor Mahan saw proper to pronounce two or three cadets deficient in the class of '48, and they failed to be commissioned in the army. So, having a life profession almost within our grasp, we did not feel at liberty to place it in jeopardy by neglecting our studies. I am sure that I applied myself as closely to my books during my first-class course as I did during any of the previous years, for Professor Mahan was liable to repeat the same thing with us. I think this feeling was pretty generally entertained by all of the class below the middle, and I am sure that the last half of the class of 1849 knew more about civil and military engineering than did the same part of any class for ten years preceding it.

At last the annual examination was announced, and we were brought up before the Academic Board for the last time. Having satisfactorily mastered all of the arts and sciences taught at that institution, the time had arrived for an order to be issued relieving us from further duty and ordering us to our homes to await the orders of the War Department. Forty-three happy fellows gathered upon the parade-ground on the evening of June 23, 1849. Benz sounded the last call that should ever assemble us together in this life. "Fall in!" was yelled out by the first sergeants, the roll was called, and the companies were marched to the general parade-ground in front of the superintendent's quarters, where the line was formed. The band passed along in front playing "Auld Lang Syne," and then returned to its place on the right. The ranks were opened, and Captain B. R. Alden, then commandant of the corps, exercised the battalion in the manual of arms; the first sergeants made their reports, and then the adjutant was directed to read the following order:

HEADQUARTERS U. S. MILITARY ACADEMY,
WEST POINT, N. Y., June 23, 1849.

Special Orders,
No. 87.

Cadets Gillmore, Parke, J. G., Benêt, Haines, Silvey, DuBarry, Perkins, Baird, Nimmo, Coggswell, Platt, McKeever, Lewis, Kellogg, J., Moore, J. C., Saxton, Wright, DeLano, McClure, Hudson, Withers, Tevis, Robertson, B., Tidball, Field, Barton, Green, D. C., Johnson, R. W., Holabird, Williams, T. G., Washington, English, McArthur, Roy, Alvord, Clark, Marshall, L. H., Reynolds, and McIntosh are relieved from duty at the Military Academy and will repair to their homes, there to await further orders.

By order of CAPTAIN BREWERTON,

(Sgd.)   CHARLES T. BAKER,
Lt. and A. Adj.

After the order was read, the cadet officers closed to the centre, marched up and saluted the commander. Those of the first class who were in the ranks were directed to "fall out," and there upon the plain we were turned loose to enter upon a new life. And what a life it has proven to many! Sunshine and shadows have been our common lot, for God in his infinite wisdom has decreed both to every member of the human family. We have each had our trials, our triumphs, and our failures. On our journey through life each has had to bridge angry, swollen streams with sore and bleeding hands, or ford them with tired and wearied feet; but through all, and over all, the protecting arms of the Almighty have been under and around us, and we have been protected from seen and unseen dangers.

As a class, none had a more prominent place in the late war. It found us in the vigor of mature manhood. All were in some way actively engaged, and yet, strange to say, only one, McIntosh, fell in that terrible struggle.

Before closing this chapter, I desire to make some reference to the faithful professors and their assistants, who labored so hard to teach us the intricate subjects we had to pass over in their respective departments. How well I remember the earnest, devoted work of Professors D. H. Mahan, W. H. C. Bartlett, A. E. Church, J. W. Bailey, W. T. Sprole, and dear old "Dad" Kendrick. How kind, considerate, and patient these professors were! How earnestly they labored to teach us all the dark, blind, and abstruse questions necessary for us to comprehend! Then I recall R. W.

Weir, Professor of Drawing, and chief dispenser and manipulator of "Venetian red and indigo," much of whose time was taken up in trying to make an artist of one young fellow who could scarcely draw a straight line with a right-line pen and ruler. Then I recall Sam Jones, John M. Jones, H. F. Clarke (Slow Trot), Fitz-John Porter, and a long list and line of other assistants. Then, too, there was W. A. Norton, my beau ideal of physical manhood, who lost his life in attempting to save others, and went down with the "Atlantic" in Long Island Sound. I remember them all with great kindness. Some have passed over to the sunset shore of that mighty ocean which rolls between time and eternity, but this feeble tribute to their memory I gratefully bestow. To the living I desire to express my thanks for their great kindness to me and to the members of the class of 1849. All of them will live in memory as long as a "Forty-Niner" survives.

CHAPTER III.

From West Point to New York City—A Happy Lot of Fellows Homeward Bound—Appointments of Class—Arrival and Service at Fort Snelling—Colonel G. Loomis, Mrs. C. O. Van Cleve, Lieutenant A. D. Nelson, and others—Boarding, Ten Dollars per Month—Grouse Shooting—Felix, the Dog—Study Medicine—The Country wants Men—Unquestioned Obedience—A. Ramsey, Governor of Minnesota.

ON being relieved the class hurried off to New York. What a change from West Point, with its strict discipline, to New York, with its unlimited freedom! At last we were at liberty to go where and when we pleased, and there were none to make us afraid. We roamed at large over that magnificent city, seeing the sights and learning something of the immense business interests of the great metropolis. A few days in New York gave us a surfeit of good things, and we began to break up and leave for our respective homes. On the train which left New York for Cumberland, Maryland, there were quite a number, but at various points some would leave, and when we reached the western end of the line only Charles W. Field and myself represented the class. From Cumberland we went by stage to Brownsville, Pennsylvania, where we embarked for Pittsburg on the "Judge McLean," a small packet which plied between those two cities. On the arrival of the boat in Pittsburg the steamer "Citizen" was at the wharf with steam up, and amid the clanging of her bell and the oft-repeated

"All aboard for Louisville," we hurried our baggage on board, secured berths, and quietly awaited our departure. The fires soon went out, the bell ceased to ring out upon the air, and we were informed that, owing to the necessity of making some repairs on the machinery, the boat would not leave until ten o'clock on the next day. There we remained from Friday until the following Tuesday evening, but our hopes were heightened each day by fires being kindled, which threw out great volumes of black smoke from the chimneys. At last the cable was cast loose, the stage plank drawn in, and we were afloat. Field left me at the mouth of the Kentucky River. I reached Cincinnati on the sixth day from Pittsburg. Our arrival was on the glorious Fourth, but on that occasion, owing to the prevalence of cholera, which was fearful in its ravages, there was no celebration of its pleasant memories. The streets were deserted, the business houses closed, and the stillness of death prevailed. In six or eight days I reached my home in Owensboro', Kentucky, having been about two weeks in making the trip from New York. At Cumberland it was evident that the stage was to be crowded. An old, sour-looking fellow, hoping to deter some of us from going on, so that he might have more room, said that it was dangerous to travel with him, as he had just recovered from a very severe attack of cholera. A gentleman replied that having just been discharged from a smallpox hospital near New York he had no fear of cholera. The old man, not wishing to run the risk of travelling with one so recently from a pest hospital, remained to take the stage the next day.

In 1849 the railroads in the United States were few and the lines very short. The growth of such roads has been wonderful. Thirty years ago I felt sure that in the progress of time two things would be accomplished,—the abolition of slavery and the construction of a railroad which would connect the Atlantic with the Pacific Ocean,—but I hardly expected to live to see the consummation of either. Both came sooner than I expected, and, strange enough, the destruction of one rendered the other possible. The abolition of slavery, brought about by war, produced the men with energy and enterprise to undertake the latter and push it to completion. Now the iron horse inflates his lungs on the Atlantic coast, and rushes wildly over prairie, through hills and dales, and slakes his thirst in the blue waters of the Pacific Ocean. Passengers are furnished with good fare and comfortable sleeping accommodations, and the passage from ocean to ocean is made without any inconvenience whatever beyond the time consumed in making the trip. The swift, eager, far-soaring intelligence of man has annihilated time and distance, and if future generations improve on our own they must look to the discovery of some method by which the air is to be used for navigation as we navigate the great deeps.

Soon after arriving at home a circus visited the town. Some of my friends prevailed on me to wear my uniform, and on being asked when the show would begin, and supposing that I had been mistaken for the clown, I returned to the hotel, where I cast off the uniform and clothed myself in citizen dress. From that day to this I do not remember to have ever worn uniform when it was not absolutely necessary.

The customary leave of absence until the 30th day of September, following graduation, was allowed, during which time the graduates were assigned to corps and regiments, and each notified to proceed to their posts, so as to be there to report in person on the expiration of their leaves of absence. About July 15 I received the following order, and fixed upon September 15 as the date of my departure from home.

WAR DEPARTMENT,
July 3, 1849.

SIR:

You are hereby informed, that on the 1st day of July, 1849, the President of the United States appointed you a Brevet Second Lieutenant in the Sixth Regiment of Infantry, in the service of the United States.

You will, immediately on receipt hereof, please to communicate to this Department, through the Adjutant-General's Office, your acceptance or non-acceptance of said appointment; and, in case of accepting, you will report agreeably to General Orders, No. 38, herewith transmitted.

GEO. W. CRAWFORD,
Secretary of War.

BVT. 2D LT. RICHARD W. JOHNSON,
   6th Infantry, Co. C.
LT.-COL. G. LOOMIS, Com'd'g Regt., Ft. Snelling, Iowa; Co. C at Ft. Snelling, Iowa.

The following is General Order, No. 38, referred to in previous order:

WAR DEPARTMENT, ADJUTANT-GENERAL'S OFFICE,
WASHINGTON, July 5, 1849.

General Orders,
  No. 38.
Promotions and appointments in the Army of the United States,

IN PEACE AND WAR.

made by the President, since the publication of General Orders, No. 14, of March 15, 1849.

* * * * * * * *

III. The following-named cadets, graduates of the Military Academy, are attached to the army, with the brevet of second lieutenant, in conformity with the 4th section of the Act of April 29, 1812, to take rank from July 1, 1849.

Brevet Second Lieutenant attached to the Corps of Engineers.
Rank.
1. Cadet Quincy A. Gillmore.

Brevet Second Lieutenant attached to the Corps of Topographical Engineers.
2. Cadet John G. Parke.

Brevet Second Lieutenant attached to the Ordnance.
3. Cadet Stephen V. Benét.

Brevet Second Lieutenants attached to the Dragoon Arm.
20. Cadet Horace F. De Lano, Company C, First Dragoons.
25. Cadet Beverly H. Robertson, Company E, Second Dragoons.
27. Cadet Charles W. Field, Company D, Second Dragoons.

Brevet Second Lieutenants attached to the Regiment of Mounted Riflemen.
21. Cadet Daniel McClure, Company B.
24. Cadet Washington C. Tevis, Company G.

Brevet Second Lieutenants attached to the Artillery Arm.
4. Cadet Thomas J. Haines, Company K, First Artillery.
6. Cadet William Silvey, Company C, Third Artillery.
7. Cadet Beekman Du Barry, Company I, First Artillery.
8. Cadet Delevan D. Perkins, Company A, Second Artillery.
9. Cadet Absolem Baird, Company M, Second Artillery.
10. Cadet William A. Nimmo, Company B, Fourth Artillery.
13. Cadet Edward R. Platt, Company H, Third Artillery.
14. Cadet Chauncey McKeever, Company B, First Artillery.
16. Cadet John Kellogg, Company G, Fourth Artillery.
17. Cadet John C. Moore, Company H, Fourth Artillery.
18. Cadet Rufus Saxton, Jr., Company E, Third Artillery.
22. Cadet Edward M. Hudson, Company I, Third Artillery.

Brevet Second Lieutenants attached to the Infantry.

11. Cadet Milton Cogswell, Company D, Fourth Infantry.
15. Cadet William H. Lewis, Company G, Fourth Infantry.
19. Cadet Thomas Wright, Company A, Seventh Infantry.
23. Cadet John Withers, Company G, Fifth Infantry.
26. Cadet Joseph L. Tidball, Company I, Fourth Infantry.
28. Cadet Seth M. Barton, Company G, Third Infantry.
29. Cadet Duff C. Green, Company B, Fifth Infantry.
30. Cadet Richard W. Johnson, Company C, Sixth Infantry.
31. Cadet Samuel B. Holabird, Company D, First Infantry.
32. Cadet Thomas G. Williams, Company B, Second Infantry.
33. Cadet Thornton A. Washington, Company F, Sixth Infantry.
36. Cadet Thomas C. English, Company K, Fifth Infantry.
37. Cadet Joseph H. McArthur, Company G, Second Infantry.
38. Cadet James P. Roy, Company B, Eighth Infantry.
39. Cadet Charles B. Alvord, Company D, Eighth Infantry.
40. Cadet Darius D. Clark, Company C, Second Infantry.
41. Cadet Louis H. Marshall, Company D, Third Infantry.
42. Cadet Samuel H. Reynolds, Company A, First Infantry.
43. Cadet James McIntosh, Company F, First Infantry.

The following-named cadets will take rank as Brevet Second Lieutenants from July 2, 1849.

5. Cadet Johnson K. Duncan, Company E, Second Artillery.
12. Cadet Edward D. Stockton, Company F, Second Artillery.
34. Cadet John W. Frazer, Company K, Second Infantry.
35. Cadet Alfred Cummings, Company G, Eighth Infantry.

* * * * * * * *

By order:
(Signed) R. JONES,
Adj't.-Gen'l.

Owing to low water in the Upper Mississippi I was delayed so that I did not reach Fort Snelling until the 4th day of October, about nine o'clock P.M. The night was dark, and when I stepped from the stage plank the first person I met was Lieutenant-Colonel

G. Loomis, who kindly invited me to his quarters, to remain until I could make permanent arrangements for myself. Of course his kind invitation was promptly accepted, and I have never ceased to be thankful to him for his kind hospitality and the interest he manifested in my welfare. He was a very pious man, and gave me much good advice. He died March 5, 1872, at Stratford, Connecticut, in his eighty-third year.

Fort Snelling is one of the oldest military posts in the Northwest. It was established by a battalion of the Fifth U. S. Infantry, under the command of Lieutenant-Colonel H. Leavenworth, in 1819. At first it was called Fort Saint Anthony. Before its completion Leavenworth was promoted and left to join his own regiment, and Colonel Josiah Snelling was assigned to the command and instructed to push the work as rapidly as possible. General Winfield Scott paid the post a visit, and was so pleased with the energy and activity displayed by Colonel Snelling that he recommended to the War Department that the name of the post be changed to Fort Snelling in honor of its builder. The recommendation was approved, the order issued, and it has ever been known by that name. With the exception of only a few months, it has been occupied by United States troops.

The original garrison came up the river in keelboats. The country was occupied by large bands of hostile Indians, and the troops had to be constantly on the alert to avoid surprise and massacre. There were no settlements north or west, and those on the south and east were many miles away and separated from the fort by an immense district of country occupied and roamed over by numerous tribes of warlike savages. Can any one conceive of the desolation and loneliness of those military pioneers? No libraries, no lectures, and no amusements outside of themselves. It was not for five years after the establishment of this post that the placid waters of the Mississippi were disturbed by paddle-wheels propelled by steam, and then only one boat a year to bring up supplies for the garrison. The post is located on a bluff, so that two sides are inaccessible to a savage enemy. The other sides were closed in by high stone walls, with loopholes for defence. These old walls, being no longer required, have been torn down, thus throwing open the entire west front and increasing the comfort and improving the appearance very much. Of the original number who came up on the keel-boats none probably survive, except Mrs. Charlotte O. Van Cleve, the wife of General H. P. Van Cleve, of Minneapolis, Minnesota. She was a mere child when her parents brought her up in 1819. Her memory of the early settlement of this part of the country is very vivid, and with her ready pen she has done much to hand down to history accounts of the stirring events of a bygone age. Although well advanced in years, she appears to be as active mentally and physically as she was twenty years ago. Mrs. Van Cleve takes a deep interest in our Indian affairs, and has expended her best efforts in ameliorating their condition. The poor, without regard to age, sex, or nationality, are always sure of her sympathy and support in their trials and troubles, and to her they appeal as to a mother. The Northwest has not produced a more noble woman, and her name deserves to be remembered by all who admire nobility of character and disinterested friendship for the weak and for the poor down-trodden of all races and conditions of men and women.

At this time there were stationed at the post Lieutenant-Colonel Loomis, Brevet Major Samuel Woods, Captain James Monroe, Brevet Captain R. W. Kirkham, Lieutenants J. W. T. Gardiner, Castor, Wetmore, Nelson, Surgeon A. N. McLaren, and Chaplain E. G. Gear. Of these, Monroe, Kirkham, Wetmore, McLaren, and Gear were married, and with the addition of the families of Henry H. Sibley, of the American Fur Company, and Franklin Steele, the post sutler, constituted the society of the garrison. Some of the most pleasant evening entertainments I ever remember to have attended I enjoyed during the winter of 1849–50. Of these, Loomis, Gardiner, Castor, Wetmore, McLaren and wife, and Monroe and wife, Franklin Steele and wife, and Rev. E. G. Gear, and A. D. Nelson have passed away, leaving behind them as a legacy to their friends sweet memories of their many noble, generous traits of character, which endeared them to all who were fortunate enough to enjoy their acquaintance and partake of their hospitality. Woods is still in the army and lives in Oakland, California, where he has amassed a large property. Kirkham made a fortune in California, resigned from the army, and now lives a life of ease and comfort near his old friend Woods.

In the fall of 1849, Nelson was a second lieutenant, notwithstanding he had passed through the Florida and Mexican wars. Promotion in those days was slow; officers rarely ever died, and few ever felt that the service could spare them, and hence none resigned. When the officers assembled together the subject of conversation was generally the incidents of the Mexican war; the same having just terminated, the events were fresh in their memories. I had not participated in the Mexican campaigns, being, during their continuance, at West Point; and it was a source of deep regret to me to know that I was not born soon enough to take part in that war, but a time came when I had all the experience I desired on the tented field.

Under Nelson's quarters a man and his wife resided and furnished him with table board. She was *au fait* in her department, and made her husband serve at the table with all the elegance of the professional caterer.

After a pleasant, but brief, period Nelson was ordered to St. Louis and I was left alone. The cook then informed me that, as she would have only one boarder, it would be necessary to raise her charges somewhat. As the pay of a second lieutenant was only sixty-five dollars per month, I was fearful that she would take it all; but on learning that she desired to raise the monthly bill to ten dollars, I felt very greatly relieved. Think of this, you modern boarding-house keepers: ten dollars a month for most excellent table board, and money made even at that price.

Among the assets left by Nelson were two splendidly-broken pointer dogs; but I had no gun, and as navigation was closed for the season, could not have one brought up from St. Louis. It would have been something unheard of for a young officer not to be a reasonably good shot, so I determined on taking lessons with an old government musket. Loading one with a handful of shot, I started out on foot followed by the dogs, who seemed delighted to know that they were in the keeping of one who was fond of shooting. After getting beyond the garrison away they bounded, and I followed as rapidly as possible. A walk of three miles brought me near Minnehaha Falls. The dogs came to a dead point. Cocking the gun I bid them "hie on," when two birds arose, flying about eight feet apart. I fired at one and killed the other, and from that day to this I have never pulled a trigger on a prairie chicken. These trusty, faithful dogs have long since departed for other hunting grounds, and if there is another existence for them I hope they have found better marksmen than I have ever been. I have often heard some miserable selfish man spoken of as "mean as a dog." Now, this is great injustice to the canine race. I have never known a mean dog. They are man's best friend, and when all others forsake him the dog is steadfast in his affection and devotion. When both are wearied, man will lie down to sleep while the faithful dog stands sentinel over him to protect him from harm.

A friend of mine who was always followed by a black-and-tan terrier was expostulated with by a lady, who said, "It is strange that a man of your good sense should allow a dog to follow you all the time." "Well, madam," he replied, "you would follow the dog; the leading mind always goes ahead." When the late war was sprung upon the country I owned a large Newfoundland dog, which bore the name of Felix. He accompanied me on many of my marches and campaigns, and never deserted his master. At night Felix remained close to my tent and was always on the alert. He lived his allotted time, and passed peacefully and quietly away. He was only a dog, but he was my friend, and a more steadfast one I never had.

The city of St. Paul, now with a population of over one hundred thousand, had then less than four hundred. Then we had a weekly mail, though not at all regular. Bad roads and weak ice caused many failures. During the winter of 1849 a period of five weeks passed without news from the States. Thus we were left to rust or eke out a lonely existence, ignorant of what was transpiring in the world at large. In the garrison there were no young officers with whom to associate, and no books to occupy my time, so I resolved on the study of medicine. Dr. McLaren seconded my resolution with great earnestness and furnished me with every facility. I applied myself closely, and on every Saturday night he would come to my room and examine me on what I had read during the week. Before I left the post he insisted upon my going before the Army Medical Board with a view to entering the medical department. This I declined to do, for I did not have that confidence in my own proficiency which he seemed to have. But on various occasions I found the knowledge I acquired to be of great service. There is a young fellow in Texas, now about twenty-six years old, who bears the name of Richard Johnson Roach, as a compliment to my professional "skill and ability."

At this time there is not a military post in the United States as difficult of access as Fort Snelling was in 1849, so young officers can get books to read and thus improve their minds and keep themselves advised in regard to the important events transpiring throughout the civilized world. I desire to say now that the young officer who reads the most, thinks the most, and obeys orders most promptly is the one who comes to the front when necessity calls for men. And when I speak of men, I refer to them as clearly and broadly distinguished from the paltry counterfeits, the petty shuttlecocks, the supple-kneed sycophants, the pert and pretentious coxcombs, the human nonentities, who are but drones in this great world-hive of ours. I mean men of iron mould and dauntless purpose, who grasp not after baubles, who bow not at the venal shrine of a false and prostituted "public opinion,"— men whose souls are not intoxicated by shallow draughts from the beaker of success, and who do not shrivel in the first heats of disappointment,—men whose spirits rise as adversities thicken, acquire fresh courage and sterner resolve with each succeeding failure, confront new perils and difficulties, new foes and trials, with unquailing front,—men who gather to their hearts more of the light and essence of heaven as the world glowers and glooms around them. The age has had enough of tinsel, is sick of a surfeiting overdose of spurious heroes and wretched charlatans, and the pure gold, the refined gold, the gold without discount or alloy, must ring in the manhood of him who seeks and yearns to fulfil its mighty requisitions now. Action,—fearless, unselfish, discriminating action, —which spurns the shackles of a gross conventionality and scorns to follow in the same dead, dreary, beaten track, in whose dust and glare gainless millions have grovelled wearily on before, must be the test of this golden purity, the standard of this high manhood's trial. How many of the young men in the army or in civil life are destined to make their marks in this world, or to leave behind them the record of useful lives with no shame to remember, no wish to forget? Think of this, young men, and let your aim be high. Proficiency in the "german" or at whist, fondness for music and the frivolities of fashionable life, will not qualify you for position when men such as I have described are called for. There may be mountains in your pathway, but you will discover that with no more certainty do the recurrent waves wear away by ceaseless buffetings and gradual encroachments the granite of their rocky shores than do persistent effort and unswerving perseverance, when sustained by calmness, probity, and intelligence, wear away the rough places in life.

There is no genius like the genius of labor. There is no reward like that which comes from energy, system, and perseverance.

Unquestioned obedience to all orders, coming from proper sources, is not only the duty of every officer, of whatever rank, but absolutely essential to the maintenance of discipline, without which the army would be a mob with no recognized leader, and upon which no reliance could be placed when great results are to be accomplished. The best-disciplined troops do the most efficient service, not only on the battle-field, but on the march and in the garrison.

The Congress of 1848-49 organized a territorial government for this section of the country, and on the inauguration of Zachary Taylor it became his duty to appoint a governor and other territorial officers. The position of governor was tendered to Alexander Ramsey, of Pennsylvania, and accepted on the 2d day of April, 1849, and on the 27th day of the same month he arrived at the scene of his official duties, and a few days subsequently he issued a proclamation declaring the Territory organized and the courts opened for the adjudication of such cases as might be brought before them. Governor Ramsey was married in 1845 to Miss Anna E. Jenks, and she accompanied him to this, then, wild and unknown country. She was a noble woman, a fit companion of a worthy man. Governor Ramsey has held many positions of honor and trust, and has always acquitted himself with credit. He was one of the best senators the State ever had. As a senator no one exercised more influence, and his personal popularity was so great that any measure he advocated was always sure to be carried out.

At this time he is in private life, honored and respected by all who know him. His early investments have made him wealthy, and now, in the evening of his life, he is surrounded by all the comforts which money can supply. He has contributed largely to every public enterprise, while the poor have always found a friend in him. "There is that scattereth, and yet increaseth, and there is that withholdeth more than is meet, but it tendeth to poverty."

CHAPTER IV.

Scout after Indians—Indian Ring—Cause of Indian Troubles—Steele and Kittson Pre-empt St. Anthony Falls—Signing False Returns—Indian Story-Tellers—Antoine Robert—Catfish Bar—Lecture in St. Anthony, Minnesota—The North Star State—Campaign to Iowa—Colonel Woods—Colonel Stevens—Post Established at Lizard Fork of Des Moines—Promoted to First Infantry—Married—Off for Texas—Generals Pitcher, Brooke, and Reeve—Wolves at Chacon—Fort Duncan.

In the fall of 1849 the Winnebago Indians became troublesome around Prairie du Chien, and it was decided to remove them to a reservation on the Mississippi River, above Rum River. The most effectual, and at the same time the most economical, way to remove them was considered to be by contract. Accordingly an agreement was entered into with a party by which he was to receive seventy dollars per head for each Indian transported to his new home.

They were easily prevailed upon to take passage on steamboats from the Prairie to St. Paul, thence by easy marches to their new reservation. As they were well fed while in transit, this was considered "a good thing" by the noble red men and their interesting wives and charming daughters.

As soon as they reached the reservation and the issue of rations ceased, they began to hunger for the flesh-pots of Wisconsin. So great was their desire to return that they tarried but a short time. Packing up their baggage they moved out on an air-line for their old homes, which they reached almost as soon as did the boat which first brought them up the river. Again they boarded the vessel and accepted the contractor's hospitality, and were soon afloat for the second time upon the broad bosom of the Father of Waters. The contractor was not long in finding out that he had "struck a bonanza." The Indians were moving in a circle, and hence there was no end to them. How much money was made and how long this proceeding continued I do not know, but this much I do know, that the river route taken in connection with the down trip by land formed an ellipse, or a circle, and was doubtless the origin of the term "Indian Ring." It is a difficult matter to locate this ring. It is everywhere, and embraces all the rascality perpetrated upon the nation's wards. It is seen in the inferior provisions furnished, for which the government pays the highest price. It is seen in the withholding of these inferior supplies until the poor Indian, half starved, starts out on the war-path to avoid starvation. It is the source and cause of nearly all of our Indian wars. It breaks up reserves and causes the removal of tribes to less hospitable locations, thus producing dissatisfaction, which too often culminates in war and bloodshed. It is the most infamously corrupt organization in the known world. Bad faith, cheating, lying, and stealing on the part of the ring brings on desperation, and the army is called on to punish the poor Indian because he murmurs at the wrongs inflicted upon him and upon his family. In another chapter I shall have something more to say in regard to the Indians and the policy which I think should be pursued by the government towards them.

When that portion of the Fort Snelling reservation lying along the Falls of St. Anthony, on the east side of the Mississippi River, was thrown open to settlement, Major Joseph Plympton was in command of the post. The mail arrived about nine o'clock at night, and Plympton received information of the proposed sale, but supposed that no one else did. He sent for Captain Martin Scott, to whom he imparted the secret, and proposed that they should make the necessary arrangements to start at daylight on the following morning for the Falls of St. Anthony, with a view to making their claim to the lands adjacent thereto. Frank Steele, the post sutler, received the same information by the "Grape-Vine Telegraph," but instead of waiting until morning, he and N. W. Kittson, Esq., provided themselves with a bag of potatoes and several days' rations, procured a sleigh, loading it with straw, boards, nails, etc., and left the fort about twelve o'clock at night. They arrived at the falls about two o'clock A.M., and in a very short time erected a house into which they placed the straw for bedding. To make their claim a valid one it was necessary that they should be actual tillers of the soil. Holes were made in the snow and the potatoes planted. Satisfied with their success, these "horny-handed sons of toil" retired for the night. Bright and early on the following morning Plympton and Scott arrived. They were invited to dismount and take breakfast, after which they were shown around the farm and particular attention called to the field of potatoes.

Steele and Kittson were masters of the situation. Thus it was that the title to the lands upon which the East Division of Minneapolis is situated passed from the United States Government to private parties.

It was only a short time after my arrival at Fort Snelling that I succeeded to the command of the company to which I was attached, by reason of the absence of the captain and lieutenants. This imposed very little duty upon me, for it was too cold to drill, and when I recall what I had to do I can only remember the signing of the morning reports and the provision returns. One morning the first sergeant brought me a return to sign for anti-scorbutics. Now be it known that I had never seen nor heard of anti-scorbutics before, but I had heard of officers signing false returns. I had no idea of being caught in any such trap, so I told the sergeant to leave the return on my table and when I had time I would give it attention. When he withdrew I took up my dictionary and looked for the word, and was not even then satisfied that it would be proper in me to sign such a paper. Hastening over to see Major Woods, he explained that it was all right, whereupon I signed the return and sent it over to the company. I remembered this circumstance many years after when I told the junior member of a court, who was framing a sentence, to use the word mulct instead of forfeit. His reply was that he never used a word about which he knew nothing whatever, "and as to that word mulct I never saw it in my life and never heard of it before."

The first active service imposed on me was in November, 1849. The Indians from one of the western reserves moved down upon the frontier and began to kill cattle and other domestic animals for food. The settlers were afraid to interpose objection for fear of being murdered; so word reached the post commander of the existing state of things, and I was detailed to take charge of twenty men, go up to Rum River, and compel the wandering ones to return to their homes. I met a few of them, and the presence of my command was soon known, when all retraced their steps and ceased to give any more trouble. There was at that time living on Rum River a Mr. Antoine Robert, a Frenchman, who had married an Indian woman and who had about his house a large number of children. Robert was without education, but a man of strong character and, for his opportunities, a very intelligent man. I learned much from him about frontier life and Indian character. He told me that his experience with the Indians had convinced him that they were the most superstitious people in the world. An old Indian will gather around him a crowd of boys and girls, and from his fertile imagination draw out the most improbable stories. In every tribe there are two or more story-tellers,—Munchausens,—and when their tales are told the young believe them, and when they grow up tell the same to their own children, not as fiction but as truth. Mr. Robert asked me if I had ever heard of "Catfish Bar," in the St. Croix River. I told him I had. "Well," said he, "that got its name in this way, and the Indians believe the story and you cannot convince them to the contrary. The Sioux for ages had waged a savage and relentless war against the Chippewas, who became disheartened by frequent reverses and, in council, resolved on abandoning the country so dear to them; but two young warriors stepped to the front and begged their people to remain until they had gone forth in battle against their blood-thirsty enemy. They called upon the Great Spirit to witness the oath, then made, that they would neither eat nor drink until after they had overtaken and avenged the wrongs inflicted upon their tribe.

"Arranging their toilets and painting their faces, they started down the river on their perilous journey. The weather was warm, and thirst and hunger began to be felt; but, true to their solemn oath, they continued their journey along the bank of the St. Croix. At length strength failed, and they sat down to look at the water they craved so much. This only aggravated their thirst, and at last one of them resolved to crawl to the bank and drink from the cool, refreshing stream. Just as he stooped down and got his lips near the water he was suddenly transformed into a catfish, and with the instincts of a full-grown fish he swam from the shore. The more he drank the larger he grew, until finally there was not water enough to float him, and he rested on the bottom and was soon buried beneath the sand, where he lies to-day, forming Catfish Bar, which ever reminds his brethren of the fearful doom that surely awaits any one who fails to keep and perform the pledges he makes to the Great Spirit."

I remained with Mr. Robert for several days, and then returned to my post. By the 1st day of December winter was upon us. Out-door exercise was impossible, and for long, weary months we remained housed, with few amusements beyond occasional visits among ourselves. It was my first experience in such high latitude, and well do I remember the severity of the weather. St. Anthony was a small village, peopled principally from the State of Maine. There was organized in the town a "Library Association," and to raise a fund for the purchase of books a course of lectures was decided upon. Of course no distinguished lecturers could be prevailed upon to come to this unsettled, hyperborean region, and hence local talent had to be called into requisition. By some means I never knew, I was invited to lecture one evening on any subject I might select. I consented, and on a night with the temperature at thirty degrees below zero I rode up and gave the good people the best talk I could. The house was filled with an intelligent audience, and my sophomoric address was received with marked attention far above its merits. I remember to have made some prophecies as to the growth of this country, and it is due to truth to say that I did not believe one-half of what I said. I remember to have told them that the time was not far distant when thousands of smiling villages would be reflected by the waves of our rivers and lakes, and the broad and beautiful prairies would in the near future echo with the sound of the reaper. The prophecy has been fulfilled, and to-day over a million of people inhabit the State; thrifty farmers have subdued the prairies, and every year harvest wheat enough not only to feed the Minnesotians, but half of Europe, and yet the State is in its infancy.

The past is the prototype of the future and furnishes the only data upon which future events can be foretold.

What, then, may be looked for by the close of this century in the way of growth and prosperity of this State? Minnesota stands to-day unrivalled in the possession of all the elements of a mighty and prosperous career, and while it is only a question of a few years when those who have made it what it is will be gathered to their final rest, the rising generation will carry on the work inaugurated by their ancestors and make this the empire State of the Northwest.

The Sacs, Foxes, and Potawatomies Indians originally occupied the territory now covered by the State of Iowa; but when their lands were desired for the use of the avaricious white man they were compelled to remove. These tribes were colonized on the west of the Missouri River. The climate was inhospitable and the game scarce. There is something pleasant in the memories of home. There our ancestors lived and died. There their precious dust reposes within the quiet walls of some cemetery, or under the shade of some old, ancestral tree, and it is there that we hope, some day, to return and again become familiar with the scenes of our childhood. The Indian being human, his heart is influenced by the same sentiment, the same emotions which move our own. Is it strange, then, that he should have the same longing desires that we have? Is it not reasonable that they should wish to return to the home of their childhood, to see the graves of their ancestors and of their own children, to drink from the same pure fountain, and to visit old and familiar places where they enjoyed the happy days of boyhood? Parts of these tribes returned to Iowa, and encamped near the village of Marengo. It is possible that they committed some depredations while in search of food. Complaint, at all events, was made against them, and the War Department was requested to cause them to be sent out of the State. To accomplish this a command was organized under the leadership of Brevet Major Samuel Woods, consisting of one company of dragoons and two of infantry, one of which I commanded. Colonel John H. Stevens was appointed sutler, and accompanied the command with a stock of goods so varied as to furnish about every article a soldier would desire on a campaign. To reach the camp of the Indians the troops were transported by river to Muscatine, thence by easy marches to the vicinity of Marengo, passing through Iowa City, at that time the capital of the State. When our command was within a day's march of the camp the Indians packed up and departed for parts unknown. Runners were sent in all directions to find them and ask for a "talk," but they would not listen to any proposition of the sort. Finally, two citizens of that country proposed to gather them all in and remove them over and beyond the Missouri River for $3.50 per head, and as this was cheaper than the government could do it, Major Woods closed the contract, which I think was carried out faithfully on the part of the contractors.

Under instructions from the War Department, Major Woods proceeded to establish a permanent post near the Lizard Fork of the Des Moines, which he named Fort Clarke in honor of General Clarke, the department commander. The name was subsequently changed to Fort Dodge as a compliment to Senator

Dodge, of Iowa. The post has long since been abandoned, and there has grown up on its site a large and flourishing city, which bears the name of the old post.

The company which I commanded was relieved from duty with Major Woods's command, and I was directed to return with it to Fort Snelling, where I arrived about September 15, 1850. On my return I found my promotion to second lieutenant in the First Regiment of Infantry, then stationed in Texas, and I began to arrange my private affairs for a change of station.

Before leaving on the campaign to Iowa there was "a promise made to me in some of the love-making nooks" around Fort Snelling, and that little matter had to be attended to. After October 30, 1850, there were two of us in the family. If she has ever had any cause to regret saying "yes," she has had the good sense never to mention it. She left a comfortable, pleasant home to share the trials, hardships, and privations of a soldier's life on the frontier, and yet through all she was never known to complain or murmur. On the contrary, she has always been a source of encouragement and comfort. A good wife is of more value to her husband than rubies. "She will do him good and not evil all the days of her life."

On the 11th day of November following, leaving her behind me, I started for Texas *via* Kentucky. I remained in my old home for a few days, and then took passage on board of a fine boat for New Orleans. At the latter place I engaged my passage on the steamer "Galveston" for Indianola, Texas, and was fortunate in having as a travelling companion Lieutenant Thomas G. Pitcher, who in the late war was a gallant and distinguished general officer. While on the steamer I had an attack of fever, and my illness increased until after my arrival in San Antonio. I shall never forget Pitcher's kindness. He ministered to my wants with as much tenderness and devotion as if I had been his brother. As long as I live I shall remember him as a true and tried friend, whose self-abnegation added greatly to my comfort if it did not really save my life. On my arrival in San Antonio, in an ambulance and flat on my back, General George M. Brooke, the department commander, directed that I should be taken to his residence. There I had the kindest attention shown me, and when I recovered sufficiently to leave my room I was the recipient of many kind courtesies extended to me by the officers stationed in that city, and particularly on the part of Colonel I. V. D. Reeve and his estimable family. These little courtesies, small in themselves, made up a silver lining to the black cloud which had overhung me for several weeks.

When I had gained strength sufficient, I was furnished with an ambulance to take me to my post at Fort Duncan. An escort was unnecessary until I had passed Fort Inge, then under the command of Brevet Colonel W. J. Hardee, of the dragoons. I remained one night at that post, and was the guest of the commanding officer. From that point to Fort Duncan required two days' travel, unequally divided on account of water. I had to camp for the night at the Chacon, where I was liable to be attacked by prowling Indians.

Hardee instructed me to allow the men to prepare their dinners near the creek, and then advised me to make my camp on the hills beyond, so that the little party, composed of four men commanded by a sergeant, would not be easily surprised. I did as he suggested, and passed the night safely. Before daylight the escort were up, had their horses fed, and proceeded to prepare their breakfast. The fumes from broiling bacon awoke me, and about that time I heard what I supposed was not less than a thousand Indians. I put my head out of the ambulance to see what the escort thought of the situation. They seemed to take no notice of the unusual noise, which I thought quite strange. They were old soldiers and had heard the yelping of prairie wolves before. The noise frightened me, and for a while every hair on my head stood straight and alone. By the time it was light enough to see the road we were on our way, and arrived at Fort Duncan about noon. Here I met Barton, Washington, McIntosh, and Reynolds, of my class, who were as glad to see me as I was to meet them. I did not feel like a stranger in a strange land, for they soon introduced me to all of the officers at the post, and I felt at home and among friends from the very hour of my arrival. The troops and the post were commanded by Brevet Lieutenant-Colonel Thompson Morris, a kind, good-hearted man and a good soldier, who required all under him to do their duty well and faithfully. He was not a martinet, but exacted a rigid compliance with the laws and regulations, and yet exacted nothing more from his subordinates than he cheerfully did himself. He had his family at the post, and his hospitable home was ever open to the officers of the garrison. A few days after my arrival his house was thrown open and the officers of the post were invited to meet me. By some strange oversight I had not been bidden to the feast. Noticing my absence, he came over to my quarters to know if I was sick. When I told him the reason I had not gone, he was very much mortified and insisted upon my going over with him. He was so pressing, and had made such ample explanation, that I could not decline, so I joined the happy throng at the eleventh hour and participated in the closing scenes of the evening,—and, by the way, the latter part of an evening's entertainment is always the most pleasant, for formality has then given way to genuine enjoyment. The appetite has been appeased, and one feels at peace with himself and all the members of the human family.

How pleasant it is to feel just in that way! Such experiences, however, belong generally to the young. When one gets to be old, and his digestive organs have become impaired by long and improper use, he is apt to be sour and morose,—liable to take offence at almost anything that is said. He ceases to be a comfort to himself, and becomes an intolerable nuisance to all with whom he comes in contact. What a fate for any poor woman to be tied to such a "living body of death!" She humors the poor fellow, and gets along with him the best she can until death comes to her relief and takes one or the other away. If we could always be young how pleasant life would be!

CHAPTER V.

War with Mexico—Sheridan's Trip to Texas—Lawlessness of People—Horse Stealing—Murder—A Justice of the Peace Resigns—Want of Order in Building Fort Duncan—General Holabird—Northers—Good State for Railroads—Officers of the First—Mexican Ladies — Bull-Fights — Striker Twomey—Anticipated Troubles—Back to St. Paul.

Fort Duncan is situated on high ground, overlooking the Rio Grande. Between the post and the river is a low, sandy bottom, say a half-mile wide, which often overflows. In the rear of the post, and extending from the river above to the river below, is a circular range of high hills. On the north, and separated from it by a deep ravine, is the town of Eagle Pass; while in front, and across the river, is the Mexican town of Piedras Negras. The great line of travel from San Antonio to the interior States of Mexico passes through this place, and this fact, probably, determined the location of the post. The soil for miles around is pure sand, which produces nothing but the cactus and the dwarfed mesquite tree. All the grain used by our horses had to be brought from the interior of Mexico, where it was produced by irrigation; while the flour and other provisions for the use of the troops were brought by steamer from New Orleans to Corpus Christi, thence by mule teams to the post.

It will be remembered that the war with Mexico was occasioned by a dispute in regard to the boundary line of Texas. Mexico claimed the Nueces and Texas the Rio Grande as the boundary line. Had we not acquired California by the war, the lives lost and treasure expended would have been lost and expended to little purpose, for the land in dispute is worthless,—absolutely of no value for agricultural or grazing purposes. Even the butter used on our tables was brought from New Orleans, and goats, which could subsist on the sparse vegetation on the hills around the post, supplied us with milk.

It was possibly on a trip to Fort Duncan when General Sheridan declared that if he "owned Texas and the infernal regions he would lease the State and reside in the other place."

It must be remembered, however, that Texas is more than three times as large as all of the New England States; that there is more good and productive land within it than in any other State of the Union. Of course in such a large body of land there must be much barren and worthless. The eastern half is fertile and productive, and produces everything man could desire. The climate is delightful. The days are warm, but the nights are cool and pleasant.

In the settled portion of the State the people are educated, refined, and law-abiding. On the frontier just the reverse may be said; that is, the people are ignorant, destitute of any refinement, and have no respect for law or order. It should be remembered that I am writing about the state of things which existed there thirty-five years ago.

While I was stationed at Fort Duncan I think I can safely say that some one was murdered in Eagle Pass or in its vicinity every day in the year. With some few exceptions the population of that town was made up of murderers and others who escaped from Mexico for safety, or who sought the boundary line, over which they could readily pass if, perchance, they were pursued by the officers of the law.

At the time about which I am now writing horse-stealing was the greatest crime a man could commit. The taking of human life was a violation of law, but by no means a serious offence against the dignity of the State.

A man, after mature deliberation, decided upon taking the life of his neighbor. His plan was to go to his house, ring the bell, and when he opened the door to stab him to death. Arming himself with a huge bowie-knife, he knocked at the door. It was opened and he plunged the deadly weapon into the breast of the man, then throwing his weight upon it he ripped him open, his bowels falling out on the door-steps. Subsequently he learned that the man he had brutally murdered was not the one he wanted to kill. The coroner's jury found that the man died by accident, and the hero of the butcher-knife went free. I did not know the above parties, but General Albert Sidney Johnston related the case to me and vouched for its truthfulness. An officer of the army, becoming angry with his commanding officer, proceeded to his quarters and killed him in cold blood. He then gave himself up to the civil authorities, was tried and acquitted. As no one can have his life placed in jeopardy twice for the same offence, of course he could not be tried by the military authorities, and hence he escaped punishment. It would take too much space to relate half the outrages which came to my notice while I was in Texas. These will suffice. In justice it should be stated that this lawlessness was condemned by the better classes, but they were powerless to put a stop to it. In the frontier towns there was absolutely no security for life or property. When a murder was committed those who witnessed it were afraid to report it, for the informant was sure to be killed in the course of time.

A justice of the peace in conversation with me summed up the matter in a few words. He had resigned his office, and I wanted to know why he had done so. He replied, "There is no use of my being judge in this county, where every man is afraid to say turkle."

The buildings at the post were constructed with little reference to each other, or to the points of the compass. Had they been deposited on the ground as the result of a cyclone there would have been no less regard for regularity or uniformity.

The commanding officer occupied a house constructed of adobes. The nearest house to it was built of stone. There were several log and mud houses scattered around without order, while the other officers were either in tents or paulin houses, pitched wherever inclination led the occupant to decide.

The only buildings in line were those occupied by the companies. These were constructed of grass, like many of the Mexican houses, and were known as thatched houses.

A small adobe house had been constructed for the use

of the bachelors' mess. The store—erected by the sutler himself—was built of adobes. Mr. Thomas K. Wallace, the brother of Captain George W. Wallace, was the sutler, and he was assisted by his brother, Mr. E. W. Wallace. They were both clever gentlemen, and added much to the society of the post. The store was well supplied with everything usually found in a country store, and the officers and soldiers could procure such articles as they required at reasonable prices. Attached to the store was the sutler's private office, which was very generally used as a club room, —at least it was there that they assembled to discuss military and unmilitary matters. And some idea can be formed of the interest taken in these discussions when I assert that the meetings often broke up in the short hours of the morning. The officers, at their own expense, erected a billiard-room and provided it with a first-class billiard-table, which afforded many pleasant hours of amusement to those who were fond of the game. Captain Wallace and Lieutenant Holabird were the best players. On one occasion they locked the door and played steadily for twenty-four hours to decide the championship.

Holabird never gave his attention to anything at which he could not excel. Hence he was a fine shot, a splendid billiard-player, and the best quartermaster in the army. To-day he is the able Quartermaster-General of the United States Army.

It was at this post that I first experienced a real, genuine Texas norther. A description of one is unnecessary except for those who have not seen or felt one. They are invariably preceded by hot, sultry weather. Suddenly there appears in the north a light, windy-looking cloud, which approaches with fearful rapidity. Within twenty minutes after the cloud is observed the storm is at hand. There is no rain, only wind, and it is so cold that one imagines it just down from an iceberg. The mercury will fall from 60° to 70° within a half-hour. The cold is not so intense as in more northerly latitudes, but the change is so great and so sudden, and the wearing apparel so light, that I have really suffered more from cold in Texas than I have in Minnesota. The northers generally continue for three or four days, during which time the air is full of dust and sand. Finally they blow themselves out, and there is a lull for a day or so, when the wind blows a gale from the south, which continues for several days, during which time the dust is driven back in blinding sheets. Houses and tents cannot be constructed close enough to exclude it. During the prevalence of a norther, as well as the returning south wind, there is dust in the eyes, ears, mouth, in the sugar, and in the coffee. In fact, it is in everything and on everything, —dust everywhere. Long before there were any railroads in Texas Colonel Backus said that it was the best country in the world for such roads, "for," said he, "any one coming out here and experiencing a norther would like to get out of the country as rapidly as possible, and would therefore patronize the railroads."

The officers of the First Infantry, with whom I was thrown at Fort Duncan, were good soldiers and agreeable gentlemen. There were no bickerings among them. The ladies at the post made the most of their opportunities, and by frequently gathering the officers together for social intercourse, kept up the good feeling so necessary in every garrison.

We were compelled to use the river water for all purposes. It was so muddy that when a glass was filled with it the bottom could not be seen. Here I learned one use to which the prickly pear could be placed. If thrown in the fire long enough to burn off the prickers, then opened and thrown into a barrel of water, it will cause the dirt to be precipitated to the bottom, leaving the water clear and pure. All water in Texas is warm, and to reduce the temperature a porous earthen-ware jar is used. It is filled and then placed where a current of air will pass over it. The rapid evaporation on the outside surface cools the water within and makes it quite palatable, although I believe that the temperature can never be reduced below 57°.

Our neighbors, the Mexicans, seemed to me to be the most indolent people in the world. Almost every day is a feast day, and almost everybody appears to celebrate it. All kinds of amusements are invented whereby a few gather in the pennies of the many. Gambling in all its phases is participated in by both male and female. Every one smokes, and the gracefulness with which a young maiden handles her cigarette is remarkable. The women are generally handsome, well formed, and graceful in their movements. They mature much sooner than the ladies in any other country. A girl at eleven years old is as much of a woman as one of eighteen is with us. They enter society at about that age, and are candidates for matrimony. I have seen a mother only eleven years old with her infant babe upon her knee.

Every year they have "bull-fights." One bull at a time is led into an enclosure, surrounded by a circular wall, on the top of which seats are arranged for the spectators. One man enters the ring and arouses the anger of the brute by shaking a red flag at him. When sufficiently infuriated he dashes at the man, who steps aside very adroitly and sticks a rosette just between the horns, where it is held by a sharp arrow-head. This goes on until all parts of his body have been decorated, and the pain from these cruel arrow-points must be intense to the poor animal. Finally the lacerated, bleeding creature is killed, and another victim is led into the ring. This cruel proceeding seems to give the people much amusement, and they cheer vociferously the barbarian in the ring. Fondness for this game is not confined to the men alone, but the best ladies of the country patronize it by their presence and appear to enjoy the barbarous sport. ' I can hardly see how a man born and reared in a Christian land could ever witness such a disgusting sight a second time. Nearly every young officer at the post would go once, but I never knew one to go a second time.

A bachelor at Fort Duncan had an Irishman by the name of Twomey, fresh from the green slopes of his native land, to look after his quarters and make his fires. A more faithful, honest man no one ever knew. His Irish bulls amused me very much. On one occasion an officer sent him to the sutler's store for a seidlitz powder. He rushed over as if it were a case

of life and death, and seeing the sutler himself said,
"Misther Wallace, the lieutenant sent me over for
your siddle and spoours." Mr. Wallace, thinking that
"siddle and spoours" was about as near seidlitz
powder as Twomey would be likely to come, sent
what was wanted, and afterwards told me of the
servant's blunder.

In the fall of 1851 I asked for a leave of absence for
the purpose of visiting St Paul in order to remove
my family to Texas. Before my leave expired, the
river closed and I could not return. I was authorized
to remain at St. Paul until the opening of navigation,
then to proceed to New Orleans and report to Captain
John H. King for the purpose of conducting recruits
to the Department of Texas. Although absent from
Fort Snelling for only a year, the officers of the garrison had been completely changed. The old, familiar
friends whom I had expected to meet had been ordered away. So I lost interest in the fort and rarely
ever visited it, although some of my most pleasant
memories are connected with that old post. Such is
army life. Here to-day and there to-morrow. In the
first twenty-two years of my married life I changed
stations twenty-three times, and at each post had to
refit anew. Looking back at my own experience I
can but wonder why any young man endowed with
ordinary business capacity, good habits, and reasonable ability should seek service in the United States
army. An old friend once said, "Love of glory took
me to West Point, and necessity has kept me in the
army." Frequent changes have their compensations
sometimes. One may be stationed at an out-of-the-

way post without any pleasant surroundings, so a change is looked for, as it may be for a better place, certainly it can be no worse. An occasional detail on detached service enables an officer to lay aside frontier drudgery for a while and revel in the comforts of civilized life, and few, if any, fail to enjoy, to the fullest extent, such opportunities. When they rejoin their regiments they enter upon their duties with renewed interest and zeal.

I really believe that the members of the human family suffer more from anticipated troubles than they do from the present ones with which they have to contend. In garrison some one will express the belief that the regiment is to be ordered to some disagreeable place to establish a new post. This thought spreads until it becomes almost real. How are we to get there, and how shall we get our furniture and household goods transported? And so they go on worrying over something that never comes. There would be a great deal more happiness in the world if every one would resolve on meeting trouble when it comes, and not before.

The present is ours, the future may never be. Then let every one meet the responsibilities of the present, and provide for future troubles and trials when they come. The world will be happier by so doing.

The winter passed, spring came, the ice disappeared from the river, the first boat arrived, and the time of my departure was at hand.

CHAPTER VI.

Trip to New Orleans—Simon, my Old Nurse—Green—Farming in Kentucky—On the Gulf—Cultivating Potatoes on Board of Ship—Fort Terrett—Colonel Bainbridge—Rattlesnakes—Turkey-Shooting—Iron and Nails—Quarters—Accidental Death of the Adjutant—Burning of Steamer "Louisiana"—Death of Colonel Bainbridge—S. D. Carpenter—His Death—Appointed Adjutant—"Major" Mills—Game—Panthers—Fort Terrett Abandoned.

THE first boat to reach St. Paul in the spring of 1852 was the "Key City." We had our trunks packed, and, bidding good-by to our friends, boarded the boat and began our long trip to New Orleans. Then there were no railroads, and the entire journey had to be made by the river. We reached St. Louis in due time, where we remained a few days, and then secured passage on the "Aleck Scott," a splendid boat, well officered and perfect in all its details. Captain Scott, the commander, had been a river man from boyhood, and what he did not know about river navigation was not worth knowing. His table was as well supplied as any hotel table at which I ever sat. The variety was great, and the articles were prepared in the highest style of the culinary art.

When five or six years old my father had among his slaves a boy by the name of Simon, about fifteen years old, whose duty it was to look after me and see that I did not fall in the well or get injured by going into dangerous places. From the time I arose in the morning until I retired at night Simon's eyes were ever upon me. Constant association begat a friendship which has not been lessened by the lapse of time. When he was about eighteen years old he became weary of home-life and asked my father to permit him to hire himself to a Captain Pease, who commanded a steamboat plying between Louisville and New Orleans. He entered the service of Captain Pease as a cabin-boy. When the boat stopped for an hour or so near our home he always came to see us, and was greeted as a friend and brother.

In the course of time he married a woman belonging to Captain Pease. My father tried to purchase her, but Pease would not sell; and, not wishing to separate husband and wife, a proposition was made to her owner to buy Simon, who had very naturally expressed a willingness to leave his old friends in order to be with his wife. The sale was made, after which I seldom had an opportunity of seeing my old friend and body-guard.

Years passed by, and I feared that he had fallen by the wayside, although I never failed to inquire about him of all persons from whom I thought I might gain any definite information in regard to his death, or, if alive, his whereabouts.

While on the "Aleck Scott" I visited the barber professionally. He was loquacious, as all barbers are. I asked him if he knew a colored man by the name of Simon on any of the boats running to New Orleans. "What," says he, "Simon Johnson?" "Yes," I replied. "Well, sir, he is the cook on this very boat." I hastened to the cook-house and made myself known to him. "What," said he, "can this be little Dick?"

On being assured that such was the case, he burst into tears and sobbed like a child. He had changed very much since I last saw him. From a small young man he had grown to be one weighing about three hundred and fifty pounds. When he had recovered himself sufficiently I asked him many questions and learned much of his life. He said, "Old Massa Johnson told me when I was a boy never to drink liquor, use tobacco, or swear, and I have through all these years followed his advice, although at times I have been sorely tempted to do all three of these. I can do almost anything any other man can do, except swim. I cannot swim a lick." I told him that my wife was on board, and he expressed a great desire to see her, and she was equally curious to see the friend of my childhood. It is needless to say that throughout the trip we were the recipients of many little delicacies prepared by his experienced hand not spread before the other passengers. From that time to this I have not seen him, but I trust that time has dealt kindly with him and that the good Lord has blessed him abundantly.

There was another slave owned by my father to whom I wish to make reference. One of our neighbors owned a woman who died ten days after the birth of her child. The infant was sick, and my father was called to attend it. The chances of its recovery were extremely doubtful. The owner said to my father, "Doctor, if you will give me a fur hat you may have that little negro." The offer was accepted and the child sent to our house. With proper care it soon recovered and grew to be a handsome boy, to whom the name of Green was given. The original owner seeing him on one occasion, and remembering that he had parted with him for a mere trifle, made another demand, and father gave him fifty dollars. This settled the title. The boy grew to be a fine-looking man, and had he received the benefit of a college education would have made a broad mark in this world.

All the negroes on our place, with capacity sufficient, were taught to read, as father believed it to be a duty to qualify each one for reading the Scriptures. Green could both read and write, and was passionately fond of books. In accordance with my father's will he, together with several others, were to be given their freedom when my younger brother reached his majority. He would have been a free man on the 8th day of June, 1850, but he died of cholera in the year 1849.

Slavery as it existed in Kentucky was not the slavery spoken of by Mrs. Harriet Beecher Stowe.

Slaves were allowed more liberty, were better fed and clothed, and they seemed to enjoy as much happiness as any portion of the human family. No one expected to make anything by farming beyond a comfortable living. The negroes raised corn, hogs ate the corn, and the negroes ate the hogs; and so it went in one continued round. Slavery no longer exists in the land, and the farther we get away from it the more hideous it seems. While it existed in the South the Southern people were hardly responsible for it. The slaves had been handed down from parents to children, and they represented just so much money, and few felt able to cut themselves loose from the degrading institution. But the country is freed from the disgrace, and all men North and South rejoice thereat.

In due time I reached New Orleans and put up at the Saint Charles, which at that time was second to no hotel in the country. In a few days I marched the recruits on board of the steamer "Fashion," commanded by Captain Baker, an old sea captain. The "Fashion" was an old craft, having been used as a government transport during the Mexican war. I hardly thought her seaworthy, but the voyage was safely made across the gulf to Indianola. On her next trip she was lost in a gale.

I noticed on the dinner-table every day curious Irish potatoes which appeared to have no skins on them. I was informed that they were raised on board the vessel and of course in the shade. The process was explained to me, and I give it here so that those who have no ground for the cultivation of this delicious esculent need not be deprived of them. Take an ordinary crate, such as is used in importing crockery, place in the bottom about six inches of straw, and in this straw place potatoes, or parts of potatoes, about six inches apart; then put on six inches more of straw, and then potatoes as before. Continue with straw and potatoes until the top of the crate is reached. Then wet thoroughly, and every day thereafter sprinkle a bucket of water over the top surface. In due time the harvest will be abundant, and as the new potatoes are required they can be taken out and will be found nice and clean and apparently without skins. At Indianola I was furnished with the necessary transportation for my command and began the march to San Antonio, which place I reached in six days.

On reporting at department headquarters I learned that the company to which I belonged, with three others, had been ordered to march to and establish a post at or near the headwaters of the Llano River, whither they had gone a month or so before. I followed up and finally reached the new camp and reported to Lieutenant-Colonel Bainbridge, the regimental and post commander. The recruits were distributed equally among the companies and my duty with them ceased.

Just why a post was established at this point no one ever knew, unless it was General Percifer F. Smith, the department commander, and he never revealed any of the reasons he may have had for doing so. We remained guests of Colonel Bainbridge and his most estimable wife for a few days, when we entered upon tent-keeping on our own account.

I had the underbrush cleared away in a small cedar grove and pitched two wall-tents, facing each other, and about ten feet apart. Between the tents stood a large cedar-tree, which, together with cedar-boughs carefully interlaced among the limbs, made a shade between the tents. One of these tents was our parlor, the other our bedroom, and the covered way between them was our dry-weather dining-room.

Here we had evidently trespassed upon the home and domain of various families of rattlesnakes, and it was several weeks before they were exterminated. One was killed just at the entrance into our sleeping apartment. It was really dangerous to go out after dark. Many were killed, and the noise probably drove others off, so that at last we were free from molestation from that source. The soil around the post was filled with fleas, which soon filled our tents and made our lives miserable. In order to get any sleep at night it was necessary to put the foot of each bed-post in a pan of water, stand on a chair to undress and to put on night-clothes, and from the chair jump into bed. In this way few of these little pests could become bedfellows, and consequently sleep was possible.

The country for miles around was devoid of timber, except some that skirted the streams. To these wild turkeys repaired every night to roost. Thousands of turkeys roosted every night within a mile of the post, and could be easily killed in any numbers required. Lieutenant S. B. Holabird, who was an excellent marksman, had a gun which carried a bullet a little smaller than a grape-shot. He would go to a roost and seek a position where he would have a dozen or more in range, and then blaze away, and the turkeys would fall like apples from a well-shaken tree. His fondness for shooting, coupled with his unerring aim, enabled him to keep not only his own family, but the families at the post well supplied with all kinds of game.

In the building of the post nothing but "iron and nails" was allowed, and the order was rigidly enforced. The troops had to cut logs, make shingles, quarry and lay stone, and, in fact, do all of the work necessary to house themselves and the officers. The company quarters were constructed of logs, and were the first erected. The officers' quarters were built of stone.

On November 8, 1852, I struck my tents and moved into my quarters, which was one room, about twenty feet square. This we divided by a curtain into a parlor and bedroom. A tent pitched near by answered for a dining-room, and one a little more remote was used for a kitchen. As the government refused us everything except iron and nails, the officers had to furnish, at their own expense, doors, sash, and glass. The floors were prepared for carpets by throwing in clay so as to raise the ground on the inside about a foot above that on the outside. This was levelled off and rammed down to make it firm and smooth. On this old papers were laid, upon which grain-sacks sewed together were placed, and on the grain-sacks the carpet was stretched. When our house was in order I remember how neat it looked, and there we were as comfortable, happy, and contented as any two mortals could possibly be.

On the arrival of the command at this place, the site was so gloomy that Colonel Bainbridge named it Camp Lugubrious. This somewhat offended the department commander, who directed it to be called Camp Bainbridge, which he said was synonymous. By this name it was known until the War Department designated it as Fort Terrett. Soon after my arrival, I was sent out with a detachment of men on foot to follow a party of mounted Indians which it was supposed would pass a certain point about a given time. Of course, we saw no Indians nor any indications of them. I was furnished with a saddle-horse for the trip, but it broke loose the first night out and returned to the post. I continued on foot, wearing a pair of thin boots, and on my return was so lame that several weeks elapsed before I was able to walk. The companies at Fort Terrett were commanded by Captains King, Granger, Carpenter, and Caldwell. King, Granger, and Caldwell, having reached the ripe old age of sixty-four years, are on the retired list. Lieutenant F. J. Denman was the regimental adjutant, and Lieutenant S. B. Holabird the regimental quartermaster. Lieutenant Denman lost his life near Fort Terrett March 2, 1853, by the accidental discharge of a gun. He was a general favorite, admired by all for his sterling worth as an officer and gentleman.

Colonel Bainbridge, one of nature's noblemen, has passed away, and his demise was attended by the most distressing circumstances. On the 31st of May, 1857, he was on board of the gulf steamer "Louisiana," out about nine miles from Galveston. The alarm of fire was given. He arose quickly, and occupied himself in arousing the other passengers, of whom there were one hundred and four. Of this number fifty-two were saved and fifty-two perished. Colonel Bainbridge was unfortunately lost. Some days afterwards his body washed ashore, and his limbs were drawn up as if in the act of swimming. It is supposed that a spasmodic contraction of his limbs was the cause of his drowning, for he was known to be an expert swimmer.

Carpenter was killed at the battle of Stone River. I saw him a few moments before he lost his life. He had his regiment, or battalion, drawn up immediately in the rear of a battery. He was not in my command, but I said to him, "Carpenter, why do you not post your regiment on the flanks of the battery? Do you not see that every shot fired at the battery will kill some of your men, whose lives might be saved by a judicious posting of them?" He replied, "I was sent to support this battery, and must do it." I did not have time to explain that, in my opinion, the supports of a battery should be on the flanks, to operate readily upon any charging column, before he received a fatal shot. He was a brave officer, and did his duty as he construed it, but, in my opinion, needlessly sacrificed his own life.

Among the lieutenants at the post I recall Huston, Underwood, Barton, and Reynolds. Huston attained the rank of lieutenant-colonel, and died a few years since. Underwood died before the war. Barton and Reynolds resigned and entered the Southern army, and both became general officers. Barton, one of the best friends I ever had, resides in Fredericksburg, Virginia, and Reynolds at some point in Missouri.

The death of Lieutenant Denman, previously referred to, caused a vacancy in the regimental staff,—that of adjutant,—and I was appointed to fill it. This appointment gratified me very much, for, aside from the compliment it conveyed, it increased my pay, and for these and other reasons I was more than thankful to Colonel Bainbridge, who conferred it. I entered upon the duty at once, and if I failed to make an efficient adjutant, it was not for want of strict attention to my duties and an earnest desire to be the friendly medium between the regimental commander and the officers of his regiment.

On taking possession of the office, I found Sergeant John Mills one of the principal musicians. His enlistment expired soon thereafter, and on re-enlisting him I found that he had served continuously for fifty years, being by far the oldest man in the regiment. He had seen the officers of the regiment changed throughout several times. So dignified was he that the soldiers always spoke of him as " Major Mills." Age had already impaired his physical energies to such an extent as to unfit him for the performance of his duty. With the consent of the regimental commander I told him that I would excuse him from all duty except such as he felt perfectly able to perform. At first he gave up attending reveille, then tattoo, and finally instruction to the drummers and fifers. After the passage of the law creating the retired-list he was appointed second lieutenant and placed thereon.

This gave him a competency, and his last days were passed in comfort, peace, and quiet. He was not married, and, as far as I know, had no friends dependent upon him. His life was so simple, so dignified, and proper, that he had the respect of every member of the regiment. He died during the war, at the ripe old age of ninety years or thereabouts, thus severing the link which bound the rising generation to one long passed away.

The country around Fort Terrett abounded with game, such as turkeys, before referred to, deer, antelope, and bear, a sure indication that the Indians had not been in the habit of frequenting that region. Wherever they go they kill or scare away the game.

The panther is common to the hills of that district of country, and they know how to subsist themselves without much effort. Deer and antelope, as a general thing, get drinking-water at about the same place every day, and in going to and from the water generally follow the same trail. The panther conceals himself at some point on the trail near the water, and when the unsuspecting deer or antelope comes within his reach he springs upon it, and there is no escape. He drags the carcass off, eats all he desires, and conceals the remainder, to be devoured when hunger overtakes him. The panther never kills for the amusement it furnishes, but only for the food he craves at the time. Once, while on a scout, I came upon the carcass of a deer still warm which had been killed by a panther, and although diligent search was made for the beast by forty or more men, he eluded us and made good his escape.

Once, when out in search of marauding Indians, I encamped on a sluggish stream skirted with timber. I permitted two of my men to go out hunting, hoping that they might kill some game, and thus relieve us for a while from the use of salt meat. After going some distance they separated. One of the men becoming weary lay down under a tree to rest, and on looking up he saw an immense panther on a limb above him. It was preparing to spring. A moment more and he expected to be devoured. Suddenly a shot was fired, and down fell the beast to the ground. It appeared that the other soldier, not knowing where his friend was, happened to look up and saw the panther preparing to spring. Taking good aim he fired, the ball passing through the heart, and the monster died instantly. Thus was saved the life of one soldier, and possibly both. It was the largest one I ever saw. I gave one of its claws to General Albert Sidney Johnston, and asked him to carry it "for luck." He did so for several years to my knowledge, and I doubt not he had it in his pocket when he fell on the field of Shiloh.

The utter folly involved in the establishment of Fort Terrett was discovered, and its abandonment ordered in September, 1853, the troops composing the garrison being returned to the Rio Grande. Regimental headquarters were established at Fort Duncan. Transportation was furnished for the movement, and the command marched by the way of San Antonio. In changing posts there is always inconvenience to the ladies, as often they have to be crowded into the public ambulances. To avoid this I always owned a private conveyance, so, when a movement was ordered, I was always ready to transport my family without any annoyance whatever. While on the march my wife and our child, only six months old, together with the nurse, occupied a tent, while I occupied the ambulance as a sleeping-apartment. A storm arose one night, the rain descended in torrents, the winds howled, the tent blew over, and there my wife sat in the merciless storm, protecting with her body the little boy to save him from drowning. I knew nothing of this until the storm subsided, when I had a large fire built to dry out our worldly goods, all of which were as wet as if they had been submerged in the river for a week. By the time the command was ready to go forward we were prepared to move with it. In due time we reached our destination.

CHAPTER VII.

Return to Fort Duncan—Lieutenant P. H. Sheridan—Lieutenant W. B. Lane and Family—Hail-Storm—Appointed to Second Cavalry—Organization of Regiment—Colonel Bainbridge's Order—Regimental Quartermaster Second Cavalry—At Jefferson Barracks—Ladies' Styles changed—Short in Property Account.

I FOUND Fort Duncan about the same as when I left it before, possibly a little more dilapidated. The old quarters were rapidly going to decay, and no new ones had been constructed. Now there were ten companies at the post, eight of infantry, one of artillery, and one of mounted rifles. The artillery company was commanded by Captain J. B. Ricketts, who subsequently became a distinguished general officer in the Army of the Potomac, where he lost a leg while gallantly leading his command into one of the many battles in which he participated. At present he is on the retired list of the army. Lieutenant H. E. Maynadier was a lieutenant in his company. The company of mounted rifles was commanded by Captain John G. Walker, who subsequently joined the forces of the South and rose to the rank of major-general. Lieutenants E. A. Carr and W. M. Davant were on duty with that company. Carr was a gallant brigadier-general in the Union army, and did good service throughout the war. Davant, in attempting to ford the Rio Grande on horseback, was carried away by the treacherous current and drowned October 1, 1855. He was just from West Point, and a young officer of great promise. Surgeon George E. Cooper was the medical officer at the post, and a very successful practitioner. Every one had great confidence in his ability, and felt sure that in case of sickness they would have the very best attention. This was the largest command with which I had ever served. Lieutenant Philip H. Sheridan was at the post, and was an active, enterprising young officer, prompt in the discharge of his duty, always ready for any undertaking that promised adventure, but if any one had been called upon to select from the lieutenants at the post the future lieutenant-general of the army, I doubt if he would have been chosen in preference to any one of the dozen lieutenants at Fort Duncan. No one saw in the modest lieutenant the future able and gallant leader which he proved himself to be when the time came for him to show his mettle and his manhood.

Men who never reach the summit of their professions always claim a want of opportunities as an excuse. Sheridan made his opportunities as he went along. He did not wait for something to turn up, but he turned up something every day. I remember him as a commander of a division in the same corps. When we would reach camp he would give his personal attention to locating his troops; then, mounting his horse, he would be off for the surrounding hills to view the country and familiarize himself with the neighborhood roads, etc. He rarely ever returned before dark, and when he retired for the night was well informed in regard to the position of the enemy and the avenues by which he could be reached. It was this habit that made him ever ready to fight a battle or pursue a fleeing foe.

Knowing the scarcity of accommodations at Fort Duncan, and the certainty that my rank would only entitle me to a place under some mesquite-tree, I procured a hospital tent, for which I gave my official receipt. I had this tent pitched over a frame, a fireplace built, and stretching our ever-useful curtain to divide the space into two rooms, we had reasonably good quarters, which could not be taken by any officer senior in rank. Now, when I recall the miserable hovel in which we lived, I am forced to the belief that happiness is relative,—that is, if we are as well off as our neighbors, if we live in as good quarters and wear as fine apparel as they do, then we are happy and contented. But if our neighbors dress in purple and fine linen and live in large, handsome houses, and we cannot do so, then it is that poverty becomes painfully apparent, and envy and jealousy entering into our hearts make us dissatisfied with our lot and therefore unhappy. We never care for a luxury until we see some one else with it. I recall the fact that we were happy and contented, and the further fact that our accommodations were as good as those of our neighbors. During the summer Captain W. B. Lane and family came to our post, and we invited them to accept our hospitality. I had a wall-tent pitched near my own, which they occupied at night. In all other respects we could easily accommodate them. They were agreeable people, and we enjoyed their visit, although we regretted our inability to do more for them. A short time since I met Lane, who is now colonel, and his wife in Washington, and they referred to our "kind hospitality which they could never forget." I mention this little incident in verification of what I have already said, that all matters of this kind are relative. They got the best we had and the best they could get at the post, and they were contented and happy. These good people were a source of great pleasure to us, and we enjoyed their brief stay very much, breaking, as it did, the indescribable monotony of garrison life. On a certain occasion we had invited a number of friends to dine with us on the following day. In the afternoon a severe hail-storm passed over the post. My wife had the servants out at once to gather up as much of the hail as possible. This she had tenderly cared for, and on the following day placed ice-cream before our guests, probably the first ever made in that part of Texas, certainly the first I had ever seen in the State.

Winter with its chilling blasts was soon upon us, and then for long weary months we had to endure the dust and the heart-chilling northers.

As for promotion, the future looked dull and dreary. I had then occupied the position of senior second lieutenant about two years with no prospect for promotion. Officers rarely ever died, and none felt that the government could get along without them, and hence there were no resignations. During the session of Congress that winter a bill was introduced to increase the army by two regiments of cavalry and two of infantry. I doubted if the bill would pass, and if it did pass, I had no political influence to bring to bear to secure advancement. My friends were not the political friends of the administration, and I did not even apply through the official channels for promotion. Hence I expected nothing, but to follow along in the same old dusty trail which I had been following for six years.

The mail arrived at the post every Thursday afternoon. The officers were generally at the post-office waiting for it. A letter was handed to me from the War Department, which I hastily opened, and it read as follows:

WAR DEPARTMENT,
March 20, 1855.

SIR:

You are hereby informed that the President of the United States has appointed you First Lieutenant in the Second Regiment of "Cavalry" (authorized by the Act approved March 3, 1855, section 8) in the service of the United States, to rank as such from the third day of March, one thousand eight hundred and fifty-five.

You will, immediately on receipt hereof, please to communicate to this Department, through the Adjutant-General's Office, your acceptance or non-acceptance of said appointment; and, in case of accepting, you will receive further instructions from the Adjutant-General of the Army.

JEFFER. DAVIS,
Secretary of War.

To FIRST LIEUTENANT RICHARD W. JOHNSON,
   Second Regiment of Cavalry,
Fort Duncan, Eagle Pass, Texas.

Accompanying this letter was the following order:

WAR DEPARTMENT, ADJUTANT-GENERAL'S OFFICE,
WASHINGTON, March 26, 1855.

General Orders, No. 4.

I. Organization of the four regiments added to the military establishment by the 8th section of the Act, "making appropriations for the support of the Army for the year ending the thirtieth of June, one thousand eight hundred and fifty-six, and for other purposes," approved March 3, 1855; and order of precedence and relative rank of the officers of each grade, as fixed by the War Department. All the officers will take rank in their respective grades from March 3, 1855.

* * * * * * * *

SECOND REGIMENT OF CAVALRY.

No.	Names and Rank.	Co.	Brevets and former Commissions.	Born in.	App't'd from.
	Colonel.				
	Albert S. Johnston........		....	Ky.	Texas.
	Lieut.-Col.				
	Robert E. Lee.............		Col. bvt., 13 Sept., '47.	Va.	Va.
	Majors.				
	William J. Hardee........		Lt.-col. bvt., 20 Aug., '47.	Ga.	Ga.
	William H. Emory........		Maj. bvt., 9 Jan., '47.	Md.	Md.
	Captains.				
	Earl Van Dorn............	A	Maj. bvt., 20 Aug., '47.	Miss.	Miss.
	Edmund K. Smith........	B	Capt. bvt., 20 Aug., '47.	Fla.	Fla.
	James Oakes..............	C	Capt. bvt., 8 Sept., '47.	Pa.	Pa.
	Innis N. Palmer..........	D	Capt. bvt., 13 Sept., '47.	N. Y.	N. Y.
	George Stoneman, Jr.....	E	....	N. Y.	N. Y.
	Theodore O'Hara.........	F	....	Ky.	Ky.
	William R. Bradfute.....	G	....		Tenn.
	Charles E. Travis........	H	....		Texas.
	Albert G. Brackett.......	I	....		Ind.
	Charles J. Whiting.......	K	....		Cal.
	1st Lieuts.				
3	Nathan G. Evans.........	F	....	S. C.	S. C.
6	Richard W. Johnson.....	G	....	Ky.	Ky.
10	Joseph H. McArthur.....	H	....	Mo.	Mo.
15	Charles W. Field.........	I	....	Ky.	Ky.
20	Kenner Garrard...........	K	....	Ky.	Ohio.
21	Walter H. Jenifer........	B	....	Md.	Md.
23	William B. Royall........	C	....		Mo.
24	Alexander H. Cross......	A	....	D. C.	D. C.
29	William P. Chambliss...	D	....		Tenn.
39	Robert Nelson Eagle.....	E	....		Texas.
	2d Lieuts.				
3	John T. Shaaf.............	I	Bvt., 1 July, '51.	D. C.	D. C.
6	George B. Cosby..........	A	Bvt., 1 July, '52.	Ky.	Ky.
11	George B. Anderson.....	G	Bvt., 1 July, '52.	N. C.	N. C.
16	Nelson B. Sweitzer.......	H	Bvt., 1 July, '53.	Pa.	Pa.
18	William W. Lowe........	K	Bvt., 1 July, '53.	Ind.	Iowa.
21	Edwin R. Merrifield.....	C	....		Mich.
25	George Hartwell..........	D	....		Wis.
29	Joseph Minter.............	E	....		W. T.
33	Charles W. Phifer........	F	....	Tenn.	Miss.
37	Robert C. Wood, Jr......	B	....	Min.	La.

* * * * * * * *

II. The relative rank of the First and Second Lieutenants of the four additional regiments is indicated by the number prefixed to the name in each grade respectively.

III. The two regiments of Cavalry will be regarded as a distinct arm, and promotions therein be regulated accordingly. . . .

IV. The foregoing assignment of the *subalterns* to companies is intended only as a temporary arrangement. The Colonels will make any changes therein which they may deem conducive to the interests of their regiments.

V. The Headquarters of the . . . Second Regiment of Cavalry will be established at Louisville, Kentucky. . . . The recruiting for the new regiments will be conducted under the superintendence of their Colonels, to whom all the officers appointed will, accordingly, immediately report, by letter, giving their address, and suggesting the places in the neighborhood where recruiting rendezvous could probably be opened to the best advantage.

VI. The four additional regiments will be uniformed and equipped as follows:

I. The 1st and 2d regiments of Cavalry as the present regiments of Dragoons, except the trimmings of the cap and coat, which will be yellow instead of orange.

* * * * * * * *

By order of the Secretary of War.

(Sgd.) S. COOPER,
Adjutant-General.

On receipt of the foregoing orders I gave up the position of adjutant, recommending as my successor my friend Lieutenant Seth M. Barton, who was duly appointed. The post commander issued the following order:

HEADQUARTERS FIRST INFANTRY,
FORT DUNCAN, TEXAS.

Orders, 1st May, 1855.
No. 23.

I. Lieut. R. W. Johnson having this day relinquished the duties of Adjutant of the regiment, it is with pride and much pleasure that the Comm^{dg}. Officer tenders to him his acknowledgments for the correct manner he has performed the duties of staff officer, as well as for his exemplary conduct and uniform gentlemanly deportment towards all with whom he has had official intercourse. Altho' it is to be regretted that the services of Lt. Johnson are lost to this regiment, nevertheless, the commanding officer congratulates him on his advanced promotion in a new corps, and extends to him his best wishes for his future military and social prosperity.

II. Until orders arrive withdrawing Lt. Johnson from this post, he will perform the duties of Ordnance Officer under the commanding officer. H. BAINBRIDGE,
Lt. Col. 1st Inft.,
Commdg.

My unlooked-for advancement was a source of great gratification, as it opened up a new life for me. Under the old order of things I hardly hoped to be a captain before I was fifty years old; now it seemed almost within my grasp. Among so many captains ahead of me, taken from the walks of civil life, surely two would find the service distasteful to them within a year or so and resign. In this event I would be a captain before I was thirty years of age.

A few days after the receipt of the notice of my appointment I received an order to proceed to Louisville, Kentucky, and report in person to Colonel Albert Sidney Johnston. I left Fort Duncan with my family and proceeded to St. Louis, where I transferred its members to a small steamboat, the only size that could, on account of low water, reach St. Paul. Seeing them safely off, I proceeded to Louisville on the steamboat "Baltimore." My wife was sixteen days in reaching her friends in St. Paul; the miserable little craft she was on broke some of its machinery every day, and at

Rock Island it was drawn out on the dry-dock for repairs.

I should mention that, having been on the frontier so long, the styles for ladies had undergone such a complete change that when we reached New Orleans my wife did not consider herself presentable in public. So, taking rooms at the St. Charles, we occupied them until the services of dress- and bonnet-makers had been secured. I could not imagine it possible for such changes in bonnets. The stylish bonnet she wore when we first went to Texas looked like a Conestoga wagon compared with the style of 1855, and the dresses —well, they bore no resemblance whatever to those worn when we went to the Texas frontier.

I reported to Colonel Johnston on the 12th day of June, and was tendered the position of regimental quartermaster, which I accepted with thanks, although I should have preferred the position of adjutant, with the duties of which office I was perfectly familiar. In an old regiment, where each officer knows his duties and his rights under the regulations, a regimental quartermaster can easily acquire a knowledge of his duties, but in this case I had to learn not only my own duties, but teach a good many others the duties devolving upon them. In old regiments the officers and men know that the public property in the hands of the quartermaster has been receipted for, and that he is held individually, personally, and officially responsible for it, but where many of the officers and all the men are new and without experience, they seem to imagine that public property belongs to any one who can get possession of it. I had to be constantly on the alert, otherwise I would have been lamentably behind when I had to account for the property for which I was responsible. As men were enlisted for the regiment they were sent to Jefferson Barracks for instruction. I was ordered to take post at that place and not only perform the duties of quartermaster and commissary, but also those of depot quartermaster. In these latter duties I relieved Lieutenant O. H. P. Taylor. To go through all the property at that depot and count every article seemed to me to be almost an endless undertaking, but I went through all the store-rooms, with the exception of the upper story of one of the storehouses. I was informed that there was nothing on that floor except old-style clothing, which had been counted and carefully packed away many years before, and that it was not considered necessary to overhaul it; that it had not been disturbed by the various quartermasters for ten years. I did not think that any one would care to purloin such old trash, and therefore I receipted to Taylor for it. Everything went along smoothly, but when the regiment was ordered away Lieutenant Charles H. Tyler was ordered to relieve me of the depot duties, who, from curiosity or prudential reasons, expressed a desire to look through the contents on that floor. Then it was that I found I had made a mistake, just such an one as Taylor had made, but he was lucky in not being responsible when the shortage was discovered. I could not ask for a board of survey to exonerate me, for I had been negligent of my duty, and hence I made the shortage good. The loss was not great, but it taught me a lesson, which I ever remembered, *to receipt for nothing that I did not see.*

Every young officer should bear this in mind, and govern himself accordingly.

I believe that it was General D. E. Twiggs who said that a quartermaster had only two duties to perform,—

1. Make himself comfortable.
2. Make every one else as uncomfortable as possible.

I think the officers of my old regiment would give me credit for doing all that I could for their comfort and that of their men. At all events, I am sure that I did not regard myself as the owner, in fee, of the property of the government placed in my possession for the use and benefit of the officers and soldiers of the regiment to which I belonged.

CHAPTER VIII.

Purchase of Horses—Mounting an Unbroken Horse—Ben McCulloch—Death of Lieutenant Witherell—Frightful Wound—Captain Chambliss—Brevet Lieutenant-Colonel W. J. Hardee—Regiment ordered to Texas—Lieutenant C. W. Field—Bad Roads—Sick—Fording Canadian—Captain Bradfute and "Bow-Legs"—Lunch at Fort Washita—Horse Race—My Wife's Stove—Captain C. J. Whiting—Arrival at Fort Belknap—Loss of a Fine Horse—At Fort Mason—Out of Bread—No Quarters—Posts of Companies—Captain at Last.

THE colonel of the Second Cavalry was authorized to send a board, composed of his own officers, to Kentucky and elsewhere to purchase horses. No limit was placed on the price to be paid, and the result was that no regiment in the army ever had such a magnificent mount. The very best horses were purchased, and, after all, they are the cheapest, for a first-class horse will last longer and do more hard work than those purchased by the quartermaster's department at a fixed price. The board was composed of experienced officers who had long served in the old dragoons, and they knew good horses when they saw them and bought no inferior ones. The company to which I succeeded as captain was furnished with eighty-five of these fine Kentucky horses; and after constant service for six years forty-four of them were serviceable when General Twiggs surrendered the troops in 1861. When these horses were received at

Jefferson Barracks I had to receipt and be responsible for them, and for their care until they were assigned to the companies. Once, on going out to the picket-line, I noticed two soldiers, both Irishmen, doing something with one of the horses. I halted to see what they were trying to do. It seems that the horse was wild and would not stand to be mounted. They covered his head with a blanket and tried and failed. One of the men stepped up on the body of a large tree, which had been felled, and instructed the other to back the horse up to him, when he would place his hands on the croup and spring into position. This was successful. The man who held the horse said, "By the Holy Moses, I never saw a man get on a horse that way befoour." The other replied, "Go way, you fool, I did not get on him 'befoour'; I got on him behind." And so he did.

Ben McCulloch, of Texas, was appointed major of the First Cavalry and Captain W. H. Emory major of the Second. McCulloch had a more exalted opinion of his military qualifications than the War Department. He felt aggrieved because he was not appointed to the command of one of these regiments, and would not accept a majority. Emory was transferred from the Second to the First, and Captain George H. Thomas, of the Third Artillery, was appointed major and assigned to the Second Cavalry. Second Lieutenant Merrifield, of Michigan, declined to accept, and James B. Witherell, of the same State, was appointed in his stead. Several other changes were made before the regiment was thoroughly organized. Witherell was a promising young man, who lost his life by getting out of his berth on one of the gulf steamers while asleep and walking overboard. His body was never recovered. It is interesting to notice the composition of the regiment as first made up. Of the officers, twenty-three were appointed from the Southern and ten from the Northern States. It has been often asserted that this was done purposely by Mr. Jefferson Davis, the Secretary of War, expecting that at the proper time the regiment would go as an organization to the Confederate army. This was six years before the beginning of the war, and a little too early for any one to predict with any degree of certainty the supreme folly of a war between the sections. Southern and Western men are accustomed to horseback riding, and the War Department evidently acted upon the thought that better cavalrymen could be procured from those two sections. The Northern States, if memory serves me correctly, had a majority of the officers in the two infantry regiments organized at the same time. Fifteen of the original appointments from the South became general officers in the Confederate army, and the regiment furnished the Union army with seven, two of whom were from the South,—George H. Thomas and myself. Four others—McArthur, Royall, Chambliss, and Eagle—were from the South and were gallant and faithful soldiers, two of whom— Royall and Chambliss—ought to have been appointed general officers. McArthur's health failed early in the war, and Eagle resigned January, 1862. Now, of the twenty-three appointed from the South it is seen that six of them remained loyal to the United States government.

Royall received a dangerous sabre-cut on the head which came near terminating his life. At the battle of Gaines' Mill, on the 27th day of June, 1862, Chambliss was wounded six times while gallantly leading his command in a charge, left on the field for dead, but through the kindness of an old friend, General John B. Hood, was taken to Richmond and tenderly cared for until exchanged. His recovery was almost a miracle. One of his wounds was frightful. Few men have had his opportunities for investigating their own internal anatomy.

Major Hardee (brevet lieutenant-colonel) was ordered to take post at Jefferson Barracks to supervise the drilling of the officers and men of the regiment. He was thorough in his knowledge of the tactics, and seemed to take great delight in teaching others. A position under him was not a sinecure, for when the officers were not drilling their own troops he had officers' drill. Between drilling their companies, reciting tactical lessons, or being drilled in the manual of the sabre and carbine, there was no leisure time for any one from reveille to tattoo. As quartermaster I was exempt from this class of duties, but preferred to take part in them so as to familiarize myself with the cavalry tactics. As soon as the regiment was fully organized, and the officers and men were reasonably well posted in their duties, we received the following order:

HEADQUARTERS OF THE ARMY,
NEW YORK, September 27, 1855.

General Orders,
No. 5.
The following movement of troops will immediately be made:

1. The Second Regiment of Cavalry at Jefferson Barracks will proceed, by easy marches across the country, to Fort Belknap, Texas, to be there disposed of by the Commanding General of the Department of Texas, who will make timely arrangements for stationing the regiment on its arrival within his command. The Commanding General of the Department of the West will give the necessary orders for the march of the regiment to Fort Belknap.

*   *   *   *   *   *   *   *

By command of Brevet Lieutenant-General Scott.

(Sgd.) L. THOMAS,
Assistant Adjutant-General.

I was required to make out a requisition for transportation for the regiment, and on the supposition that each company would have to take a supply of clothing, camp and garrison equipage, I estimated that it would require one hundred and twenty-nine six-mule teams for the use of the regiment and one ambulance to transport any sick we might have on the march. This requisition was approved by Colonel Johnston and forwarded for the approval of the War Department. The Secretary of War considered the estimate excessive and cut it down just one hundred wagons, or, in other words, allowed us twenty-nine wagons and one ambulance. All company property, the surplus baggage of the officers, and the company laundresses were sent by water to Indianola, Texas, and Lieutenant J. H. McArthur was placed in charge of this singular collection. Mules, wagons, and harness were supplied and the necessary teamsters detailed from the companies, to whom was issued a complete outfit. All things being in readiness, the colonel issued his order for the movement to begin, and on the 27th day of October, 1855, the regiment started out on its long journey. The mules were young and unbroken to a great extent, and consequently our progress was necessarily slow. Duty generally required me with the train, so Lieutenant C. W. Field was detailed to go ahead each day, select a proper camping-ground, and provide forage. This duty he always performed satisfactorily to the regimental commander, as he never failed to have the forage on the ground by the time the troops arrived.

The rainy season was upon us and the roads became fearfully heavy, so that often I could not get the train in before dark, although the teams belonging to the headquarters, which always went at the head of the train, generally reached camp with the column. Four ladies accompanied their husbands on this march, being the wives of Colonel Johnston, Captain Oakes, Captain Palmer, and my own. Each lady was furnished by her husband with a carriage-ambulance, conveniently constructed so that the seats and their backs, when laid down, formed a good bed upon which to sleep, if the non-arrival of the teams made it necessary. When I recall the difficulty we had in getting twenty-nine wagons along, I can see the great wisdom in reducing my estimate. The trip was made in two months, and if we had a train of one hundred and twenty-nine wagons it would have required twice that length of time. At some time during the night I always succeeded in getting the train up, with one exception, and on that occasion the teams were mired, the wagons were down to the hubs, the night was dark, and it was just simply impossible to move. I directed the teamsters to unharness, feed, and encamp for the night.

I rode forward to camp and reported to Colonel Johnston. Next morning, at six o'clock, he called at my tent to instruct me to return and hasten the train forward. My wife informed him that I had gone back at three o'clock. After that he never thought it necessary to give himself any concern in regard to the duties devolving upon me.

By nine o'clock I had every team in camp, where we remained all day to rest the mules, so that they would be better able to continue the march the following day. When I recall the hardships, vexations, and annoyances which I had to endure and overcome, I pity a quartermaster who has to conduct a large train through a country so much of which is underlaid with quicksand. For the first month out it rained almost every day, and I was wet "to the skin" every time it rained. Exposure brought on sickness, and I continued to grow worse until finally I had to give up and take to my ambulance. I could not turn over my responsibility to any one on the march, so I asked that Lieutenant N. G. Evans might be detailed to assist me. I gave him the key to the safe and he disbursed the money and took charge of all of my duties. I was so sick that it was thought advisable to leave me at some frontier town in Missouri. To this I would not consent, preferring to accompany the regiment to being left to the care of some country physician. With the seats laid down I occupied one side of the ambulance and my wife and two little boys occupied the other. With careful nursing I soon began to improve, and finally resumed my proper duties. I found that Evans had been remarkably careful in his disbursements, as I knew he would be, and my cash balanced to a cent, while all the property for which I was responsible was duly accounted for. I knew Evans well, and was never associated with a more honorable, companionable gentleman. He died since the war in South Carolina, his native State.

One night the regiment encamped on the Canadian River, and Colonel Johnston directed Captain Bradfute to accompany me in search of a crossing-place for the command. The water was not deep anywhere, but the river was wide, and there were quicksands in the bottom. In crossing such a stream it must be done in a hurry, for if there is a halt the horses go down at once. We found what we took to be a splendid ford, and on the following morning, when we pulled out of camp, Bradfute, mounted on his favorite horse, "Bow-Legs," conducted the head of the column to the proper place. When he reached the river "Bow-Legs" refused to enter. Closing the spurs upon him, he plunged in and went out of sight, but soon came to the surface and swam to the shore. In passing over that place the evening before, the movements of the feet of our horses had put the sand in motion, and the result was the formation of a deep hole where shallow water previously existed.

In crossing this stream many buffaloes have lost their lives. If they ever stopped to drink—and many would do so—the sands would wash from under them, and they would sink so deep that they could not extricate themselves, and would of course die of starvation. As far as we could see above and below our crossing, which was safely effected, the bleached bones of the head with horns attached were to be seen in great numbers.

We had to pass through Fort Washita, and the exact time of our arrival was known, so Mr. Samuel Humes, the post-sutler, had a bountiful repast in readiness for the officers of the regiment, to which he had invited the officers of the garrison and the visiting officers who were there in attendance upon the sessions of a general court-martial. There must have been fifty officers to partake of his hospitality on that day. Many of these officers I had known before, and when the champagne began to flow a more jolly set of fellows I do not remember to have ever seen. I do not wish to be understood as saying that there was an excessive use of champagne, for such was not the case, but sparkling wine always develops wit and good humor among gentlemen.

With cavalrymen a discussion in regard to the fleetness of the horse is always in order. Evans had a thoroughbred Glencoe colt, which he named "Bumble-Bee." He had purchased him from a fine stable in Kentucky, and always boasted that he could outrun any horse in the regiment, or the picked horse at Fort Washita, a proposition that any one would accept in regard to the Washita horses, as there were none at the post except those belonging to a light battery. It should be remembered that horses for artillery purposes are selected more for their fitness as draught animals than for the turf. Lieutenant O. D. Greene (now general) became somewhat annoyed at Evans's boasting and bragging, and he offered to run a battery horse against his celebrated charger. The race was made up, conditioned that each officer should ride his own horse. The word go was given, and "Bumble-Bee" dashed forward like the wind, and, of course, won the race, as every one supposed he would. I have always admired Greene's pluck in not allowing Evans to go unchallenged.

We passed a few days at the fort, and then reluctantly bade the good fellows good-by, and resumed our march. On the evening of December 23 we encamped on a beautiful prairie. The air was as soft and balmy as spring. Our tent was pitched to the north to catch any cooling breezes coming from that quarter. During the night a norther came upon us, and it was the severest one I had ever witnessed. Water froze in our tents. So intense was the cold and so fierce the wind that Colonel Johnston determined not to move forward on the following day. My wife and children remained in bed as the only place where they could be at all comfortable, while the cook and myself attempted to get breakfast. About noon there was a lull in the storm, and I had the tent repitched, facing southerly.

On the following morning it was "bitter cold," but the command moved out and made a short day's march. On the 27th day of December we reached Fort Belknap, having been just two months on the march. Here we encamped in the brush without sufficient fuel, and the suffering was very great, not only with the men, but with our animals. I had a very fine horse which was tied to a small sapling near my tent. In his frantic endeavor to find the warm side of that bush he kept going around it, winding up the halter-strap, until he could go no farther; then in his struggles to free himself he broke his neck. He was an unusually fast walker, being able to walk five miles an hour. I felt his loss very keenly, for I could not replace him at any price.

My wife, who was a good campaigner, conceived the idea before we left Jefferson Barracks that a small sheet-iron stove could be used advantageously on the march, and while I did not think favorably of it, yet I had one made according to her instructions. We would set it up inside of the tent and put the pipe out in front near the front tent-pole. This was really a great comfort, although the front of the tent had to be kept open. On one occasion Captain C. J. Whiting made us a visit, and suggested an improvement. It was to rip a seam of the tent about eight inches and open it as wide as possible, stitch a tin plate to the tent, so as to cover the opening, and then make a round hole in the centre of it just large enough for the stove-pipe. He did it himself, and after that we got the full benefit of the radiating surface of the little stove. With dry wood we could make it red hot in a few moments, and when we were about to break camp it was taken out first and emptied, and by the time the tent was taken down and rolled up the little heater would be cold enough to pack in the wagon. Her pocket stove, as I termed it, was afterwards imitated, and became very popular in the regiment.

A few days after the regiment arrived at Fort Belknap an order was received from the headquarters of the Department of Texas, directing the colonel to send Major Hardee with four companies to establish a camp near the Indian reservation on the Clear Fork of the Brazos, and to proceed with the remaining six companies to old Fort Mason. Hardee arrived at his post January 3, and the colonel, with the six companies, reached Fort Mason on the 14th. With the timely notice given to the department commander, it was reasonable to suppose that we would find provisions and stores at Fort Mason, but such was not the case. The only bread that the officers and troops could get was made of corn crushed in a mortar. Such food, in time of war, is admissible, but in a time of profound peace such culpable neglect should have secured the punishment by court-martial of the guilty party. This condition of things continued to exist until the already jaded teams were despatched to San Antonio. In due time they returned, freighted with provisions, and about the same time a wagon-train arrived, bringing up the company property which had been sent from Jefferson Barracks.

There were not sufficient quarters at Fort Mason for the officers and the troops. Colonel Johnston took possession of a building, being two rooms connected by a covered way between them, but was too unselfish to occupy the entire building. He kindly asked me to occupy one of the rooms with my family. The passageway between his apartments and mine was used in common, as we entered our respective rooms from it. It occurred to him that if the passage-way was closed in it would give him another room, and he directed me to have it done. It did not occur to him then, and probably never did, that the closing up of the passage-way would compel me to egress and ingress through a window. I soon had this, however, converted into a door, and enclosed the back porch for a dining-room. The front room we used for a bed-chamber, parlor, and library all combined, and while the accommodations were decidedly limited, yet they were so far superior to anything we had had since leaving Jefferson Barracks that we felt quite comfortable indeed.

While the march to this post had veteranized both officers and men, Colonel Johnston never allowed a day to pass at Fort Mason that the companies were not out for drill. Soon scouting-parties were sent out at regular intervals, so that a company or detachment was absent all the time. Some of these commands overtook roving bands of Indians, and never failed to punish them severely. All the officers were young and ambitious, and the enterprise and energy displayed by them soon established a fine name for the regiment, and convinced the Indians that they could not depredate upon the people of the frontier with impunity.

Colonel Johnston was placed in command of the Department of Texas on April 1, 1856, and after that, I believe, he never served with his regiment. From commanding the Department of Texas he was assigned to the command of the Utah expedition, and subsequently to that of the Department of California.

He was one of the most unselfish men I ever knew, and one of the most just and considerate to those under his command. The officers of the regiment not only respected but loved him. His desire to make the Second Cavalry the finest regiment in the army was seconded by every officer of whatever rank under his command.

For the better protection of the frontier the companies of the regiment were distributed, about June, to various parts of the State, as follows: Companies A (Van Dorn's) and F (O'Hara's) were detached to form a camp near the Colorado River. Companies B (E. K. Smith's) and G (Bradfute's) were to remain at Fort Mason. Company C (Oake's) was ordered to Fort Clark. Company D (Palmer's) to Camp Verde, Company K (Whiting's) to Fort Inge, and Company I (Brackett's) to Camp Sabinal. The regimental headquarters remained at Fort Mason. With such a small command, the duties imposed upon the regimental quartermaster were very light. Some time in August Captain O'Hara, of Company F, sent in his resignation, to take effect December 1. On that date, therefore, I was entitled to promotion, Evans having been promoted by the resignation of Captain Travis. On September 30 I forwarded my resignation as regimental quartermaster, so as to be able to transfer all public property in my possession, and make up all of my returns in time to permit me to assume command of my company on the very day I was promoted. Lieutenant J. F. Minter succeeded me, and to him I transferred all my public responsibilities.

Since my connection with the Second I had been little more than a wagon-master, employed to discharge duties which might have been performed by a citizen. When I laid aside the duties of that office, which I never liked, I felt as if I was entering the military service for the second time. I removed my family to

Camp Colorado, and entered enthusiastically upon the legitimate duties of an officer and soldier. I had reached that rank which would ever exempt me from duty with mules, broken harness, and the accumulated trash and rubbish which drift into the storehouses in charge of a post quartermaster.

I had been with my company only two weeks when Major Van Dorn ordered me to proceed on a scout to the head-waters of the North Concho. Rationing my command for twenty days, I moved out on the 18th. Lieutenant A. Parker Porter, who had just joined Van Dorn's company from West Point, was directed to accompany me. Whenever Van Dorn sent a command out from his post, he invariably furnished the commander with a rough map of the country, drawn by himself, and with such notes as he thought might be of service. On this occasion I had such a map. About the place he indicated I struck the North Concho and then coursed up it. The weather was cold and the fuel scarce, only a light fringe of small growth of willow along the edge of the stream. I made short marches, and when we encamped for the night the men would catch the greatest quantity of fish, more than sufficient for the use of the command.

On December 21 I encamped about five miles from the head spring of the river. Up to this time no indications of Indians had been seen, and I was about determined to retrace my steps, but, on looking at my little map, I found that Van Dorn had written around what represented the head spring, from which flowed the river, the words, "Big Indian fight."

So I concluded to move on to that point. On nearing the place I observed a large number of mules and ponies, and, moving the company so as to cut the Indians off from their horses, we got in upon them before they knew anything about our advance. The animals were surrounded, and we proceeded to operate against the enemy, who had sought safety in a dense chaparral. Lieutenant A. P. Porter, with a part of the command, went on one side of the thicket, while I, with the other portion, went in on the other. We killed three outright and mortally wounded others, who were carried off by their comrades. I lost two of my men, and captured a Mexican who had been with the tribe from childhood. Gathering up the saddles and other property of any value, I started back by the way of Fort Chadbourne, where I lay by one day. The company had a splendid old soldier for first sergeant, but occasionally he would indulge his appetite for drink. On such occasions I tried not to see him. On the day the command moved homeward from Chadbourne, and while the column was in motion, he came to me and said, "Captain, don't you think I had better kill this captive, for he will certainly make his escape?" I asked him why he thought so, and he replied, "He has been looking around at the hills all day." I told him that I thought he would not escape, and that when I wanted him killed I would give the necessary orders. With our captive and captures we rode into the post and reported to Major Van Dorn, who was very profuse in his compliments to all engaged in this little affair. Lieutenant Porter behaved with great coolness. He was a gallant young officer, and had he not died of disease during the war would have made his mark.

This little affair was referred to by General Scott in orders as follows:

HEADQUARTERS OF THE ARMY,
NEW YORK, November 13, 1857.

General Orders,
No. 14.

I. . . . In announcing to the army the more recent combats with hostile Indians, in which the gallant conduct of the troops, under, in most cases, circumstances of great hardship and privation, is entitled to high approbation, the General-in-Chief takes occasion to notice all those of a similar character, not mentioned in his general order, No. 4, of the current series, which have occurred since the beginning of last year, and to which, since the publication of that order, his attention has been directed. They are too interesting to be omitted.

In the order of time the cases are as follows:

* * * * * * * *

XVI. . . . December 22, 1856, Captain R. W. Johnson, with twenty-five men of Company F, accompanied by Second Lieutenant A. P. Porter, all of the Second Cavalry, after a march of seven days from Camp Colorado, Texas, came upon a part of Saneco's band of Comanche Indians, near the head of the main Concho, charged upon and drove them into the chaparral; dismounted and followed them in, killing three, wounding three, and capturing thirty-four horses and all their camp equipage. In this sharp conflict Bugler Campion and Private Lamb were killed by arrow-shots through the heart, and Sergeant Gardnier and Private McKim slightly wounded.

* * * * * * * *

By command of BREVET LIEUTENANT-GENERAL SCOTT,

IRVIN MCDOWELL,
Assistant Adjutant-General.

CHAPTER IX.

John McLoughlin—Uncertain Habits—Trailing—Signs—Snakes, Owls, and Prairie Dogs—Happy Family—Sam Cherry—Lieutenant C. W. Phifer—Back to Fort Mason—Regiment ordered to Utah—Order countermanded—Brigham Young sends Salt to General A. S. Johnston—Johnston's Threat to hang next Man with Flag of Truce—Van Dorn's Wichita Expedition—Camp—Battle—Complimentary Orders.

THE government employed at our post a Delaware Indian, known by the name of John McLoughlin, as guide for scouting parties. He knew the country well and could always tell where water could be found, either from personal knowledge or instinct, and I could never tell which. A day or so before I would start out I would send him word, so that he could prepare his rations and arrange his toilet for twenty or thirty days. As soon as he received notice he would go on a private spree and be so drunk as to be unable to move out with the command, but he was sure to overtake it at the end of the second day's march. Noticing this to be his habit, I once said to him, "John, why do you always get drunk before starting on a scout?" He replied, "Maybe so for, captain, thirty days before I can get some more whiskily." He never carried any with him, and when he would overtake the command would be sober, and a more faithful guide I never knew. The great advantage of an Indian as a guide was found in his ability to follow a trail which to an inexperienced eye would never be discovered, or, if seen, soon lost. Indians, in travelling in war parties, never ride together, but scatter out so as to render their trail as indistinct as possible. In passing over rocky hills, where the hoofs of their ponies or mules make little or no impression, one unaccustomed to following them would lose all trace of the trail they made. I never knew John to lose the trail, and he explained to me how he could not only follow it easily, but see the course of it some distance ahead. Getting down on the ground, he said, "You see here a stone which looks black; now that stone has been turned over by the foot of a horse or mule. Had that surface always been uppermost, the rains would have washed it clean and the sun would have made it look bright and fair. Now look ahead and you can see a black line of stones,"— which I could easily recognize when my attention was called to it. "Now look beyond the stones; you see what appears to be a light streak in the grass. Some animal has passed along there, and his feet have turned the grass, and the underside looks light." This business he had made a study of, and I do not remember that he ever failed to find the last end of a trail, unless the Indians were too far ahead. When we would strike a trail he would say, "Indians passed three days," two days, or so many hours before. If they were several days ahead of us we rarely ever overtook them, unless, in fancied security, they would stop to rest. John was a fine shot, and when he fired at a deer or antelope we were sure of fresh meat. When he brought a deer into camp he would cut off the head and neck and give the carcass to the troops. The head and neck he would skin, take out the eyes and remove the nostrils, then pass a small stick up the neck and into the head, build a large fire, and plant the other end of the stick in the ground near it, and as one side became cooked he would turn it, bringing another surface to the fire. When the cooking process was complete he would take up the stick and remove away from the fire, stick it in the ground, sit down near it, and with his knife cut off pieces and begin to eat. When he had eaten all he wanted with his knife he would remove the front bone of the head and eat the brain. I expressed a desire to dine with him when he killed the next deer, and he was very anxious that I should; so in a few days I was informed that all things were ready for the feast. I do not think I ever enjoyed a dinner more than the one I took with this Indian. The meat taken from the neck was delicious, and the brain was food fit for a king. If a white man should kill a deer he would throw away just the part that this epicure of the forest and plain would prize more highly than any other part of the animal. He always slept near me. One night he was asleep. I awoke him and asked him to point to the north star, which he did with the accuracy of the magnetic needle. I laughed and said, "John, you are lost." He looked around to satisfy himself and remarked, "John no lost, but captain lost." I have heard of an Indian who could not find his tepee, and when asked if he was lost, replied, "Indian not lost, but tepee lost."

For some superstitious reason Indians, generally, will not kill snakes. On scouts John was habitually near me, and if he saw one would invariably call my attention to it. On one occasion he called, "For captain, snattlesake." I went to him at once, and found one of the largest reptiles of the kind I had ever seen. It was lying coiled up and ready to spring. Stooping down, I discharged one of the barrels of my revolver, and the ball passed through each coil, making as many holes through it as there were coils. This reminds me of another snake-story. Captain R. S. Granger (now General Granger) and myself were out hunting one day while we were stationed at Fort Terrett, and as we were following an old beaten buffalo-trail a rattlesnake passed across it just in front of us. Granger fired and cut the serpent into two parts, about equal in length. That portion to which the head was attached continued on, while the tail part remained in the path, and rattled with as much force and effect as if nothing had happened.

Snakes of this kind exist in great numbers in Texas. It is not an unusual sight to see rattlesnakes, prairie-owls, and prairie-dogs occupy the same hole in the ground, and some have gone so far as to say that there exists perfect friendship between them. This I am inclined to doubt. My impression is that the snakes live on the young dogs, which are produced very rapidly, at least sufficiently so to furnish the snake with a comfortable living without the trouble of hunting around for it.

"As wise as a serpent" is a scriptural expression, and I believe the Texas rattlesnakes are wise enough not to disturb the old prairie-dogs, realizing the fact that they are the source whence comes their daily food.

Under the tuition of John McLoughlin I learned to be a very good trailer myself, but there was one thing he could not teach me. He seemed to be able to determine the location of water by the general direction of the hills and the relation the valleys sustained towards them. This I could never do; but he never failed. If I asked him how far it was to a water-hole, he had a habit of saying, "That depends for, Captain, how you go; if you ride a lame mule, it is twenty miles; if a good horse, it is only ten miles." His unit of measurement was time, not distance at all. At another post I had as a guide Sam Cherry, an American, who had passed the greater portion of his life on the frontier, and who, by the way, was a good trailer. I never heard Sam confess ignorance on any subject. He had an answer for any question propounded to him, whether it was on the ordinary affairs of life, or in the deep fields of science and philosophy.

The Indians use the brain of an animal in tanning the skin. Just the effect of the one upon the other I did not know, so I asked Sam, and he gave me this very lucid explanation:

"The tissues of the brain combined with the fatty substance of the hide forms a most searching compound, which cleanses and tans the skin thoroughly. The Indians use it without being able to account for it on scientific principles," continued Sam; "but I can never do anything without knowing the whys and the wherefores, and hence I studied it out." Both of these guides were fine horsemen, and never seemed to weary in the saddle. Their endurance was simply wonderful, and their courage there were none to dispute. Lieutenant Phifer, a gallant and brave young officer of my company, went out from camp with John McLoughlin, in search of game. Not returning in time, a detachment was sent out to look for them. In the dim twilight Phifer discovered the party, and, supposing them Indians, turned to John and said, with a view of ascertaining if he could be relied on in an emergency, "John, fight or run?" John replied, "Heap fight, Lieutenant."

Rather than show the white feather, he was ready to make war against any number of hostiles. After that Phifer never doubted his courage or his loyalty.

On February 22, 1857, my company (F) was ordered to march to, and take post at, Fort Mason. I arrived at the latter place on March 1, following. On the 18th of May I was ordered out in search of any bands of Indians which might be prowling around the country. I was absent until June 14, having pursued a small war-party, but failed to overtake it. From September 28 to October 28 I was engaged in like manner.

On February 12, 1858, the post of my company was changed to Fort Belknap, where I arrived February 21.

After Colonel Johnston reached the neighborhood of Salt Lake City, and assumed command of what was known as the Utah Expedition, he asked that his regiment might be sent to him. His request was granted, and the companies were concentrated at Fort Belknap preparatory to a long march for that remote region. Then there were no railroads, and all movements in that section of country had to be made by marching overland. The Mormons, finding a resolute, determined man at the head of affairs, decided to relinquish their warlike attitude and sue for peace. In weakness the government yielded, and the necessity for the regiment in Utah ceased to exist; the order was therefore countermanded, and the commanding general of the Department of Texas was instructed to dispose of it as he thought proper. The troops of the Utah Expedition passed the winter of 1857-58 at Fort Bridger, where, from the want of clothing suitable for the climate, and from insufficient rations, there was great suffering. The army was supplied with beef on the hoof, but there was no salt to be had. By flag of truce, Brigham Young sent Johnston a quantity of salt, but he returned it with the message, "If you dare to send another party to me under a flag of truce, I will hang the last one of them."

There is an old Eastern custom by which salt is sent to an enemy as a peace offering, and it was doubtless in compliance with this custom that suggested it to Brigham Young; but Johnston had no confidence in him, and feared that it might be a mean way of endeavoring to poison his command, and rather than run any risk, he preferred his beef without salt.

While the regiment was together, General Twiggs thought the occasion opportune to organize an expedition against the Northern Indians. Accordingly, Brevet Major Van Dorn was instructed to take command of eight companies, and proceed to the Wichita country, establish a camp, and then operate against the Indians as he thought advisable. This command, of which my company was a part, marched from Fort Belknap on September 15, 1858, and arrived at or near the Wichita Mountains on September 23. A camp was established, to which Van Dorn gave the name of Camp Radziminski, in memory of an officer of our regiment of that name, who died of disease a short time before.

Van Dorn at once sent out his Indian scouts to ascertain the location of any large or small bodies of hostile Indians. They returned in a few days with the information that a large camp of hostile Comanches had been discovered near Wichita village. "Boots and saddles" was sounded, and the command was off within an hour. General Twiggs, in general orders, said,—

XVIII. October 1, 1858.—Near the Wichita village, Brevet Major Van Dorn, captain Second Cavalry, commanding A, F, H, and K companies of his regiment, after a forced march of ninety miles in thirty-six hours, came, a little after daylight, upon the camp of the hostile Comanches, consisting of one hundred and twenty lodges, and between four and five hundred Indians. He immediately charged upon it, and after a most desperate struggle of an hour and a half, during which there were many bloody hand-to-hand conflicts, achieved a most decisive and important victory.

Fifty-six Indians were left dead on the field; one hundred and twenty lodges were burned; over three hundred animals taken; a large quantity of supplies appropriated or destroyed; and the surviving Indians dispersed among the mountains in a destitute condition.

With this victory, it is painful to record the death of Second Lieutenant Cornelius Van Camp, Second Cavalry, an active young officer of exceeding promise, once before named in this order for his gallantry, who was shot through the heart with an arrow while charging the enemy.

Sergeant J. E. Garrison, of Company F; Privates Peter Magar and Jacob Echard, of Company H, were also killed. Private Henry Howard, of that company, missing; supposed to have been killed.

The following were wounded:

Company A.—Brevet Major Van Dorn, severely, four wounds; Corporal Joseph P. Taylor, dangerously.

Company H.—Private C. C. Alexander, severely; Sergeant C. B. McClellan, Corporal Bishop Gordon, and Bugler M. Aborgast, slightly.

Company F.—Privates C. C. Emery and A. J. McNamara, severely, and W. Frank, slightly.

Company K.—Private Smith Hinckley, slightly.

The sutler, Mr. J. F. Ward, was slightly, and the special agent in charge of the friendly Indians, Mr. S. Ross, was severely wounded. They had volunteered for the expedition, and are deserving of great praise for their gallantry in the action.

The officers with Major Van Dorn were Captains Whiting, Evans, and Johnson; Lieutenants Phifer, Harrison, Major, and Porter. Acting Assistant Surgeon Carswell was the medical officer. These officers, together with the non-commissioned officers and privates of Companies A, F, H, and K, Second Cavalry, are entitled to great commendation for their gallantry.

The friendly Indians,—Delawares, Caddoes, etc.,—under Mr. Ross, rendered essential service both before and during the conflict.

One of Van Dorn's wounds, we feared, would prove fatal. He was shot from the side, the arrow passing through him in the region of the navel. It was supposed that it had passed through the cavity of the stomach, but fortunately it proved to be only a flesh wound. As soon as he could be moved on a litter, we returned to our camp. After our horses were allowed to rest for a day or so, I was ordered to proceed to the mouth of the Salt Fork of the Brazos, cross it, and proceed up to its head. After having made a long day's march without crossing any small tributary, from which I expected to get fresh water for the men and horses, and darkness overtaking the command, I resolved to go into camp. I instructed the men to get ice from the river and melt it by the fire, as the water thus obtained would be much more fresh than the water taken from the river. Soon Bugler Patrick Larkin returned and informed me that the water in the river was fresh and good. It is strange that the only fresh water tributary of the Brazos is called the Salt Fork. Throughout the trip we had good water, but saw no Indians, nor had there been any on the stream for many years, judging from the remains of the old camps I discovered. On this trip I had to abandon several horses, which, for want of proper forage, broke down and could go no farther.

Many of the horses thus abandoned recover, and unite with the bands of wild horses which inhabit all remote parts of Texas and the adjoining Territories. I have seen some of these, and they were as wild as any in the wild herds, and could not be approached. In these herds of wild horses there seems to be a single color in each. I have seen all bays, all blacks, and all sorrels, and, by far the handsomest, all spotted or calico horses. I have often chased what I supposed to be parties of Indians, only to find out, after miles of rapid travel, that I was following wild horses. Whence came these wild animals? Indian tradition assigns the origin of these wild bands, or herds, to certain Spanish stock brought into the regions inhabited by them by the Jesuit fathers in the first days of the missions. The round bodies, the clean limbs, delicate ears, and beautiful manes and tails certainly suggest an Andalusian pedigree. A stallion controls each band, and jealously keeps his charge from all others. While grazing they move about at random, but the stallion is ever on the alert, and a snort from him is the danger-signal, when they close in compact mass and break away, like one huge body, for a place of safety. In these flights the stallion in charge is ever in rear, at the post of danger. In the raising of stock, the sexes about equal each other. It has been said that among the wild horses about three-fourths of the male colts are killed by the mature stallions when they are foaled. This I do not believe.

The wanton, reckless, and wicked destruction of the buffalo in past years is a sure guarantee that their days are numbered. Soon the breed must become extinct. The area of country occupied by them is becoming more and more contracted every year. The robes are becoming more valuable, which stimulates the hunter in his efforts to kill all he can, just for their hides. The most determined enemy to the buffalo is the Indian, who cannot, or will not, comprehend that the extinction of the buffalo means his extinction also. Without the buffalo the poor Indian will be wholly dependent upon the agent for supplies, which means starvation, if the future can be judged by the past. With the disappearance of the buffalo, the Indian must go, unless some more humane method, or policy, be adopted for his government and protection.

CHAPTER X.

On Leave of Absence—Trip on Overland Stage—Visit to Kentucky—Back to Fort Mason—Scouting—Engagement with Indians—Buffalo—Barnard's Capture of a Wild Buffalo—Loss of his Coat—Scarcity of Water—Artesian Wells—Camels introduced into Texas—Lieutenant Beale's Estimate of Them—What became of the Camels—Secession—Lieutenant-Colonel R. E. Lee—Base Betrayal of General Twiggs—Governor Houston deposed.

In February, 1859, I applied for a leave of absence for the purpose of visiting my family, at that time in St. Paul. The indulgence was granted, and I returned to Fort Belknap, which was on the line of the Overland Mail Stage from San Francisco to St. Louis. I boarded the first stage which arrived. The roads were hard and firm, and the gentle undulations of the prairies made the riding both easy and agreeable.

The company was replacing the mules along the line with wild, unbroken mustangs, picked up in the country. At one stand there were hitched to the stage four of these animals, all wild, never having been harnessed before. It took eight men to do it. One held each animal by the bridle; another fastened the traces. The passengers were called upon to take their places, the driver, a daring, reckless fellow, mounted his box, adjusted his reins, raised his whip, and bid the holders let go. Then he laid the whip on unceasingly at every jump. We reached the next station—ten miles distant—in just forty-five minutes. At the end of this ten-mile dash they were as calm and docile as if they had been in use for years. Then we were furnished with a fresh team, and experienced the same rapid travelling. In five days and nights we reached the end of the Pacific road from St. Louis, where we took the cars for that city. I remained in St. Louis a day, and left for La Crosse by railroad. At La Crosse I took the stage again for St. Paul, and on the ninth day from Fort Belknap reached my final destination. Here I met my third son for the first time, then eight months old.

After the opening of navigation I went with my family to Kentucky, where I passed the greater part of my leave of absence, only allowing myself time to reach my post before its expiration. On reaching San Antonio I found that the company to which I was attached was stationed at Camp Cooper, on the Clear Fork of the Brazos. I did not care to go there, so I asked General Twiggs to order the company to Fort Mason. I did not expect him to comply with my request, but he did so.

Taking my family to that post and locating them, I hastened on to join my company and conduct it to its new station.

I left Camp Cooper November 27, and arrived at Fort Mason on December 9, 1859. From December 22 to 29 I was out in pursuit of Indians, and again from January 30 to February 25, 1860.

On April 22, 1860, I left Fort Mason for an extended scout, taking with me forty men, supplied with twenty days' rations. I made a long and tiresome expedition, and, finding no Indians, decided to return home by the way of Fort Chadbourne. While there it occurred to me to send twenty men, whose horses were lame or partially broken down, directly to Fort Mason, and with the other twenty men make a circuit in another direction, hoping to come up with a small party of Indians. When within a day's march of home the guide, who was just in front of the column, halted, and then began circling around, as if scenting a trail. The column was halted, and I joined him, when he told me that the Indians had passed only a few hours before. At once we started on the trail, which was followed for three days, making about sixty miles each day. Just before sunset, on the third day, I heard an unearthly yell; it was the danger-signal given by the Indian on the look-out. Looking up, I saw their horses grazing. These were surrounded at once. The band of Indians had halted in a circular chaparral, in the centre of which was a good spring, and there they felt themselves very secure, for they could be reached only by one narrow path, which was protected by their rifles. Making them believe that the command was withdrawing, intending to leave them alone, some came out to the edge of the chaparral, and were picked off by the sharpshooters. The Indians were estimated at about forty, just double the force under my command. They had no animals to care for, and my men had to look after their own horses, as well as those we had captured. Soon the blackness of darkness closed in around us. With the men I had I tried to picket around the chaparral, but the pickets had to be necessarily far apart. About nine o'clock a heavy rain and wind-storm came up, which continued through the night, and thus they were enabled to escape, for none of them were to be seen next morning when we were ready to renew the fight. During the war I often thought of this skirmish, and resolved that, if it ever became my duty again to fight Indians, I would take with me on every expedition a mountain howitzer, to be used in cases like the one I have just described. In this little affair we certainly killed five and wounded others, and captured the horses, saddles, and other property of the entire party. On the day following, I marched for my post. Our rations were out, and it became necessary for the men to subsist on mule meat. I did not have to partake of it myself, for some one of the command would kill a bird or catch a fish every day, and these were generously given to me.

I wish to say here that I do not believe that a superior lot of men could have been found in the army than those constituting Company F. About forty of them weighed from one hundred and forty to one hundred and fifty pounds each, and from these I always selected the men to accompany me on Indian expeditions. Each was an excellent horseman, afraid of nothing, never tired, and always cheerful, and always willing to endure fatigue and hardship, if I exacted it of them. The strictest discipline was maintained in the company, and every man in it knew that if he offended, punishment would surely follow; but, if orderly and well behaved, the largest liberty, consistent with proper discipline, would be allowed him. Every effort was made to stimulate their pride, by letting them understand that the company must be considered the best in the regiment, and to do this it was necessary that each one should be thorough in drill and discipline, and at all times on his good behavior.

There was one thing I always noticed when scouting over the hills and plains of Texas. Indians and buffalo are rarely ever found in the same neighborhood. On some of the scouts I made I have travelled for several days at a time with buffalo always in sight. Of course, not immense herds, but isolated buffalo could be seen on distant hills at all times. They seem to have a military organization among themselves. The cows and calves herd together while away off on the hills, in all directions, the old and experienced males are posted on outpost duty. Upon these sentinels the main herd relies for information in regard to approaching danger, and as they are always on the alert, no herd can be surprised. Whenever we desired the flesh of one, either the guide, or one of the men, mounted on a fleet horse, would charge into the herd and select a young heifer, which would be shot and killed. I never allowed the destruction of more than was necessary for our use, regarding the wholesale butchery of them as wrong for sundry reasons. The small calves are easily captured and domesticated, but old ones can never be tamed.

I met a gentleman in Texas by the name of Barnard, who had been on the frontier many years. He told me that at an early day he was driving an ox-team from one frontier settlement to another. When a long way from any habitation he encamped one night under a large but solitary tree on the prairie. That night one of his oxen died. With one he could not proceed on his journey, and just what to do was the most important question he had ever been called on to decide. Finally, he concluded that his only hope was to catch a buffalo and make him useful, and he imagined that curiosity would lead some of them to come around to make the acquaintance of his surviving ox. Fastening one end of a strong rope to the root of the tree, with the other end he climbed up among the branches and awaited developments. At last a buffalo came near and he threw the noose around his neck. The animal reared and pitched around at a fearful rate, but the more he struggled the tighter the rope was drawn; and finally, not being able to breathe, he fell exhausted to the ground. Barnard descended hurriedly, and in a moment had the yoke over his neck, and the process of harnessing a wild buffalo was complete. When all things were ready he loosened the rope around the neck, and the buffalo began to breathe slowly. In a few moments he was on his feet, gave a snort, and Barnard said, "From that day to this I have not laid my eyes upon the ox, buffalo, or wagon, or any part of either." I do not vouch for this story, but give it as it was related to me.

Scarcity of water was the most serious obstacle in the way of successful military operations in Texas. Railroads had not then penetrated that State and the Territories beyond, and hence all supplies designed for the troops in New Mexico and Arizona had to be hauled by mule-teams from the coast. On the usual line of travel between San Antonio and El Paso there were several distances of about eighty miles each between water-holes or streams.

These were long drives, and the poor animals suffered untold misery for the want of water. It was usual to start on these journeys over the deserts about sundown, drive all night and until the beginning of the intense heat of the following day, then lie by until the cool of the evening and renew the journey. On the approach to the water the jaded mules would prick up their ears and start on a full run, instinctively knowing that soon their great thirst was to be quenched in the waters of some cooling stream.

To overcome this great drawback to successfully transporting supplies, and with the hope of being able to do something calculated to develop the country, Mr. Davis, then Secretary of War, prevailed upon Congress to make an appropriation for the purpose of boring a series of artesian wells. Brevet Captain John Pope, now major-general, was placed in charge of this enterprise, and bored several to great depths, but did not succeed in getting water to flow to the surface, and hence that plan failed of success.

It then occurred to Mr. Davis to introduce into this country a large number of camels, to be used in transporting supplies over these destitute regions, as they can go for several days without water.

In 1857 a number of them were brought in government vessels from the borders of the Mediterranean, and on their arrival sent to Texas, being a climate more like that of their native land than any other portion of the United States. It seems that some of these were placed in charge of Lieutenant Beale, commander of an expedition to explore for a wagon-road from New Mexico to California. In his report he says,—

An important part in all of our operations has been acted by the camels. Without the aid of this noble and useful brute, many hardships which we have been spared would have fallen to our lot; and our admiration for them has increased day by day, as some new hardship, endured patiently, more fully developed their entire adaptation and usefulness in the exploration of the wilderness.

At times I have thought it impossible they could stand the test to which they have been put; but they seem to have risen equal to every trial, and to have come off from every exploration with as much strength as before starting. Unsupported by the testimony of every man of my party, I should be unwilling to state all that I have seen them do. Starting with a full determination that the experiment should be no half-way one, I have subjected them to trials which no other animal could possibly have endured, and yet I have arrived here, not only without the loss of a camel, but they are admitted, by those who saw them in Texas, to be in as good condition to-day as when we left San Antonio. In all our lateral explorations they have carried water, sometimes for more than a week, for the mules used by the men, themselves never receiving even a bucketful to one of them. They have traversed patiently, with heavy packs, on these explorations, countries covered with the sharpest volcanic rock, and yet their feet to this hour have evinced no symptom of tenderness or injury; with heavy packs they have crossed mountains, ascended and descended precipitous places where an unladen mule found it difficult to pass, even with the assistance of the rider, dismounted and carefully picking its way. Leaving home with all the prejudice attaching to untried experiments, and with many in our camp opposed to their use, and looking forward confidently to their failure, I believe, at this time I may speak for every man in our party, when I say there is not one of them who would not prefer the most indifferent of our camels to four of our best mules, and I look forward hopefully to the time when they will be in general use in all parts of our country.

Now, it should be remembered that the best results were not expected from those imported, but from their offspring reared in this country. The war came on before the matter could be fairly tested, but I think the

Secretary of War at that time is entitled to the credit of having taken a step which, had it been fairly tried, would have resulted in a complete revolution of the transportation question over the arid plains of Texas and the Territories beyond.

I do not know what finally became of those at Camp Verde, Texas, but am of the opinion that they fell into the hands of the Confederates, although I have recently read an article on this subject from a correspondent of the New Orleans *Times-Democrat*, which I reproduce for the information of the reader, with the remark that I am clearly of the opinion that it is one of those wild frontier stories so easily gathered from the frontiersman and Indian:

> In the Hualpias can also be found that phenomenal animal on American soil, the Arabian camel. In the early sixties the government purchased about 100 head of these natives of the desert, thinking that they could be utilized in the long stretches of arid travelling on the Western trails. For some reason, never thoroughly understood, the experiment was considered a failure, and these animals—average cost price $1000—were offered to the highest bidder. Some were sold, but a great many escaped to the hills and plains of unknown Arizona. The Hualpias region received not a few of them, and here, in a climate where the sun shines as hot as on their native saharas, and no bad substitute for the sirocco blows in its season, they throve and multiplied. The Indians of the Hualpias are familiar with the "new buffalo," as they call the camel, and tell marvellous tales of its speed and endurance. Though the animals originally purchased by the government were of the carrying or burden variety, their sojourn in the Hualpias has developed in their offspring all of the characteristics of the dromedary or saddle-camel of the Arabs. Lighter and cleaner in form than its progenitor, the present camel of the Hualpias can proudly challenge comparison with the ancient and gentle strain from which springs the pride of the sheik and the pet of the Arab household.

The camel of the Hualpias affects principally a region still in the east of the great horse range, but within the Hualpias hills. They prefer the sheltered valleys to the open stretch of plain, and their favorite food is the fruit of the wild peach-tree that grows in the utmost profusion in their favorite habitat. In the early fall the fruit falls to the earth, and is soon, by the action of the rarefied air of the section and the sun, dried as well as though human hands had superintended the operation. It is then that the transplanted camel feeds the most greedily upon it. The animals do not herd together in any numbers, the male, female, and their own particular offspring forming a select circle of their own. The section in which these eastern exiles have found a refuge and home is as remote and unknown to this city as it was in 1872. The Hualpias Indians keep the secret from all white men but the ubiquitous and scheming Mormon. In this region lie almost unlimited possibilities, and the time is coming when the Hualpias hills will give prosperous homes to thousands of families, among whose beasts of burden the Arabian camel will hold a proud prominence.

In the early days of 1861 it was evident that the Southern States intended to secede from the Union and establish for themselves a separate and distinct government, the chief corner-stone of which was to be human slavery. Their rights had not been questioned. No wrong had been done to either one, yet in their madness and folly they were determined to pursue that course regardless of consequences. South Carolina led off in this treasonable effort to dissolve the Union, and other States made arrangements to follow her in her mad career. Texas began to organize troops to overpower the Federal army. At all the posts in the department suspicious-looking men lurked around. Lieutenant-Colonel Lee, afterwards the leader of the rebel army, was in command of Fort Mason. He called on me one day and stated the case fully; said he was determined to defend his post at all hazards, and asked me if he could rely upon my support, to which I replied, "Yes, as long as I hold a commission in the Union army, I shall be loyal to its flag." This seemed to gratify him very much, and he then and there divulged to me his plan of fortifying the post. Before he began to carry it out an order summoned him to Washington to confer with General Scott, who entertained an exalted opinion of his ability, and who desired his advice and services in the approaching contest. The last time I saw him was when I went to the ambulance which was to bear him away, and said, "Colonel, do you intend to go South or remain North? I am very anxious to know just what you propose doing." He replied in these words, "I shall never bear arms against the United States,—but it may be necessary for me to carry a musket in defence of my native State, Virginia, in which case I shall not prove recreant to my duty." The driver cracked his whip, and as he drove off Colonel Lee thrust his head out of the ambulance and said, "Good-by. God bless you."

These were the last words I ever heard him speak and the last time I ever saw him. Colonel Lee was one of the most agreeable men I ever knew, handsome, courteous as a knight, pleasant and entertaining in conversation. He was universally beloved by all the officers of his regiment, and all regretted his departure.

While these things were going on around our post others were taking steps to tie the army hand and foot, and force a surrender to the insurgents. General Twiggs, who was on leave of absence, finding that a crisis was soon to be reached, and fearing that Colonel Waite, who was commanding during his absence, might not be willing to do just as the rebels wished him, surrendered his leave, returned, and assumed command. Now, it is well known by every officer who was in Texas that a concentration might have been made, and in that case we could have defended ourselves against all the militia the State of Texas could have brought against us. It was this possible concentration by Colonel Waite that Twiggs feared, and hence his return. It was said that, after his return, the rebel leaders in San Antonio were greatly encouraged, still they feared to make a formal demand for the surrender of all the troops and property of the government. To encourage them he visited the hotels where these men were generally to be found, and openly and boisterously proclaimed that "If any old woman armed with a broom-stick demands a surrender, I will accede to her demand." Thus emboldened, the demand was made, and the most disgraceful surrender the world has ever known was then and there agreed to. I have understood that an effort has been made to relieve him from the stigma that should ever attach to his name for this outrage, but when that is done let Benedict Arnold's treasonable memory be vindicated also. Perish the thought that Twiggs, Arnold, and Judas Iscariot, a notorious trio, should ever be canonized as patriots, pure, noble, and true. On the contrary, let their names be handed down to posterity together as traitors of the deepest, darkest hue. No one can estimate the damage Twiggs did to our cause by basely trailing the flag of our country in the dust, and surrendering the immense supplies of arms, ammunition, clothing, camp and garrison equipage. It is said that he frequently telegraphed and asked for orders, which the War Department neglected to give. What more orders did he want than the following article of war:

ARTICLE 52. Any officer or soldier who shall misbehave himself before the enemy, run away, or shamefully abandon any FORT, POST, or GUARD which he or they may be commanded to defend, or speak words inducing others to do the like, or shall cast away his arms and ammunition, or who shall quit his post or colors to plunder and pillage, every such offender, being duly convicted thereof, shall suffer death, or such other punishment as shall be ordered by the sentence of a general court-martial.

In his peaceful surrender is there any doubt in regard to his abandonment of dozens of forts and posts? Is there any doubt whatever that he laid himself liable to the penalty imposed in this article?

Oh, no, there can be no pardon for him, and his name must go down to posterity as infamous, and alongside of that of Benedict Arnold. I have a great deal of charity for many men who drifted away into the rebellion, but for General Twiggs none whatever. He knew his duty and did it not. He was a traitor while holding a commission under the government. Every State in the Union had a better right to withdraw than Texas. That State was bought by the government, and while the United States did not own the people it did the soil. When it was admitted a debt of ten millions was paid by the United States government, and it was permitted to retain all of the public lands within its boundary-lines.

The United States paid dearly for the purchase, and all it had to show for the money expended was the ownership of the soil, and the State had no right whatever to secede. Such was the opinion of Sam Houston, the father of the State. He was governor of Texas at the time, and was called on to take the oath of allegiance to the Confederate States. This he declined to do. The Convention arbitrarily removed him, and inaugurated the lieutenant-governor. Houston could not prevail upon those hot-headed rebels to stop and consider before they went too far. He was hooted at and threatened, and, finding himself helpless, withdrew to his farm on the Brazos, where he soon died a heart-broken patriot. He told the people just what would be the final outcome, and in the light of subsequent events he seems to have been endowed with the spirit of prophecy, for the predictions he made were verified, though in greater degree. It would have been far better for the people of Texas had they yielded to his advice. They did not, and the grief which he predicted would come upon them, came sooner and more severe than he had anticipated. The institution of slavery about which they went to war soon ceased to exist. It is said that those whom the gods wish to destroy they first make mad. The madness of the people in the early days of the war was evident. There never was a people who rushed into war so foolishly as those of the South. They seemed to think that the North would quietly and peaceably submit to a dismemberment of the Union without raising their hands in its defence. How foolish! How idiotic!

CHAPTER XI.

Governmental Policy towards the Indians—Give them Lands in Severalty—The Wealth of the Crows—General Sheridan's Views on the Indian Question—Schools should teach English—Sioux Best Warriors—Comanches Best Horsemen—All Good Marksmen—Names—Indian Wives are Servants—Brave Act of an Indian—Opinion of Commissioner of Indian Affairs.

From the earliest settlement of this country the vacillating course pursued by the government towards the Indians has been one of imagined expediency rather than one of justice. When the whites were greatly in the minority, the fear of the tomahawk and the butcher-knife suggested a very liberal course to be pursued towards them. They were petted and toyed with,—in fact, allowed to do about as they pleased. From that time to the present they have been fed and fattened at public expense; and if the government had attempted to deprive them of their manhood and make paupers of them all, no more sure way of accomplishing it could have been devised than the one which has been followed. It is a misuse of words to say that the government has had an Indian policy. We have never had a policy calculated to elevate, ennoble, and lead these poor untutored children of the forests and the plains to a higher civilization. They are assembled on the reservations, where all interests are in common, where there is no incentive to strive to attain to any higher position intellectually, morally, or financially. Their wants are partially supplied, and they know they will be, hence their only ambition is to attain eminence as hunters and to live lives of indolence and immorality. Among all the tribes into which I have been thrown this same condition of things exists, with the exception of the Cherokees, Chicasaws, and Choctaws.

As a general thing, Indians cannot recognize the act of one white man as the act of a single person; but if a white man does them a wrong, it satisfies their savage natures to wreak vengeance upon any other white man. Hence it is, when the missionary goes among them and by earnest, persistent effort succeeds in planting in their hearts some knowledge of the Saviour of men, suddenly they see some unprincipled white men stealing the rations belonging to them and their tribes, then at once the missionary is characterized as a thief also, and all of his patient work goes for naught. Can we Christianize these poor deluded savages with the machinery of the government? It cannot be done through the instrumentality of the agencies as at present conducted. There are many good men employed on the various reserves who treat these people with great fairness; but their labors are futile unless all those associated with them are in full sympathy, and earnestly and faithfully labor to better the temporal and spiritual condition of these unfortunate beings.

The Indians in this country occupy an anomalous position. They are regarded as a separate nationality, above and beyond all law, owing no allegiance to the country, unprotected by the laws, and not amenable to them.

There is a solution to this question. It is not new, but has been urged from time to time for a century. Far better for all concerned had the policy been adopted long since; but it is not yet too late. Give to each family a home, a tract of land large enough for the wants of an ordinary-sized family, and say to the head of each, this is yours, and it can never be taken from you; but to protect you against land-sharks who will seek to cheat, wrong, and defraud you, you will never be permitted to sell your land,—at least until after you have shown yourselves capable of guarding your own interests. You may leave it to your children or set aside portions of it for their exclusive use during your lifetime, but you can never dispose of it outside of your family. Now, here is a team, spade, shovel, hoe, rake, plough, and such other agricultural implements as you will require in the cultivation of the soil upon which you must depend for a living. You know that the game has disappeared, you can no longer trust to the uncertainties of the chase, and so you must work as your white brothers are compelled to do. You must be governed by the laws, and their protecting mantle will be thrown over and around you. After a certain time all assistance will cease, and by that time you must be self-sustaining. You must enter the race of life as the white man has done. If you work, God will reward your labors with abundant harvests, and they will be your own. You can sell your surplus, and, with the money obtained therefrom, purchase other articles for your family which you cannot produce on your farm. By strict economy you will soon be above all want. Your days of idleness and dependence are over, and henceforth you will be regarded as a human being, a citizen of the United States, and entitled to the respect of all men just in proportion as you deserve it.

The Crow Indians are the wealthiest people on the face of the earth. This tribe numbers about thirty-three hundred, and own about 20,000 horses, ponies, and mules, and in round numbers about 5,000,000 acres of land. Of what earthly use is such a large body of land to a people who neither sow nor reap? Set aside for their use land sufficient for each family, sell the remainder, and give them the interest of the amount realized by the sale annually, or oftener, if thought advisable. From the report of Lieutenant-General Sheridan for the year 1885 it would seem that this is the plan he proposes. He says,—

> On account of the rapid growth of our Western settlements the army is obliged in some places to protect white people from Indians, while in other places it is protecting the Indians in their persons or properties from the whites. The Indians are the richest people in the country as communities. Their reservations include some of the best lands; if divided among the heads of families, each family would have thousands of acres. If I may be permitted to suggest, I would recommend that each family be given and located on three hundred and twenty acres now provided for them by the law in case of actual settlement. The government should then condemn all the balance of each reservation, buy it in at one dollar and twenty-five cents per acre, and with the proceeds purchase government bonds, to be held in trust by the Interior Department, only giving to the Indians each year the interest on the bonds for their support. Let this money, if you please, be disbursed the same as the money appropriated last year by Congress. The practical working would be about as follows: The Crow Indians, for instance, have nearly 4,800,000 acres of land. There are not more

than thirty-three hundred of them, and counting five persons to a family,—large estimate,—they could be settled separately on two hundred and thirty acres for each family, and then have 4,500,000 acres left, which the government could buy of them when condemned.

If the proceeds were invested in government bonds, and the interest used for their support, it would be more money than is now appropriated by Congress for their yearly maintenance. It would be their own money, and take the question of annual appropriations for them out of Congress.

The first great lesson to be taught these sons of the prairies is "that all men are created equal, that they are endowed by their Creator with certain unalienable rights, that among these are life, liberty, and the pursuit of happiness," and that true happiness can only be attained by following some honest industry. When the laws are made to govern and protect them, as they do all other races of men, they will feel that they are a part and parcel of the government, not a nationality separate and distinct. Schools among them should teach the English language,—" the language of civilization and of progress." Time should not be wasted in teaching them their own language. They can learn the English as readily; and when they can speak it, there will be a closer sympathy with the whites. Separated at their own homes, they can be more easily instructed by the missionary and taught that the races whose God is the Lord are more prosperous and more happy than those who know Him not. The various tribes should be transferred to the War Department. It is often asserted by well-disposed persons that the turning over of the Indians to the War Department means their annihilation by the sword and the musket.

How absurd! Are not the officers and soldiers men like all others? Are they not as humane and as careful of human life? Have they not done as much for the temporal good of the Indian as any other class of men? Look, if you please, at the Cherokees, Chicasaws, and Choctaws. These tribes were colonized by the army. The army took charge of them when they reached their present home; and where among all the tribes has there been such progress in civilization, education, and religion? They are making rapid strides forward, and the time will come when their civilization will be such as to demand the admission of their Territory into the Union as a State. They have an able system of laws, which are faithfully executed; and our States would do well to incorporate some of their statutes among their own. I point with great pride to the noble work of the army with these tribes.

The expeditions made in the State of Texas against the Indians, referred to on previous pages, were rendered necessary by the absurd policy of herding them together on reservations. Young men can never rest in idleness, and what more natural result could be expected than the organization of small parties to make forays against the settlements?

The Sioux are the best warriors, but the Comanches are by far the best horsemen. They seem to be able to cling to the side of a horse like a fly, and hurl arrows under their horse's neck at their enemy on the opposite side. A Comanche can run his horse at full speed and readily pick up anything from the ground, such as a hat, a bow, or an arrow. In this feat the only contact apparently between the Indian and his horse is his heel, which clings to the back of the animal.

They are fine marksmen, and can shoot an arrow with unerring accuracy. As soon as the boys are old enough to spring a bow they begin to practice, and it is astonishing how readily they familiarize themselves with its use. The women, also, are generally expert in the use of the bow, and in the Wichita battle did effective service with the rifle. Once I witnessed a number of boys shooting at dimes ten paces off, and I do not remember that a single one missed his aim. They enjoyed the sport very much, for each one hitting a dime was permitted to keep it. It was real fun for the boys, but expensive to those who furnished the targets.

Just how the Comanches preserve any knowledge of relationship I do not know, for each member of a family has a name without any reference to any other member of that family. For instance, the man whose name is Buffalo-rising-in-the-grass may name his son Crazy-horse, and the latter may name his son Antelope.

Now, when Antelope dies there is a meeting of the head men of the tribe, and the name of Antelope is changed to something else; and the word agreed upon is duly promulgated to the members of the band, after which the original name never passes the lips of any one of them. This is probably a compliment to the memory of the deceased.

I have seen the head men assembled in council, and although in rags and covered with the accumulated dirt and filth of years, yet they act with as much coolness and dignity as would the crowned heads of Europe, if assembled to consider weighty questions which were agitating the people of the civilized world. No women are permitted to be present on such occasions. To them the woman is inferior and is regarded more in the light of a beast of burden, whose place is the kitchen or in the forest gathering wood for winter's use. The wife of an Indian is his servant, and there is no drudgery so laborious, no service so humiliating and degrading that he will not demand it of her. She recognizes her subordination, and never raises objections to anything required by her lord and master. Such is savage life. The higher the human family rises in the scale of civilization, the more deference is paid to woman. Among educated and refined people in America she is queen, and all men bow to her as they should.

In Texas we rarely ever heard of Indians attacking any organized force where there was the slightest chance of defeat. When pursued by superior numbers, they invariably attempted to escape by flight, and this gave rise to the belief that they were all cowards. I do not believe they were,—for when driven to the wall they would fight with desperation. A party of soldiers, on the 26th day of August, 1860, encountered a number of Indians near the head of the Clear Fork of the Brazos. They were moving with their women and children when attacked. The fight was a running one; and when it became evident to the head men that the entire party would be killed or captured, an old Indian, himself badly wounded, made a stand, resolved on selling his life as dearly as possible. Taking a position in a small thicket, and by keeping up a constant fire, the command was forced to halt, thus enabling his comrades, women, and children to escape. The brave old savage was wounded about twenty times before he was finally despatched, and managed to kill and wound quite a number of the soldiers. Before his death, the guide called to him, in his own language, to surrender and his life should be spared; but his reply was, "Surrender? Never! never! Come on!" Such courage, such a spirit of self-sacrifice, deserved a better fate. What could better illustrate the courage and the nobility of character than the conduct of this savage? To save others he voluntarily offered up his own life; and it was not lost in vain, for his comrades made good their escape. An examination of his body revealed his terrible wounds, more than half of which would have proven mortal.

The report of General J. D. C. Atkins, Commissioner of Indian Affairs, has just been published, and the views he expresses are so much in harmony with my own that I embody a part of it. He says,—

It requires no seer to foretell or foresee the civilization of the Indian race, as a result naturally deducible from a knowledge and a practice on their part of agriculture, for the history of agriculture among all people and in all countries intimately connects it with the highest intellectual and moral development of man. The increased interest in agriculture manifested since the opening of last spring and the preparations on several reservations for a still larger increase of acreage in farming are among the hopeful signs of Indian progress and development. This brings me directly to the consideration of the practical policy which I believe should be adopted by Congress and the government in the management of the Indians. It should be industriously and gravely impressed upon them that they must abandon their tribal relations and take lands in severalty as the corner-stone of their complete success in agriculture, which means self-support, personal independence, and material thrift. The government should, however, in order to protect them, retain the right to these lands in trust for twenty-five years or longer, but issue trust-patents at once to such Indians as have taken individual holdings. When the Indians have taken their lands in severalty in sufficient quantities, and the number of acres in each holding should vary in different localities, according to fertility, productiveness, climate, and other advantages, then, having due regard to the immediate and early future needs of the Indians, the remaining lands of their reservations should be purchased by the government and opened to homestead entry at fifty or seventy-five cents per acre. The money paid by the government for these lands should be held in trust in five per cent. bonds, to be invested as Congress may provide, for the education, civilization, development, and advance of the red race, reserving for each tribe its own money. If this policy were adopted systematically by the government, it would be strange if in five years from this inauguration and establishment there should be an Indian of any tribe in the whole country who would refuse to accept so favorable and advantageous a measure. Every step taken, every move made, every suggestion offered, everything done with reference to the Indians, should be with a view of impressing them that this is the policy which has been permanently decided upon by the government in reference to their management. They must abandon tribal relations. They must give up their superstitious ideas. They must forsake their savage habits and learn the arts of civilization. They must learn to labor and rear their families as white people do, and to know more of their obligations to the government and society. In a word, they must learn to work for a living, and they must understand that it is their interest and duty to send their children to school. When the farm and school have been familiar institutions among the Indians, and reasonable time has intervened for the transition from barbarous or a semi-civilized state to one of civilization, then will the Indian be prepared to take on himself the higher and more responsible duties and privileges which appertain to American citizenship.

For this General Atkins deserves the thanks of every one who desires to see the condition of the red man improved, and this embraces all of our people not included in the hated Indian ring.

The present commissioner is the first one who has had the boldness and independence to advocate a policy so wise, so just; and may we not hope that his sage counsel may be heeded by Congress, and that henceforth we shall have an Indian policy which will elevate and ennoble rather than degrade this poor down-trodden people?

CHAPTER XII.

March to Indianola—Embarkation on "Empire City"—Captain R. S. Granger—Major A. K. Arnold's Valuable Assistance—Brigades Organized on Ship-Board—Sea-Sickness—Arrival at Havana—Carriage-Drive around the City—Call on the Captain-General—Visit to Cigar-Factory—Political Boss—Joining in the Rebellion—Arrival in New York—Trip to Carlisle Barracks—New Mount—Rebel Women—War, etc., etc., etc.

LET us return to the surrender. Before a demand was made upon General Twiggs there was a public meeting held by the citizens of San Antonio, and a "Committee of Safety," composed of seven members, appointed to demand the surrender and to arrange the details. Public property at the various posts, not required for the transportation of the troops to the coast, was to be turned over to some one to be designated by this committee of safety. The various commands were to leave their posts on specified dates and march to Indianola. These dates were so arranged that not more than one thousand men would be at any one point at the same time. This was done evidently to prevent any resistance being offered to this disgraceful transaction. At Indianola transportation and arms were to be turned over to the representative of the Confederate government. A general murmur was heard throughout the department in opposition to surrendering the arms, and this murmur reaching the ears of General Twiggs, he saw the possibility of trouble and bloodshed, and had the terms so modified that the troops could leave *with the honors of war*, bearing their arms.

Major Fitz-John Porter was designated to superintend the embarkation of the troops and to provide transportation for that purpose, and to his zeal and energy the government is indebted for the safe departure of the troops in that State.

In the absence of Lieutenant-Colonel Lee and Major Van Dorn from Fort Mason, the command of the two companies of cavalry and the band of the regiment devolved on me, and March 29, 1861, was the date fixed for this command to take up the march to Indianola. Early on that day I moved the column, and when out a mile or so looked to the rear, and the dense, heavy smoke which I saw revealed the fact that the old post was on fire. As it then belonged to the Confederate States, I had no particular interest in it, and never inquired how the fire originated, although I shrewdly suspected that it was fired by some of the men of my command. In due time I reached San Antonio, where I was joined by Captain R. S. Granger, who was in command of two companies of the First Infantry. Our commands were not joined, but we marched practically together. For several days before reaching Green Lake, the point of rendezvous, it appeared to me that Granger wanted to get his command there ahead of mine, as he always encamped a mile or so in advance. Supposing that he knew something that I did not know and that he had some object in pushing ahead, I resolved to beat him at his own game. Accordingly, on the day both of our commands were to reach the lake, I had reveille at one o'clock. At two o'clock "Boots and Saddles" was rung out on the early morning air by my ever-faithful bugler, Larkin. I passed Granger's command before his reveille, and all were sleeping sweetly and soundly. I reached Green Lake at ten o'clock, and was informed that my command just completed the load for the "Empire City;" and the commander directed me to move at once to Indianola, turn over my horses, and board the steamer. Granger arrived soon after, and had to go into camp to await the arrival of other troops to make up a load for another vessel. At sundown on that day we were afloat on the broad bosom of the gulf, *en route* to New York *via* Havana. At eight o'clock, on the following morning, Van Dorn arrived in Matagorda Bay with an improvised gun-boat, and openly violated the terms of the surrender by capturing and paroling all of the officers and men who had not left the State. Granger was paroled, and was not exchanged for a year or so, thus losing rank and experience, both of which I had received long before he entered upon active duty. I have often thought how lucky it was to conceive the idea that Granger was seeking an advantage over me. It may have been, and doubtless was, all imagination on my part, but it was a very happy conception, as it turned out. Just here I recall the difficulty we experienced in boarding the steamer, which, as it was anchored outside of the bar, had to be approached by a small lighter. Upon this craft I had my wife and children, and when we came alongside of the "Empire City," it seemed that a mighty wave would raise the lighter just as the steamer sank down in the hollow between two waves, and *vice versa*. Men could manage to get aboard, but how the children were to be transferred puzzled me. At last Lieutenant A. K. Arnold, now major of the Sixth Cavalry, took one of my little boys under his arm and climbed up and deposited him safely, then came back and took another. I remember how adroitly it was done. No professional sailor could have done it more handsomely. His kindness took a great weight of anxiety from my shoulders, and I have always remembered him with great kindness, and will continue to do so as long as I live. This circumstance recalls the fact of the rapidity of the flight of time. One of these little boys has children now larger than he was when Arnold climbed the rope ladder with him under his arm.

There were on board of the "Empire City" parts of the Second Cavalry and Third Infantry. Colonel Oliver L. Shepherd of the Third Infantry was the senior officer, and the next in rank to him in his regiment was Captain George Sykes. The senior officer of the Cavalry was Captain C. J. Whiting. Shepherd assumed that this was the largest command ever concentrated together since the Mexican war, and so he organized it into a brigade, designating Sykes as chief of infantry and Whiting as chief of cavalry. When we reached deep water, and billows rolled high, the organization was not maintained, as most of the officers retired to their state-rooms, and remained there until we were safely moored in the harbor of Havana. The roughness of the ocean never affects me, so I had to discharge the duties of these high officials in addition to my own. I doubt if any other officer of that command descended to the apartments occupied by the men. However, the duties were light and did not burden me. While I never became sea-sick, there is a very uncanny odor about an ocean vessel, and I am always glad to leave one and take to the land which is my natural element.

Judging from the effects on others, I am satisfied that sea-sickness is a most distressing malady, and that both gentlemen and ladies suffering from it would just about as soon die as live. Ladies who are usually very particular about their toilets become careless, almost to a total disregard of their raiment, leave the doors of their state-rooms open to get fresh air, without reference to passers by. These same ladies, not so suffering, would make as much noise should a male member of society pass in front of their open door before their toilets were completely made, as they would if a mouse invaded the precincts of their stateroom. Men are even worse, and their elongated faces and pain-distorted features are quite sufficient to make those around them sick even if the storm-tossed ocean failed to accomplish it.

For a long time I thought sea-sickness was more the result of the imagination than the motion of the vessel, but this theory was disposed of when I saw young children, too young to think about such matters, as deathly sick as the men and women around them.

As our vessel neared the harbor of Havana, the United States flag was raised on the mast and beautifully and majestically floated upon the breeze. As soon as our colors were recognized, a gun was fired from Moro Castle, signifying a hearty welcome into that grand and beautiful harbor. The powerful engine was again put in motion, the "Empire City" quivered in all her parts and soon began to move forward into the blue waters surrounding the city. At once we were besieged by a fleet of small boats filled with curiosity seekers in the main, but several contained health and custom-house officers. An American called out from one of these small crafts, "Fort Sumter has been fired upon." Then sank the heart of every one on that vessel. Up to this time none of us could believe that the extreme folly of the Southern people could go so far as to inaugurate a civil strife, the results of which no one could foretell; but our hopes were dashed to the ground and our thoughts turned to the magnitude of the terrible contest upon which we were soon to enter. Our vessel was delayed for several days in taking on coal and water, during which time we visited all places of interest in that queerly-constructed city.

Colonel Shepherd, thinking that it would be an act of courtesy for all of the officers to call in a body on the captain-general, wrote him a note asking what time would be most agreeable for him to give us an audience. He designated the time, and in full uniform all of the officers marched to the place designated. Colonel Shepherd, who spoke Spanish fluently, made a neat little speech, saying how proud we were in being able to pay our respects to such a distinguished personage, etc., etc. When he had finished he paused a moment for a reply. The captain-general, straightening himself up, spoke, to the great surprise of every officer, as follows, in the purest and best English: "Gentlemen! I am rejoiced to see you individually and collectively, and nothing in my power shall be omitted to make your visit to this city pleasant and agreeable. I bid you be seated." Shepherd looked a little disappointed at the turn matters had taken, but thereafter he was particular to speak the best English he could command.

This brings up the thought that the English language will ultimately be the universal language of the world. In all civilized countries no education is considered complete that does not embrace it, and it is becoming in more general use every year.

The natives of Cuba seem to be the happiest people in the world, although in almost every square in the city squads of foreign troops are quartered to preserve order. No native can serve in the army nor hold any civil office. They are not allowed the right of suffrage; but notwithstanding these deprivations they are light-hearted, contented, and happy.

I hired a volante to take my wife to the "Captain-General's Garden," and to visit other places of interest. These vehicles looked odd enough to me. The horse is hitched at the end of the shafts at least fifteen feet in front of the seats provided for the passengers. A man mounted on horseback rides at the side of the horse in harness to guide and direct him through the narrow streets of the city, and it is perfectly wonderful how easily they can turn the short corners and avoid collision with other vehicles. All the drivers I saw were negroes, none of whom could speak a word of the English language.

In the garden we saw many pieces of statuary, many varieties of fruit, beautiful fountains, birds of variegated plumage, lovely drives, and cool, inviting shades. Perpetual summer reigns in that beautiful island, and the bright seasons come and go without change enough to distinguish one from another.

If Cuba rested under the shadowy sheen of our own banner, it is there that I should like to make my permanent home. But no true American can entertain the idea of making a home under a foreign flag.

I visited the largest cigar factory in the world, and saw hundreds of ragged, dirty-looking men engaged in making fragrant Havanas. These men looked untidy, and when they thrust their dirty fingers into small boxes containing filthy paste to finish up each cigar, I then and there resolved that I would never again bite off the end of another cigar, but remove it with a knife. In fact, cleanliness and possibility of contagion clearly require all smoking to be done through an amber mouth-piece. But why smoke at all? It is an expensive, dirty habit, injurious to health, and no good whatever was ever known to result from it; on the contrary, it is a narcotic poison, which is slowly but surely saturating nearly all of the young men in the country, the natural tendency of which is to shorten their lives. The clothing of all those who indulge in the needless, vulgar, filthy habit is so saturated with the fumes of tobacco as to offend the delicate nostrils of ladies and all gentlemen who abstain from the use of cigars. Parents do not appear to know that their boys begin to smoke when very young, and when they are twenty the habit is fastened upon them. Not long since I saw a little Irish boy, about twelve years old, puffing away at a cigar with an earnestness worthy of something better. I said to him, "My son, do you want to know how to make money?" "Yes," he replied, "that is the sort of a fellow I am." "Well," said I, "if you will stop smoking and save all the money you would otherwise expend for cigars, by the time you are as old as I am you will have money enough to buy a farm." With a motion of his head which signified his contempt for me, he remarked, "I don't want any farm; I am going to be an alderman and a political boss."

All things being in readiness we sailed from Havana, encountering some rough weather, but reached New York in safety, where we found the greatest excitement existing in consequence of the bombardment of Fort Sumter and the firing upon the volunteers in the streets of Baltimore. The very capital of the nation was threatened by an armed force from Virginia. As we steamed into the harbor of New York, it was easily seen that from every house-top, dome, and steeple the stars and stripes floated to the breeze. Everything wore the aspect of a gala day, and the people seemed to be on one grand picnic, little thinking of the solemnity of the occasion. Without thought of the trials, troubles, and bloodshed through which our people had to pass, they rushed wildly about, apparently imagining that the war was to be terminated by "three cheers and a tiger." There were sad hearts on our vessel. There were a number of officers from the South who left us here to join the troops of their respective States; and when I recall the bitterness of their sorrow at severing the ties which had bound us together, I realize fully the fact that they were not the promoters of the war, had no desire to engage in it, and only left us under the mistaken notion that their allegiance was due first to the States in which they were born. I have always thought that those officers who left us were harshly criticised for their act. Joining in rebellion against a government like ours cannot be justified, but it should be remembered that their friends were in the South, and it was quite natural that some should leave the Federal army and join them even if they had been sure of overthrow and defeat. This actuated many, and I know of many who left and at the same time condemned the action of the Southern States. It was an easy matter for a man in the North to be loyal, for his friends and property interests were there; but it required patriotism of high order for one to stand by the Union and take up arms against his father and his brothers. Strong appeals came to me, one of which I recall: "Can it be possible that you are to remain with the Yankees and take up arms against the soil which holds the sacred ashes of your father and mother? Can it be possible that we are to meet on opposite sides and fight and possibly kill each other?"

Let us then be charitable to those who left, many of whom went against their own convictions of right under the pressure of family influence. I could mention many who were carried away just by the influence from the homes of their childhood, and who, when they handed in their resignations and bade us good-by, wept bitterly over the thought of breaking up old and tried friendships. There is one singular circumstance connected with the selection of sides by many of the officers, and I have never heard it mentioned by any one. Every Northern officer married to a Southern wife joined in the rebellion against the United States, and every Southern officer whose wife was from the North remained loyal to the government. I do not say that these wives had any influence upon the loyalty or disloyalty to the government of their better halves; I merely mention the fact and let each reader decide the matter for himself.

The cavalry on board the "Empire City" was ordered to Carlisle Barracks for a remount, where it arrived April 27, 1861, and united with the other companies of the regiment, under the command of Major George H. Thomas.

CHAPTER XIII.

Poor Horses—Grinding Sabres—Taking Oath of Allegiance—How to Dispose of Wife and Children—Union, Constitution, and Enforcement of Laws—Firing Harper's Ferry—General Patterson at Chambersburg—Living on the Fat of the Land—Fed by Patriotic Men and Women—Philadelphia City Troop—Where to Cross Potomac—Falling Waters—Mr. Lincoln, etc.

On the trip from New York to Carlisle Barracks we passed through a village of Dunkers. These people, like the Quakers, do not believe in settling difficulties by force of arms, yet they comfort and encourage those who do go to war by supplying plain food to combatants who pass near them. In this village a committee had been formed to board every passing train, upon which there were troops, with baskets filled with sandwiches for distribution. One of these men asked an officer from what State the troops came. He replied, "This is the Second Cavalry, from Texas." The word Texas seemed to grate upon his nerves. He looked wildly around to see if Texas had captured the Union, and then with a rush jumped from the train. The Dunkers had no bread for soldiers from Texas, even if they were loyal United States troops.

When our companies reached Carlisle Barracks great confusion existed, as is the case when cavalrymen have no horses. A cavalry soldier is incomplete without his horse, and we had yet to provide a remount. Simon Cameron, Secretary of War, gave a contract to some of his friends to supply about one thousand horses. These were brought in from day to day for examination by a board of our own officers. Such as were approved were accepted and paid for by the quartermaster. It was spring of the year, and the animals brought in had thrown off their winter coats, were well groomed, and looked sleek and fat. When enough had been received they were distributed among the companies, as far as possible making the color in each company uniform. As soon as we began to use these animals on the hard pikes of Pennsylvania, Maryland, and Virginia we found that many worthless horses had been palmed off upon us by the good people of Pennsylvania, who were much more anxious to get high prices for their stock than they were to make the cavalry efficient and thus more readily put down the rebellion. The horses in my company, at the end of the third day's march, had swollen legs, many were lame, and the company was practically on foot. The contractor who furnished this mount must have made an independent fortune in this his first contract.

While we were yet at Carlisle Barracks I went out to the carpenter's shop one day and found one of our captains superintending the grinding of the sabres of his company. I asked him why he was doing so, and he replied, "To more readily cut off rebel heads." In a few days this officer went off to settle his family, and, falling in with some of his relatives, was induced to send in his resignation, and within ten days he was in the rebel army, where he became a very distinguished officer, as he would have done in the Union army had he not fallen under the influence of his friends. If he had remained loyal, his fine record and commanding appearance would have secured promotion and he would have been one of our great leaders. Knowing this officer as well as I do, I have always regretted his final determination, believing that the natural affection of his heart was on the Union side; but when he went over he did so with all his heart, mind, and soul, and was as true in his allegiance to the South as the needle to the pole. About this time each officer began to suspect the other. No one knew who would be the next one to leave, and some few were suspicious of the loyalty of all the others. The loyalty of one officer was suspected by another because in placing the stamp on a letter he had inadvertently turned Washington's head downward instead of upward. This suspicious one thought that "no loyal man would turn the image of the Father of his Country upside down."

Every officer of the army had taken the oath of allegiance to the United States Government on entering the service, but the Washington authorities directed that it be again administered. This was thought to be an uncalled-for insult to every officer in the army, and I spoke to Major Thomas in relation to it. His reply was, "I do not care a snap of my finger about it. If they want me to take the oath before each meal I am ready to comply." So we were again sworn to "bear true faith and allegiance to the United States of America against all her enemies and opposers whomsoever."

We were soon to move against the enemy, and the

disposition to be made of my wife and children was a subject of deep moment. Neither of us had homes to which they could go, and it seemed like abandonment to leave them at a hotel or boarding-house among strangers. But something had to be done, for it was certain that they could not accompany me in the field. I finally decided on taking them to my brother's, in Owensboro', Kentucky. There they were surrounded by rebels, and one woman, who passed for a lady, once said to my wife, "I would like to see the Ohio River run red with Yankee blood." My wife was a native of a Northern State, and as I was a loyal man of course I was classified among the Yankees. Unlady-like expressions of this character coming to her ears every day—not, of course, from any member of my brother's family—made her life miserable, and she wrote to me that she could endure it no longer. That same night I rode forty miles on horseback, so as to take the morning train for the West. In three days I was with her, and in three days more my entire family was comfortably quartered at the Jones Hotel, in Harrisburg; surrounded, it is true, by strangers, but they were loyal people and friendly. That short trip to Kentucky served to intensify, if possible, her loyalty, while her brief experience strengthened me in my love for the Union and in my hatred of treason and non-combatant traitors, both male and female. I have respect for a man who will brave the dangers of the battlefield in defence of his principles, but none whatever for one who is too cowardly to fight for what he believes to be right.

It will be remembered that in 1860 there were four

Presidential candidates,—Lincoln, Douglas, Breckinridge, and Bell, the last named being the candidate of the American party, whose platform was brief but comprehensive: "The Union, the Constitution, and the enforcement of the laws." I was a sympathizer with Breckinridge, believing that he had been wrongfully defeated for the nomination in the National Convention, in Charleston. After the election was over and Mr. Lincoln was declared elected and civil war seemed imminent, my brother, Dr. John M. Johnson, a senator in the Kentucky Legislature, who had been a warm supporter of Mr. Bell, wrote to know how I stood on the political questions of the day. He was anxious to know if I was going to bear arms against the South. I replied, "I stand to-day where you stood last November, on 'the Union, the Constitution, and the enforcement of the laws.'" This was the platform upon which I stood throughout the war. From early boyhood I learned to venerate Mr. Clay, and his political views were mine because they were Mr. Clay's. When the Whig party was wiped out of existence I drifted, naturally enough, into the Democratic party, where I have ever been, though not an "offensive partisan" by any means; yet I generally find it consonant with my feelings to vote the straight Democratic ticket, and will probably continue to do so unless a new party is formed embracing the better elements of both.

While we were hastening our preparations for taking the field, the rebels were equally active, and soon appeared in threatening attitude near the nation's capital. To save it from capture the first troops organized were sent forward to Washington as rapidly as possible. The six companies of our regiment first mounted were hurried off in that direction. Companies A, C, F, and K, being the last companies to arrive at Carlisle Barracks, were the last to be supplied with horses and placed upon a war footing.

Simultaneously with the appearance of a rebel force in front of Washington, General Joseph E. Johnston, in command of a force variously estimated, marched to and took possession of Harper's Ferry. This was a very important point, as the United States Government had an arsenal there, with all the machinery necessary for manufacturing arms. The storehouses were well filled with muskets, ammunition, etc., etc. We had a small command at Harper's Ferry, which, on the appearance of such overwhelming numbers, fired the public buildings and withdrew. The fires were extinguished, presumably by the citizens, and no great damage was done to either buildings or stores.

The presence of Johnston's force created consternation in Pennsylvania, as it seemed to threaten invasion of that State, and the good people called loudly and lustily for an army to be interposed between them and the enemy. It was not the Macedonian cry of "Come over and help us," but come over and save us from the invasion of a terrible army with banners.

When the rude bullets of the enemy whistle around our uncovered heads, it is astonishing how popular the soldier becomes.

> "God and the soldier all men adore,
>   In times of war, but not before.
>   When the war is over and all things righted,
>   God is forgotten, and the soldier is slighted."

In response, however, to the earnest and persistent call for troops, a force was concentrated at Chambersburg, and General Robert Patterson, a veteran of the war of 1812, and also of the Mexican war, tendering his services to the United States Government, was commissioned major-general and assigned to that command. As no army is complete without cavalry, Patterson asked that the four companies of our regiment, then at Carlisle Barracks, be assigned to duty with his command. His request was granted, and George H. Thomas, who had been promoted to the position of colonel of the regiment, was ordered to move at once with companies A, C, F, and K to Chambersburg and report to the commanding general. These companies had been held in readiness to move at a moment's notice, so there was no delay. The command moved out, passing through a number of small villages whose patriotic inhabitants always met us with the good things of life. On that march no soldier was compelled to subsist on the government ration, but all lived on the very fat of the land furnished by the patriotic men and women along our route. On May 27, 1861, we reached Chambersburg and encamped in a beautiful piece of open woodland adjoining the town. Thomas was assigned to the command of a brigade, to which the four cavalry companies were assigned.

The Philadelphia City Troop, composed of the very flower of Philadelphia society, volunteered for ninety days and was assigned to duty with our cavalry. The troop was commanded by Captain James, and his lieutenants were Price and Camac. Price was not with the troop, being on staff duty elsewhere. To give an idea of the character of this body of men, it was said that each member was a man of reasonable fortune. All were men of education and refinement. Hon. Samuel J. Randall was first sergeant. These men submitted to regular military discipline with the air of veterans, and were as good soldiers as any with whom I met during the war.

The officers of the old army, who had for so many years learned to lean upon General Scott,—the greatest soldier the country had produced up to that time,— began now to realize that this grand old man would soon be compelled, on account of infirmities incident to age, to retire from active duties. In looking over the army officers from whom his successor would doubtless be selected, I confess that great doubt and uncertainty rested upon all. Who could possibly fill his place was the question uppermost in the minds of many. At the same time we who had learned to rely upon the great ability of Clay, Webster, and Calhoun, and a few others to extricate us from every national difficulty, looked to the United States Senate to see upon whose shoulders their mantles had fallen. Alas! their places were vacant. Mr. Lincoln, whose patriotism no one doubted, was an untried man. Truly the future looked dark and foreboding in the early days of 1861.

Experience has taught the nation a lesson. When God requires a people to do a great work, He invariably furnishes the man or men to carry it out. When Sherman, Sheridan, and all that long list and line of distinguished military men have passed away, in God's own time He will not only supply others, but greater ones, if necessary to meet the exigencies He may create.

The perpetuity of the American Republic does not depend upon any one man or any number of men. When Mr. Lincoln was cruelly and brutally murdered, after having enwrapped himself in the love and affection of every loyal man and woman in the land, the government moved right on in its accustomed orbit without vibration or perceptible friction. The Senate in 1861 was composed of men of obscurity compared with those master-minds to whom I have referred, but there was a number who proved themselves equal to the emergency, and will be regarded as men of great ability, whose names will ever be associated with the downfall of the great rebellion. And so it is: God furnishes not only soldiers, but statesmen to carry on the work He requires of nations and of peoples.

It was at Chambersburg that I first served with volunteers. While there I found it to be dangerous to be out of my tent after "taps." It is usual to challenge a passer-by, and if no reply is made then fire at him. But the volunteers reversed the order of things,—they fired first and challenged afterwards. Often the stillness of the night would be broken in upon with—Bang! "Who goes there?" The sentinel would kill his man first and then inquire who he was. Of course, the men were new and soon learned better. The greater part of them went into the three years' service and made most excellent soldiers; but while they were learning their duty, woe unto those who passed their posts after "taps."

While at Chambersburg a controversy arose between the general-in-chief and General Patterson in regard to the point at which the command of the latter should cross the Potomac into the State of Virginia. Patterson urged to be allowed to cross at Leesburg, but he was overruled and directed to cross the river at Williamsport. I shall always believe that Patterson was right and the general-in-chief wrong. In crossing at Williamsport, McDowell and Patterson were placed on exterior lines, while Beauregard and Johnston occupied interior lines, thus enabling them to unite and defeat McDowell, and with equal ease they might have turned against Patterson and driven him out of the Shenandoah Valley, thus defeating every organized force and leaving Washington a matter of easy capture. It mattered not at which place Patterson crossed, so far as Johnston's army was concerned, for in either event he would have threatened the rebel line of communication, and the evacuation of Harper's Ferry and the occupation of Winchester by Johnston would have necessarily followed. If, however, Patterson had been at Leesburg he would have been within supporting distance of McDowell, and could have joined him sooner than Johnston could have effected a junction with Beauregard. If Patterson's plan had been adopted the Federal army would have been victorious at Bull Run, and not been required to suffer a humiliating defeat.

CHAPTER XIV.

Battle of Falling Waters—Consolidation of all Mounted Regiments—Thomas appointed Brigadier-General and ordered to Report to General Anderson in Kentucky—Appointed Lieutenant-Colonel of Kentucky Cavalry—Mr. Lincoln's Kind Interest—Beau Hickman—Commodore Vanderbilt's Son—Visit to the Theatre.

SOON after crossing into Virginia the advance arrived at Falling Waters, where "Stonewall" Jackson, then not so distinguished, was encountered and defeated. Our column pushed on to Martinsburg. Here an order was received from General Scott, directing General Patterson to press General Johnston so closely as to prevent him from reinforcing Beauregard, and announcing the fact that McDowell was to move against the enemy in his front on the following Tuesday. Patterson was instructed to occupy Johnston until after that day, when he was authorized to transfer his troops and headquarters to Charlestown. A forward movement was ordered, and he marched to Bunker Hill. For several days reconnoissances were made in the direction of Winchester. On the Thursday following the Tuesday upon which the battle of Bull Run was to have been fought, the writer was sent forward in command of a body of infantry and cavalry to ascertain if Johnston was still at Winchester. Finding him there in force, on the following morning Patterson moved his army to Charlestown, and Johnston fell back and joined Beauregard on Sunday evening in time to participate in the closing battle of that day. The Federal army was put to flight, the country disappointed, and the heart of the enemy filled with joy unspeakable at his apparent success. It is an astounding fact that, notwithstanding Patterson's army was within telegraphic communication with Washington, nothing was heard of the delay to offer battle on Tuesday, nor of the result of the battle on Sunday, until the arrival of the Philadelphia newspapers in our camp on Monday morning.

Patterson's army was composed almost entirely of three months' men, whose terms of service expired about the last of July; and when they were "mustered out," General Patterson was honorably discharged, and returned to his home in Philadelphia.

The battle of Bull Run, terminating as it did, inspired the Southern people with hope and courage. In all parts of the South the wildest enthusiasm was manifested. Young and old flocked to the cities to enlist under the Confederate banner and prepare for war. About this time the Legislature of Kentucky called for General Anderson, the hero of Fort Sumter, to take charge of the Union troops in that State. President Lincoln acceded to the request, and ordered Anderson to the command of that department, designating General W. T. Sherman as his associate.

On the 3d of August, Congress passed a law consolidating the dragoons, mounted rifles, and cavalry into one arm of service, to be known as cavalry. The First and Second Dragoons became the First and Second Cavalry, the Mounted Rifles the Third Cavalry, and the First and Second Cavalry became the

Fourth and Fifth. The same act authorized an additional regiment, which was known as the Sixth. This consolidation wrought great injustice to many of the old officers of the dragoons and rifles who had to take rank under those whom they had formerly ranked. To illustrate: J. P. Hatch entered the army four years before I did, but in the new regiment I attained the rank of captain before he did in the rifles. When we were united, he had to take his place on the lineal list below me. In other cases the apparent injustice was even greater. There were many reasons why we opposed the consolidation. The reputation made by the Second Cavalry the regimental officers were extremely proud of, and now it seemed that we had to begin over again under a new name. The same feeling, doubtless, prevailed in other regiments.

On August 17, Colonel George H. Thomas was appointed brigadier-general of volunteers, and ordered to report to General Anderson, at Louisville. Soon after he left I received a letter from Hon. James S. Jackson, the member of Congress from the district in Kentucky in which I had formerly resided, informing me that he was going back to his State to raise a regiment of cavalry, and wanted me to accompany him and accept the position of lieutenant-colonel. At once I rode into Washington to confer with him. The only way this could be done was to get a leave of absence, to enable me to accept the position. I called on Adjutant-General Thomas and submitted the question to him. He objected, as I expected he would, said that regular officers if permitted to accept volunteer commissions would break up the army,—that the proper place for all regular army officers was with their companies, etc., etc. I left him convinced that one or the other of us was wanting in common sense, and I was charitable enough to myself to believe that I was not so wanting. With a sorrowful heart I proceeded to Jackson's rooms to report progress. "Well," said he, "Dick, we won't give it up yet. To-night we will go up and see Mr. Lincoln." At the designated hour I was on hand, and soon we were ushered into the presence of the President. Jackson stated the case, and Mr. Lincoln said, "Come up in the morning at ten o'clock, and I will go over with you to see Mr. Thomas." But said I, "Mr. President, I have seen him, and he objects on the ground that so many regular officers are leaving their commands that it will break up the army." "Well, well," said Mr. Lincoln, "we will go to see him any way." Promptly at ten o'clock we were again at the Executive Mansion. As I approached the President he extended his hand and said, "Good-morning, my Confederate friend." For a moment I wondered why he had addressed me as his Confederate friend, but soon learned that as Kentucky was balancing between the United States and the Confederacy, and as both of us hailed from that State, we were naturally "Confederate friends." We proceeded at once to General Thomas's office, where the President became spokesman. He said, "General Thomas, I would like to have a leave of absence granted to my Confederate friend, Captain Johnson, to enable him to accept the position of lieutenant-colonel of a Kentucky cavalry regiment." "It cannot be done," said Thomas. "But," said Mr. Lincoln, straightening himself up until he looked to be fifteen feet high, "I have not come over to discuss this question with you, General Thomas, but to order you to give the necessary instructions." "Ah, well," said Thomas, "it will all be right." Then I knew it would be. In less than an hour I had my order in my pocket. In the course of the evening I stepped into a tailor-shop to get measured for a lieutenant-colonel's uniform, and directed that it be sent to me at Louisville, Kentucky. On reaching the pavement I was accosted by a rather seedy-looking fellow by "Helloa, colonel!" I remember thinking, how can it be possible that my promotion is known so soon? Have I jumped in a few moments from an obscure captain to a colonel, and become so generally known that even this seedy-looking fellow knows me? He continued, saying that his supplies were cut off by the attitude the South had taken, and that he did not have money enough to buy medicines. He remarked, "You don't seem to know me, which argues yourself unknown." As quick as flash the thought came over me, this is none other than Beau Hickman, and such proved to be the case. I asked him what was the extent of his necessities, and he replied, about fifty cents. He was so modest in his demand that I gave him the money and passed into the hotel.

Seating myself in a good, comfortable chair to watch the crowd coming in and going out, a dapper young man came up to me and asked if I was Colonel Johnson, to which I replied affirmatively. He said, "I am the son of Commodore Vanderbilt, and am here out of money. I would like to borrow fifty dollars until morning, when my father will send me a large remittance." I wondered to myself if it could be possible that there was anything about my personal appearance that made this fellow believe that I was from the country, and therefore easily imposed upon. I was genteelly dressed, had seen a great deal of the world, and did not feel like a greenhorn by any means. I replied that I was to leave the city early in the morning, yet if he would send a despatch to his father and have him telegraph back that his draft would be honored I would get the money for him. He left saying that he would do so at once. From that time to this, it is needless to say, I have not seen Commodore Vanderbilt's son.

Probably there is a period in every boy's life when he is not very well informed in regard to the ways of the world. My father was a physician as well as a minister of the gospel, and taught me that the theatre was the "very gate of hell." So deeply had he impressed this thought upon my mind that I had never attended one, fearing that his satanic majesty might seize upon and hold me as one of his permanent boarders. On my way up the Ohio River, *en route* to West Point, I fell in with quite a number of Western merchants on their way East to purchase goods. At Wheeling we left the boat to take the stage over the mountains, but had to remain over night. After tea one of them proposed that we should all go to the theatre. I was ashamed to decline, and so went with them at the proper time. I cannot now recall the play, but remember well the closing scene. It represented a violent storm at sea. Angry and portentous clouds darkened the heavens. A vessel in sight was tossed by the mighty waves, which were lashed into a fury by the heavy winds. Lightnings flashed and thunders rolled. At last the electric current struck the vessel, and calcium lights were thrown upon it. This being the closing scene, the rowdies began to rush out. Seeing the commotion, it flashed across my mind—it is real, the house is on fire. With a bound I started for the door, riding over men, women, and children. I heard some one say, "He is crazy." I did not stop to refute the charge, but kept on until I was out in the pure open air. In double-quick I hastened to the hotel, and there awaited the return of my friends. When they came in, I asked if there were many lives lost in the conflagration. Then it was that I learned it was only a scenic display. It was many years after this that I met Commodore Vanderbilt's son.

Arranging all of my affairs in Washington, I returned to my company in order to turn over the public property for which I was responsible, and, having accomplished that, I took the first train for the West, reaching Louisville on the evening of September 17, 1861. I found the wildest excitement prevailing, occasioned by the seizure of the up-bound train from Nashville by General Simon B. Buckner, who had embarked his command thereon and was at that time *en route* to Louisville,—in fact, expected during the evening. After taking tea at the Galt House I walked out on the street, where it seemed that the entire population had assembled in groups to discuss the situation. It did not take long to ascertain that a large majority of them hoped to fall into Buckner's hands before the following morning, their sympathies being with him and against the government which had protected them so long. Well do I remember that memorable night. All was excitement, chaos, and confusion. Fast-fleeting clouds were passing, occasionally obscuring the light of the moon, and in a moment the darkness was that of night, and the next almost as light as day. It appeared to me then that this alternate light and darkness very fitly represented the disloyal and the loyal elements at that time in the city. The rebels were bright and joyful over the approach of General Buckner with his command, while the loyal people were in the dark valley of sadness and sorrow at the apparent prospect of falling under rebel rule. Many of the Union men, instead of taking up arms to defend their homes and their firesides, fled across the river, seeking safety in the State of Indiana. Indeed, it was a dark, gloomy night to every patriotic heart in Kentucky. As the train neared Elizabethtown, by a fortunate circumstance it was derailed, and by the time all things were ready to move forward General Buckner concluded not to attempt the capture of the city, but to halt and encamp in the neighborhood of that village. General Lovell H. Rousseau, one of the original Union men of Louisville, had established Camp Joe Holt on the Indiana side of the river, and enlisted a regiment which was known as the Louisville Legion. During the evening of the 17th he was ordered to move two regiments across the river. With the measured tread of disciplined soldiers they marched through the streets to the Nashville depot, where transportation was furnished to take the command to the Rolling Fork of Salt River. When the legion was known to be between Louisville and General Buckner's command, the Unionists felt more secure. On the following day the home guards, composed of a number of independent companies of Louisville, were called out and placed under my command. In compliance with instructions, I moved to Lebanon Junction and established a camp. Of the composition of this command and the services performed by it I shall have more to say in a succeeding chapter. In a few days troops came pouring into Kentucky from Ohio, Indiana, and Illinois; and the home guards, being no longer required, were disbanded and I was ordered to proceed to Owensboro', the designated rendezvous of Jackson's cavalry. It was expected that it would be the First Regiment, but in some way it became known as the Third Kentucky Cavalry.

During all this time I had been expecting my uniform for which I had been measured in Washington, but it came not. I wrote to the tailor, who informed me that it had been sent by express weeks before. I had the agent of the company send what he called a "tracer" in search of the box. It was found in Pittsburg, where it had been seized by some over-officious official as "contraband of war." Being marked Lieutenant-Colonel R. W. Johnson, First Kentucky Cavalry, Louisville, Kentucky, the official imagined that it was a uniform for a rebel, and hence he seized and held it. On proving my loyalty, which required considerable correspondence, the box was finally forwarded, and I received it after my arrival in Owensboro'. Our regiment and another had taken possession of the fair grounds. Recruits flocked in rapidly, and the prospect was flattering for an early organization. Before the companies were filled to the maximum I determined on returning to Harrisburg to remove my family to Kentucky again, intending to rent suitable accommodations in Louisville. On my arrival in that city I reported to General Sherman, who had relieved General Anderson in the command of the department, and he informed me that he had on the day previous recommended me for promotion to the rank of brigadier-general; in fact, he showed me a despatch from President Lincoln, in which he said, "In compliance with your request, I will appoint Wood and Johnson to-morrow." This was a rank I had hardly hoped to attain, and the thought uppermost in my mind was, am I competent to discharge the duties? Of this I was satisfied,—that I should do the best I could; and I was greatly encouraged to hope for success, judging by many of the appointments which had been already made. I thought if some of those who had been commissioned could command a brigade of men, I certainly ought to be able to do so. I telegraphed to my wife to hold herself in readiness to move at a moment's notice; so when I arrived in Harrisburg she was ready, and without delay we set out for Louisville. My commission dated from October 11, 1861, and I accepted it on October 14, 1861. At once I asked for the appointment of Henry Clay, of Kentucky, as captain and assistant adjutant-general United States volunteers, and his assignment to duty at my headquarters. Clay was the son of Lieutenant-Colonel Henry Clay, who was killed at the battle of Buena Vista, Mexico, and the grandson of the immortal Henry Clay, the orator and statesman. Young Clay was a man of fine promise. His education had been thorough, and he was a gentleman in every sense of the term. Exposure in camp brought on typhoid fever, from which he died. The following is a copy of the letter communicating to me my appointment as brigadier-general United States volunteers:

WAR DEPARTMENT,
October 11, 1861.

SIR:

You are hereby informed that the President of the United States has appointed you Brigadier-General of Volunteers in the service of the United States, to rank as such from the eleventh day of October, one thousand eight hundred and sixty-one. Should the Senate at their next session advise and consent thereto, you will be commissioned accordingly.

Immediately on receipt hereof, please to communicate to this department, through the Adjutant-General's Office, your acceptance or non-acceptance of said appointment; and, with your letter of acceptance, return to the Adjutant-General of the army the OATH herewith enclosed, properly filled up, SUBSCRIBED and ATTESTED, reporting at the same time your AGE, RESIDENCE, when appointed, and the STATE in which you were BORN.

Should you accept, you will at once report, by letter, for orders, to Brigadier-General W. T. Sherman, at Louisville, Kentucky.

THOMAS A. SCOTT,
Acting Secretary of War.

BRIGADIER-GENERAL RICHARD W. JOHNSON,
U. S. Volunteers.

CHAPTER XV.

Report to General McCook—Assigned to Command a Brigade—Measles—Board to Examine Incompetent Officers—Mill Springs—Enter Nashville—Army well supplied—Shiloh—Bulger—General Grant's fondness for Horses.

AGREEABLY to instructions, I reported to General Sherman in person, and he directed me to proceed to the front and report to Brigadier-General A. McD. McCook. As soon as Sherman relieved General Anderson he began the concentration of troops on Nolin Creek, on the line of the Louisville and Nashville Railroad. McCook named this camp in honor of the owner of the soil, Camp Neven. It was at this camp that I reported for duty, and it became a grand school of instruction for both officers and men.

Camp Neven will long be remembered by the troops stationed there. Here they learned for the first time something of the hardships of a soldier's life. Change of diet, wet, cold, and disagreeable weather, produced disease, and at one time the camp was little more than one vast field-hospital. McCook assigned me to the command of the Sixth Brigade, composed of the Fifteenth and Forty-ninth Ohio Volunteers, Thirty-second and Thirty-ninth Indiana Volunteers. The field-officers of the Fifteenth were colonel, Moses R. Dickey; lieutenant-colonel, ———; major, William Wallace; those of the Forty-ninth, colonel, W. H. Gibson; lieutenant-colonel, Blackman; and major, Lewis Drake.

The field-officers of the Thirty-second Indiana Volunteers were colonel, August Willich; lieutenant-colonel, H. von Trebra; and major, Schnackenburg. This regiment was composed of Germans only. The Thirty-ninth Indiana was officered as follows: Colonel, Thomas J. Harrison; lieutenant-colonel, F. A. Jones; and major, John D. Evans. These were the officers and regiments with whom and with which I had to do. Daily drills, by company, by regiment, and by brigade, began at once. When sufficient progress had been made, I gave orders for a review. Willich came to my tent to know what he should do with his baggage on review. I told him that it would not be necessary to bring out his wagons and teams. "Oh," said he, "general, I do not mean wagons; but I want to know what I shall do with my baggage, the doctor and the chaplain." The command went through with the ceremony very creditably.

Measles I had always understood to be a disease of childhood, and that few children ever escaped it. It astonished me to find that so many men had escaped it when boys to have it at Camp Neven. At one time there were so many men down with that disease that drills had to be discontinued. Cold, wet, disagreeable weather caused it to assume a dangerous character, or rather to run into some other malady which proved fatal. From my brigade alone I lost quite a large number by death, and as many more had to be discharged on surgeon's certificate of disability.

The field-officers to whom I have referred were all that I could wish for. They were intelligent, anxious and willing to learn, and took great interest in the welfare of their men. Through their indefatigable labors the troops were brought to great perfection in their duties. They were orderly and well behaved, both in camp and on the march; and on the battle-field none fought with more coolness and bravery.

On the 9th day of December, 1861, McCook ordered me to move forward with my brigade to Mumfordsville, on Green River; and on the 17th his entire command moved up, and here for long, weary weeks we floundered around in a sea of mud, which for military purposes was called Camp Wood, in honor of the father of General Thomas J. Wood, an old resident of that place, and one whose loyalty had never been questioned.

Here examining boards were appointed to examine into the qualifications of the officers, with a view to ridding the service of incompetent and unworthy ones. In these examinations great injustice was often done through prejudice on the part of regimental commanders. There was one brought up before the board of which I was the president. I was satisfied that he had incurred the displeasure of his colonel, and that otherwise he was a good soldier. He seemed so anxious to serve his country and so mortified that he should be summoned to appear with the incompetents that I made up my mind he should not be driven out of his regiment, and so he was not reported against. I watched him closely ever after, and found that my estimate of him had been correct. The last time I remember to have seen him he was commanding his company with an empty sleeve, having lost his arm in an act of heroism sufficient to immortalize his name.

In selecting surgeons and assistant surgeons for regiments, affection or partiality, rather than fitness, often dictated the appointments, and it became necessary to get rid of some of those who did not know the sartorius muscle from the femoral artery. The medical director on McCook's staff had a board ordered to examine such cases as he might send before it. This board was singularly constituted,—two line-officers and the medical director. The line-officers were not supposed to be suitable judges of the qualifications of a physician, while the only one on the board who was supposed to know anything about the subject was the one who ordered the doctors before the board. Of course, they might have just as well sent in their resignations when notified to appear before a board so constituted, for their days were numbered.

The greater part of a year had now passed with but one battle fought, and that was an inglorious defeat of our army. The country was becoming anxious. The longer we delayed, the better prepared would the rebels be when we did move against them. Mr. Lincoln was anxious that something should be done, yet he did not know just how or where to begin. He did not feel like ignoring the commanders in the field by ordering a movement at once, feeling assured that they ought to know when they were ready to strike. But our drooping spirits were greatly elated by the victory achieved by General George H. Thomas at Mill Springs, where the Confederate commander, General Felix A. Zollicoffer, was killed and his army dispersed. When compared with subsequent battles, Mill Springs was a small affair, but it was a beginning, and the troops fought nobly. The country was rejoiced, and a feeling prevailed that our army thereafter was not to be idle. In the mean time Sherman had been superseded by General Don Carlos Buell, regarded in army circles at that time as one of the ablest generals in the Federal service. He was a fine organizer and disciplinarian, and seemed to grasp the magnitude of the rebellion, and the means necessary to suppress it. It has been said that Sherman was relieved because he gave utterance to his views that two hundred thousand men would be required in order to thoroughly stamp out the rebellion. Some said, "Sherman is crazy," but after all he was right, and spoke words of wisdom, which a few pig-headed men could not comprehend. Go to any insane asylum, and each inmate will insist that all the world is crazy, and he only is sane. Possibly it was a parallel case that caused the sanity of Sherman to be questioned.

Soon after this the army was put in motion in the direction of Nashville, and General Grant notified the commander at Fort Donelson that he proposed "to move against his works without delay." He carried his threat into execution, and captured the entire garrison except Generals Pillow and Floyd and their staffs. When it became evident that Grant would compel a surrender, Pillow, who had no taste for prison-life within the walls of a "Northern bastile," turned the command over to Floyd, and he, for a similar reason, relinquished in favor of General Buckner, who was too honorable to run away and abandon the command to its fate, but like a true soldier remained to share its fortunes. Pillow and Floyd escaped by boat to Nashville, where they arrived on the Sabbath morning while the good people were in attendance upon divine service. Congregations were dismissed without the usual benediction, and all who could get away left before the arrival of the dreaded Yankee.

Floyd remained in Nashville long enough to cut the wires of the suspension bridge, and precipitate that grand structure in a shapeless mass to the bottom of the river. The rear of the column of fugitives was scarcely out of the city when Buell, with his magnificent army, arrived on the north side of the Cumberland River. Boats were procured, and the work of crossing began at once. By nine o'clock at night the troops were all over, and Nashville was in the possession of the Union army. The Federal army found a very bitter feeling prevailing in Nashville against the Yankees. From the breaking out of the war, orators, poets, the press, and the pulpit had united in instilling into the hearts of the masses the most deadly hatred against the Federal government. The soldiers were characterized as hirelings and scoundrels, worse than the old Norsemen, who had been the terror and the shame of the world. The people had been told that when the Sunny South was disgraced and humiliated by the tread of mercenary soldiers, barbarities, atrocities, and outrages worse than those ever perpetrated in the deepest, darkest night of heathenism would be heaped upon them by the Northern horde. Buell tried conciliation, and we soon found that his course had a happy effect upon those who had previously been so bitterly opposed to the general government.

I shall never forget the night we crossed the river and entered Nashville. A cold rain had been falling nearly all day, and when evening came the mercury fell below the freezing point. My brigade crossed after dark, and had to march out several miles on one of the pikes to the camp designated for McCook's command. My clothes, which had been thoroughly wet all day, were frozen on me, and of course every officer and soldier in the command was in the same plight. Arriving at the place, I was shown an open field in which to encamp for the night. This field was enclosed by a stone fence, which we could not burn, and there was no wood in sight; hence we could have no fires. In the absence of fire without, it was thought advisable to kindle one within; accordingly, two barrels of whiskey were delivered to the brigade commissary for issue to the men. This seemed to arouse their drooping spirits, and they were enabled to endure the storm until morning. After pointing out to the regimental commanders where to bivouac their men, I observed a tent near by in which there was a light, and I went to it, hoping to find it occupied by an acquaintance or by a gentleman who would invite me to share it with him. I found the occupant to be a recently-appointed major in one of the new regular regiments, and I proceeded to thrust myself upon his hospitality. There was room enough in the tent for the major, myself, and staff, yet he seemed to regard us as intruders. Possibly we were, but the case was too desperate to stand on dignity or ceremony. Had he been an old officer, or a clear-cut, thoroughbred gentleman, he would have gladly shared his tent with us; but he was neither, and therefore ignorant of the usages common among gentlemen, and especially among soldiers. The true soldier will divide his last crust of bread or share his blanket with a comrade; for there are no ties that bind members of the human family so closely together as those forged in the furnace of common privations, common hardships, and common dangers.

For some reason unknown, the Senate refused to confirm his appointment, and soon he "disappeared from history."

On the following morning General McCook selected suitable camping-grounds for each brigade, and soon they had immense log fires, their clothes were dried, the seething camp-kettle told of coffee, and the patient soldiers soon forgot the hardships and trials of the night before. On our way out from Nashville, on the previous evening, I noticed a young soldier struggling along without shoes. His feet were bleeding, and he was suffering from the intense cold. I had him mount my extra horse and ride into camp. Not a word of complaint was uttered by him, and I was astonished to see a man under such trying circumstances so light-hearted and happy.

We read of the terrible hardships of the soldiers of the Revolution, but there were often cases in the war of the rebellion where there was as much suffering and as many privations as were endured and experienced by those brave and patriotic men to whom we are indebted for the liberty and freedom we enjoy. In the Revolutionary war none of the troops were properly supplied, and all suffered. In the war of the rebellion supplies were abundant, and cases of suffering were rare and only temporary.

When we remember the size of the army, it is wonderful how thoroughly the wants of its members were supplied from the very beginning of the war. If subsistence stores were at any time scarce, it was not for the want of them, but for the temporary derangement of our modes of transportation, which could not be foreseen or guarded against.

After a short delay General Buell moved his army south. On reaching Columbia it was necessary to construct a bridge before the troops could cross Duck River, and while encamped at that point I had a violent attack of typhoid pneumonia, and my brigade surgeon informed me that my restoration was contingent upon more care and greater comforts than I could have in camp, so I was granted a sick-leave, and returned to my family in Louisville. Colonel W. H. Gibson, of the Forty-ninth Ohio, being the senior colonel, commanded the brigade ably and well during my absence. A few days after I left Columbia, General Buell received a despatch from General Grant to hasten to his relief on the wooded banks of the Tennessee.

Cutting down the transportation to the lowest limit, and leaving behind any and everything which would impede his progress, Buell moved with great rapidity. When forty miles away the booming of cannon was distinctly heard, and served to nerve the soldiers to extraordinary effort to reach the battle-field, that they might share in the glory to be achieved by our arms. Buell with his command arrived very opportunely on the memorable field of Shiloh. A great deal has been said and written about the management of the campaign leading to this conflict and about the battle itself. There are parties who contend that our troops were surprised and many captured in their tents, and this has been repeatedly denied over and over again. Without espousing the cause of either side, I can say that, in my opinion, and in the opinion of many others, Buell's timely arrival saved General Grant's army from overthrow and defeat, if not from complete and thorough annihilation itself.

This battle was fought on the 6th and 7th days of April, 1862.

On April 10 the news was received in Louisville, and although still far from being a well man, I took a steamer for Pittsburg Landing, where I arrived on April 14. The troops were still encamped on the battle-field, and everywhere were to be seen unmistakable evidences of the fierceness of the conflict. Our dead had been decently buried. The enemy, before retiring, attempted to bury their dead within their own lines, but so imperfectly was it done that in many instances the bodies were not covered, and arms and feet projected from under the light covering of earth placed upon them. The stench was terrible, and it became necessary to detail parties to go over the field to cover up completely partially-exposed bodies.

General H. W. Halleck had arrived on the field and assumed control of all the forces. General Grant was assigned as "second in command," a position about as important as the fifth wheel to a wagon. He felt keenly the degradation, but submitted like a true soldier, trusting to the future for vindication, and in due time it came. Had he asked to be relieved, it would have been granted, and that would have been the last of Ulysses S. Grant.

A few days after my return I mounted my horse to ride over the battle-field. When out some distance I met a gentleman mounted on a cream-colored horse who said to me, "You have the only horse in this army which I prefer to my own." Supposing him to be some horse-fancier who either wanted to swap horses with me or buy mine, I said that I could not entertain the idea of parting with my horse. He is as good as he looks, and the best-broken horse I ever owned. He is fast, sure-footed, and handsome, and his gaits, either walk, trot, or gallop, are all easy. I could not replace him, and therefore he will die mine. The gentleman introduced himself as Grant. "What," said I, "General Grant?" "Yes, that is what they call me." It was the first time I ever met the general.

While on the subject of horses, let me say that they are very much like men, either brave or cowardly, sensible or foolish. The horse upon which I was mounted when spoken to by General Grant, was both brave and sensible. He was not afraid of brass bands, and he would not flinch if a cannon was fired within a few feet of him. Such a horse is invaluable. "Bulger," as the groom called him, from his beautiful form, graceful carriage, and proud aristocratic appearance was better known throughout the army than his owner. I was not astonished that General Grant, a fine horseman, should fancy him on sight. It is said that General Grant, while he was President, fancied a horse he saw in a butcher's wagon. He purchased the animal for two hundred dollars, and had him delivered at the President's stables. A few days after this he took Senator Conkling to see his purchase. After Conkling had examined all his points, Grant asked him what he thought of the horse? Conkling replied, "I would rather have the two hundred dollars." "That is just what the butcher thought," replied the President.

CHAPTER XVI.

March on Corinth—Conflict May 27—Rebel takes Oath of Allegiance—March to Bridgeport—Buell falls back to Louisville—Perryville—Rosecrans relieves Buell—Buell's Court of Inquiry—General Milroy and the Woman's Cow—Safe Places—Courage, Wounds, etc., etc.

WHEN General Halleck had made his arrangements, and had learned all about the country between Shiloh and Corinth through his corps of spies, he caused an order to be issued for a general forward movement of his entire army.

The roads were in a wretched condition, and to make them passable for our artillery and baggage-wagons, miles and miles of "corduroy" had to be laid. This required much time, and our progress was necessarily slow. The roads gave abundant evidence, by the abandoned wagons and other property, of the demoralization of the Confederate army when it fell back. After many days we arrived in front of Corinth, and within artillery range of the centre of the village. There were attached to our army about four hundred pieces of artillery, including light batteries and heavy siege-guns, and why Halleck did not let loose those dogs of war has ever been a mystery to me. I believed then, as I believe now, that Beauregard and his entire army was completely at our mercy, that the last one of them could have been captured, or at least a sufficient number of them to practically destroy the usefulness of his army and break it up forever.

Beauregard replaced his artillery by Quaker guns, —that is, cannon made of wood,—and our army was held at bay by this formidable array of Quaker artillery while he was engaged in moving his stores and munitions of war. His evacuation was perfect, and he carried with him everything of value. Halleck captured many pieces of wooden artillery and a dirty, filthy town, and a few men who preferred to remain and be captured. This was considered a great victory, and throughout the North there was great rejoicing. Then followed a report that General Pope had captured about thirty thousand prisoners, or thereabouts, which caused still greater rejoicing. This last report, which had little or no foundation in fact, was the subject of some disagreement between Generals Pope and Halleck, but just how it was settled, if ever, I am not advised. One thing is certain, and that is, only a few willing prisoners were taken at the capture of Corinth. On the day before the evacuation (May 27) my brigade was warmly engaged with some troops in its front. The firing was very heavy on both sides, but we drove the enemy to his intrenchments, and could have driven him beyond had there been a general movement of the entire line from right to left.

Whenever a citizen of the country was arrested for disloyalty, the oath of allegiance was generally administered to him, and then he was permitted to go his way. This was of such frequent occurrence that it became a by-word with the men. On one occasion a fellow called out, "I have got a rattlesnake. What shall be done with him?" A dozen voices cried out, "Administer the oath and let him go home."

A good story was told of a deserter from "Stonewall" Jackson's command. He came into the Federal lines, and wanted to know what he should do to become a loyal citizen. The officer showed him the oath to which he would have to subscribe. After reading it over, he said he could take the oath, which was then administered. "Now," said the reb, "am I entitled to the same privileges to which any Northern man is entitled? Am I to be henceforth considered one of you?" Being assured that such would be the case as long as he maintained his loyalty, the reb coolly replied, "Then, didn't 'Stonewall' Jackson give *us* thunder down on the Rapidan?"

McCook's division remained in camp near Corinth until June 6, and then moved and established a camp two miles south of Corinth. Here it remained until June 10, when, in conjunction with the other divisions of General Buell's army, it moved eastward into Tennessee. This movement threatened the very vitals of the Confederacy, and Bragg saw at once the necessity of compelling Buell to fall back.

As the Confederate commander did not feel strong enough to make a direct attack on the Federal army, he resolved to accomplish by strategy that which he was unable to do by force of arms. For this reason the invasion of Kentucky was planned.

Bragg crossed the Tennessee River at or near Chattanooga, ascended the Cumberland Mountains, thence down in the Sequatchie Valley, from which position he could strike for Nashville or Louisville, as circumstances might seem to direct. Buell saw at once that this movement threatened his entire line of communication. It was evidently Bragg's intention to move on Nashville, but by the rapid movement of Buell he kept his army at all times between Nashville and the rebel army.

Bragg, finding it impossible to reach Nashville without fighting a desperate battle, changed his plan, and deflected his course and marched upon Louisville. This movement was promptly met, and for some days it seemed doubtful which army would be the first to reach the Ohio River. Again great excitement prevailed throughout the city. The disloyal element was in high glee, and again Union men fled to some point of safety north of the Ohio River, instead of arming themselves and aiding in repelling the advancing enemy. Finally, suspense was at an end, for Buell and his tired and dusty veterans reached Louisville and took possession of the city. Bragg had been fairly beaten in the race, and taking a position at Perryville, awaited further movements of Buell. He did not have long to wait, for in a few days the troops moved to meet him. This meeting took place near Perryville, and resulted in one of the fiercest battles of the war. I have no desire to enter into any discussion of the particulars of that bloody struggle. Errors have been persistently charged upon some of the gallant gentlemen who figured most conspicuously upon that occasion. But I will say that, in my humble judgment, if any errors were committed there, they were the results of honest misapprehension of fact, and were the errors of men who have proven their mettle and chivalry in the midst of conflicts as terrible as ever shook the earth or crimsoned the soil of the battle-field. By an unfortunate circumstance all the troops were not engaged at any one time, the result of which was a partial failure,—that is, the victory was not as complete as it should have been. Our army held its ground, and the enemy fell back. Had Buell's plans been carried out thoroughly, I am satisfied that he would have crushed Bragg's army and rendered it useless for future operations.

The government became dissatisfied with Buell's management, and General W. S. Rosecrans, whose brilliant exploits in Mississippi had brought him prominently to the front, was designated as his successor.

A court of inquiry was ordered at General Buell's request, and it sat for many months. Finally, the record was forwarded to Washington, where it was 'pigeon-holed" and never published. In fact, it is said that the original proceedings were mysteriously withdrawn from the files, and had it not been that the short-hand reporter kept his notes, nothing would have ever been definitely known in regard to the action of the court. A duplicate copy was obtained and published by order of Congress, from which it appears that Buell's management was sustained throughout.

I was a great admirer of General Buell, and regarded him as one of our ablest generals. He was firmly convinced that great achievements could only be expected from thoroughly disciplined troops, and hence his great desire was to have an army of men governed by law and orders, upon whom he could rely in great emergencies. He was opposed to unnecessary destruction of private property. He felt that we appeared among the Southern people as the representatives of good government, and that it was a part of our duty to show them that the old government of the "stars and stripes" was better than the one proposed by the Southern disloyalists. There were a few men in our army who believed in the destruction of everything by fire and sword, and these men were opposed to Buell because he was opposed to their mode of warfare, which was destructive of all discipline. These "do as you please" soldiers did much to prejudice public opinion against him and to demand his removal. Buell saw at once that the war was a peculiar one. We were not fighting a foreign foe, but a people with whom we hoped again to live in peace and harmony; and to accomplish this, our duty called us to oppose with all our might every armed force within our reach. The destruction of their armies and their materials of war only concerned us. Horses, mules, and such articles as our army required the laws of civilized warfare authorized us to take.

When the historian sits down to write the history of the rebellion, after its principal actors have passed away, the services of General Buell will be recognized, and his splendid campaigns will serve as lessons to students in the military art; and when the names of those who so cruelly pursued him shall have been forgotten, his name will shine brightly on the pages of our national history. The grandest mistake of his life was his resignation. He should have remained, and time would have righted all things, and he would have stood among the greatest of our leaders.

I remember, after the battle at Chattanooga, we found a large number of houses on Lookout Mountain. The destruction of these buildings seemed to be the great desire of some men. I saw, in the future, that we might want them for hospital purposes, and I stationed a guard to protect them. Some scribbler to a Northern paper said that my sympathies were with the rebels because I protected these houses. True enough, they were occupied and used by our sick and wounded whose fevered brows were fanned by the cool breezes of that high elevation. I saw a little farther into the future than some of the men who denounced me for being opposed to their destruction, and many a poor sick soldier was doubtless restored to health by the pure mountain air he there enjoyed.

I remember seeing an article in some newspaper about General Milroy and a rebel woman. Both armies had occupied her farm, and in consequence every article of subsistence had been taken from her, until finally all she had left was an old cow, upon the milk of which she subsisted. Milroy, or some of his command, took the cow. She went to see the general to request that old "Pidey" might be returned to her. He received her with great cordiality. She stated the object of her visit. Milroy, straightening himself up, said, "Madam, you can't have the cow; this rebellion must be put down." "All right," said the old woman, "if you can put down the rebellion with my old cow, go on and do it." I do not vouch for the truthfulness of the story. I give it just as I read it in one of the newspapers of the country during the war.

I have often tried to determine in my own mind, by

inquiry of many persons who have been participants in battles, as to the safest and the most dangerous places on battle-fields. I am satisfied that the solution of this problem depends to a great extent on the character of the enemy. In Indian warfare, as they have no baggage, no base of supplies, and no lines of communication, they are free to attack in the front, on the flanks, or in the rear. So one place is as safe or as dangerous as any other. But with a civilized foe, about equal in number with the opposing force, the commander cannot divide his command into many attacking parties. The front and flanks are about all to which he can give attention, and hence there are a few points of comparative safety, although these are not posts of honor.

Strange as it may appear, in my opinion the safest place within the range of the enemy's guns is on the skirmish line. Here the men are widely separated; and, in order that they may be killed or wounded, deliberate aim must be taken, and the chances of missing under the excitement incidental to battle are very great. When masses fire at each other they are in such a hurry to deliver their fire that as a rule the aim is too high, and the bullets go whistling over the head, to fall into the ranks of the reserve, or among the teamsters of the baggage train. In a battle where masses meet each other, a position in the main line is preferable to one in the reserve for the above reason; and if you are in the main line you are liable to strike an easy place where the fighting is not so severe. If in the reserve, you are called into action only to replace some command which has been driven back by overwhelming numbers, and you have to take position under difficulties, and confront an enemy already flushed with partial success.

Before any of the great battles were fought I heard many officers and soldiers express the fear that, when the critical moment arrived, they might find themselves so wanting in courage they would run away from the field. Here is a case of this character, from the experience of a private soldier:

"On one occasion my file-leader, or the man who stood in front of me in the ranks, turned and said, 'If you see me attempt to run, or if I show the white feather, knock me down. I feel now as though I was going to bolt, and I believe if I have a chance I will go like lightning. If I start grab me, kick me, pound me, but don't let me run.'

"The fight came on, and the line at the flanks went back and back, and the centre began to falter. The man who had been in front of me was beside me. As the sweeping rebel line came down on us he said, with ghastly face, 'Let's meet them half way.' He sprang forward with a whoop, and that part of the line went with him. There was an awkward and furious struggle, but in five minutes we were pursuing the Confederates through the cornfield; and in rare exhilaration of spirits the man who had been afraid he would bolt was conducting himself after the manner of a frolicksome dog.

"He told me afterwards that he spent in that cornfield with bullets whizzing about him the happiest minutes of his life. He was happy because he had proven himself a better man than he thought he was. He was hysterically happy because he discovered that after all he was not a coward, and after that he never had a doubt of himself. He had none of the daring that made men rejoice in a fight, but he had that sort of self-control that made a good sharp-shooter, that made a man to be depended on in the crisis of battle, that made a good volunteer to charge a battery, and he made a reputation as a man of rare and indomitable courage."

Pride, if nothing more, will generally carry a man into battle, although there are cases of constitutional weakness that even pride cannot overcome, but these cases are rare indeed.

The great trouble with a man who goes into battle for the first time is that he imagines every gun of the enemy is aimed at him, and if his position is charged upon he alone will have to receive the shock. He fails to recognize the fact that weak men combined together make a solid, compact phalanx that cannot be overturned or driven at pleasure. It is the gentle raindrop which precedes the flood, and by uniting with others makes up the rushing, seething torrent. It is the little rivulet which sings its way along, gathering strength as it proceeds, until finally it is lost in the deep, broad waters of the mighty river.

It is the aggregation of men that makes irresistible armies. When the soldier has been disciplined to understand that he is only a drop in the army with which he serves, and that "in union there is strength," he moves forward to the contest with the steady tread of the veteran.

Some one whose time could not have been valuable has ascertained the number killed and the ammunition expended in a number of battles.

Calculating the weight of the bullets and dividing by the number killed, the quotient he found to be two hundred and forty-three. From this he drew the conclusion that it required two hundred and forty-three pounds of lead to kill one man. If this be true, surely the risk in battle is not very great.

I have noticed a great difference between a wounded Indian and a wounded white man. The former believes that his condition in the happy hunting-grounds depends upon the number of his enemies he has slain, and hence when he feels that he has received a mortal wound he is nerved to desperation to increase the number of his dead. The white man has no such belief, and his thoughts turn to other matters "beyond this vale of tears." He has no longer any use for his musket, and almost invariably his thoughts turn to her who gave him birth, and his last words are, generally, a message of love to her. I would rather attack five able-bodied Indians than one whose wound is such as to prevent his escape and still allow him the use of his arms and hands, for as long as he has an arrow in his quiver, or a bullet in his pouch, he is a dangerous and formidable enemy.

CHAPTER XVII.

The Battle of Stone River—Colonel Thomas E. Rose—Author of Tunnel under Libby Prison—Makes his Escape and Reaches the Federal Lines—Rose at present in the United States Army.

THE unsatisfactory termination of the battle of Perryville decided the President on making a change in the commander of the Fourteenth Army Corps, and General W. S. Rosecrans, whose brilliant exploits in Mississippi and elsewhere had brought him prominently before the country as a great and successful commander, was selected to relieve General D. C. Buell.

On assuming command, Rosecrans found Bragg and his army in full retreat, which continued until he had reached Murfreesboro'. It has always seemed to me that a great mistake was made by Bragg, as the line of the Cumberland River would have been much more easily defended than the position he took at Murfreesboro', which offered no natural defences whatever. General Rosecrans occupied Nashville on the 7th of November, and from that date to the 26th of December was untiring in his efforts to get the troops under him in readiness for an active, vigorous campaign. Every department of the staff was busily occupied, while Rosecrans, through a corps of faithful, energetic scouts, was informing himself in regard to the character and resources of the country, the position and strength of the enemy, and the avenues by which he could be reached. General Bragg did not expect a winter campaign. He had established his army in winter-quarters at Murfreesboro', and supposed that the Federal army would remain in Nashville all winter. In order that the cavalry could be more easily supplied with forage, and for the purpose of threatening the communications of Rosecrans, Bragg despatched the greater part of that force under its skilful and able leaders to West Tennessee and Kentucky. The absence of these important forces was seized upon by Rosecrans as the opportune time to move forward; so accordingly, the day following Christmas, the Federal army, in "all the pomp and circumstance of glorious war," marched forth to meet the enemy.

It was positively known that the forces of Polk and Kirby Smith were at Murfreesboro', and that Hardee's corps was on the Shelbyville and Nolansville turnpike, between Triune and Eaglesville. The Federal army moved in three columns, in accordance with the following instructions of General Rosecrans:

McCook, with three divisions, to advance by the Nolansville pike to Triune. Thomas, with two divisions (Negley's and Rousseau's), to advance on his right, by the Franklin and Wilson pikes, threatening Hardee's right, and then to fall in by the cross-roads to Nolansville. Crittenden, with Wood's, Palmer's, and Van Cleve's divisions, to advance by the Murfreesboro' turnpike to La Vergne.

With Thomas's two divisions at Nolansville, McCook was to attack Hardee at Triune, and if the enemy reinforced Hardee, Thomas was to support McCook.

If McCook defeated Hardee, or Hardee retreated, and the enemy met us at Stewart's Creek, five miles south of La Vergne, Crittenden was to attack him. Thomas was to come in on his left flank, and McCook, after detaching a division to pursue or observe Hardee, if retreating southward, was to move with the remainder of his force in pursuit of him.

Here it will be well to understand that the Fourteenth Corps, for convenience, was subdivided into three parts,—the right wing, the centre, and the left wing. These subdivisions were commanded by McCook, Thomas, and Crittenden, in the order named, and each was composed of three divisions. The second division, commanded by the writer, was composed of the following troops:

First Brigade: Brigadier-General A. Willich, commanding.—Forty-ninth Ohio, Colonel W. H. Gibson; Fifteenth Ohio, Colonel Wallace; Thirty-ninth Indiana, Lieutenant-Colonel Fielding Jones; Thirty-second Indiana, Lieutenant-Colonel Eckelmeyer; Eighty-ninth Illinois, Lieutenant-Colonel Hotchkiss; Goodspeed's First Ohio Battery.

Second Brigade: Brigadier-General E. N. Kirk.—Thirty-eighth Indiana, Colonel J. B. Dodge; Twenty-ninth Indiana, Lieutenant-Colonel Dunn; Seventy-seventh Pennsylvania, Lieutenant-Colonel Houssam; Seventy-ninth Illinois, Colonel Reed; Thirty-fourth Illinois, Lieutenant-Colonel Bristol; Edgarton's Battery, First Ohio Artillery.

Third Brigade: Colonel P. P. Baldwin.—Sixth Indiana, Lieutenant-Colonel Tripp; Fifth Kentucky (Louisville Legion), Lieutenant-Colonel W. W. Berry; First Ohio, Major Stafford; Ninety-third Ohio, Colonel Charles Anderson; Simonson's Indiana Battery. Major Klein's Battalion, Third Indiana Cavalry, was on duty with the division.

I have been thus particular in giving the composition of my division, in order that the gallant men whom I had the honor to command at the battle of Stone River may have justice done them even at this late day. I have always supposed that truth would ultimately vindicate itself, but in the evening of a life prolonged beyond the average, I am forced to say that error, when once well on its way, is very difficult to overtake and correct.

> "Truth crushed to earth will rise again,
> The eternal years of God are hers;
> But Error, wounded, writhes in pain,
> And dies amid her worshippers."

This is good poetry and good sentiment, but my experience teaches me to doubt its truthfulness.

A pebble dropped in mid-ocean creates a circular ripple, which goes on and on and never ceases. Another pebble dropped in a second after creates a like ripple, but the latter never overtakes the former, and so error starting first outruns the truth.

At six o'clock on the morning of the 26th, Davis's division moved out on the Edmonson turnpike with orders to march to Prim's blacksmith-shop, and thence by a country road to Nolansville. Sheridan moved at the same hour on the direct road to Nolansville, followed by my division. Skirmishing was kept up all day by the advance, and the entire command of General A. McD. McCook encamped on the hills beyond the town of Nolansville. It had rained almost incessantly the first day out, and the roads had become muddy and difficult of travel, but the enthusiasm of the men was very great at the prospect of meeting the enemy in an open combat. At daylight on the 27th the command moved forward, Stanley, with the cavalry, in advance, followed by my division. When about two miles out the advance became engaged with the enemy's cavalry, which was supported by artillery. The firing becoming quite brisk, the column pushed rapidly on until ascending a ridge, when it was opened on by shot and shell. A proper disposition of the troops was made, and the line moved cautiously, yet quickly forward, overtaking the cavalry, which was steadily pushing the enemy back. Soon the advance met the Confederates in force. Edgarton's battery was placed in position, supported by the Thirtieth Indiana. The battery was skilfully handled, and soon silenced the guns of the enemy and drove them beyond the range of our artillery. While Edgarton's battery was playing upon the enemy, I directed Baldwin's brigade to take position on the right of the road. The First Ohio, Major J. A. Stafford, and the Sixth Indiana, Lieutenant-Colonel Tripp, in deployed lines, supported by the Louisville Legion, Lieutenant-Colonel W. W. Berry, and the Ninety-third Ohio, Colonel Charles Anderson. Simonton's battery was posted on the road. My first brigade, General A. Willich, was held in reserve. Owing to the dense, heavy fog which settled down upon us, any movement we might make was hazardous, so it was deemed advisable to wait for it to rise, which it did about eight or nine o'clock. We then moved forward for the balance of the day in the same order. About four o'clock we ascended a high hill which overlooked the town of Triune. Here the enemy was in plain view in line of battle, with the centre in the town, and the flanks extended to the right and left. Edgarton's and Simonton's batteries were brought into action, and did good service, disabling one of the enemy's guns. The Sixth and Twenty-ninth Indiana, and Thirty-fourth Illinois charged upon the enemy's battery, but the artillerists did not stand to receive the bayonet. Just about this time it seemed that the flood-gates of heaven were opened. The rain descended in blinding sheets, rendering pursuit out of the question. The storm continued about an hour, after which the pursuit was resumed until darkness closed in upon us. We encamped for the night about two miles south of the town of Triune, where we remained on the 28th awaiting developments.

Under instructions from General McCook, I sent Willich's brigade to determine whether the enemy had retired to Shelbyville or to Murfreesboro'. This reconnoissance was extended seven miles to the front, and developed the fact that Hardee had retreated to Murfreesboro'. This fact settled in our mind where the great battle was to be fought. On the 29th, McCook's command was again in motion on the Bole Jack road. Baldwin's brigade of my division was ordered to remain at Triune as a corps of observation, taking a position on the north bank of Wilson's Creek. One company of Klein's cavalry and a section of Simonton's battery were left with this brigade. This position was only temporary, designed to protect the right flank of McCook's command. On the night of the 29th I encamped with Kirk's and Willich's brigades near the Salem road, and within five miles of Murfreesboro' and near Davis's division. On the 30th, McCook advanced his command, Sheridan's division covering the Wilkinson pike and Davis in line on Sheridan's right. My division was held in reserve. McCook directed me to order Baldwin to join his proper division, which he did about dusk on the 30th. The operations of the day had forced the enemy to develop his entire line of battle, and when night came we rested upon our arms in readiness for a heavy battle on the following morning. In the rear of McCook's main line was a large, open cotton-field. Sheridan and Davis were on the south side of this cotton-field, while I was directed to go into camp in the timber on the north side, placing my command in the rear of the centre of Davis's division, looking well to my right flank. During the evening, General McCook received a message from General Davis, in which he expressed some uneasiness in regard to the safety of his right flank, and requested that a brigade be sent from my division to take position on his right, and McCook so ordered. I directed Kirk's brigade to take position on Davis's right, and instructed him to refuse his right flank. Soon Kirk asked for troops to be placed on his right, and I sent Willich's brigade, instructing him to throw his right well to the rear. On the north side of the cotton-field, and just in front of my reserve brigade, with which I was encamped, an ordinary country road was laid out, and upon this road Willich had his headquarters, distant from mine about a half-mile. I mention this distance because it has been asserted by some camp followers that my headquarters were a mile and a half in rear of my line.

In the course of the evening General Rosecrans furnished General McCook with an order to the effect that a great battle was to be fought on the following day. "If our right was attacked, it was to fall back slowly, contesting the ground, and our left was to cross Stone River and move into Murfreesboro'. If the enemy failed to attack, we were to do so at a signal to be given by General Rosecrans." McCook called his division commanders together and explained to each one what was expected of him. On retiring from General McCook's headquarters I called my brigade commanders around me and explained the order, and when they left each understood thoroughly what was required of his command. The line of the entire army in its relative position was this: The right of Wood's division rested upon the Nashville pike, and his left on Stone River; Palmer's was on Wood's right; Negley's on Palmer's right; Sheridan on Negley's right; Davis's on the right of Sheridan; and Kirk's and Willich's brigades of my division on the right and rear of Davis's division. The reserves of each division were in the rear of their respective divisions. General Rosecrans desired to create the impression that he was massing his forces heavily on our right. Accordingly he allowed no fires to be built by the troops in line, but had immense log fires made away off to our right, and Lieutenant-Colonel Langdon, of the Second Ohio, who had an immensely heavy voice, was sent out to these fires to give commands locating imaginary divisions, brigades, and regiments. Now this plan would have succeeded with an unenterprising enemy, but Bragg knew as many of the tricks of war as Rosecrans. Feeling assured that where we professed to be strong we were really weak, Bragg, during the night, massed a force consisting of Cleburne's and McCown's divisions of infantry, flanked by Wharton's cavalry, opposite to the right of our army. These divisions of the Confederate army were composed of four brigades each. Desiring to be entirely correct in regard to the troops opposed to me, I sent a copy of our official map of the battle-field to Major-General B. F. Cheatham, a distinguished officer of the Confederate army, and asked him to indicate thereon the position of the Confederate troops, which he kindly did, and returned to me with the following letter:

BEECH GROVE, COFFEE CO., TENN., October 18, 1885.

DEAR GENERAL,—I received your letter last evening, and, in reply, will say that Polk's corps was composed of two divisions, commanded by General Withers and myself. Withers's, not having been in the battle of Perryville, was stronger than mine, was placed in the front line, his right resting on the Nashville pike, and extended a little north of west to the old road to Franklin. My division was formed in the rear of Withers's. Cleburne was on my left, and west of the Franklin road. McCown was on the left of Cleburne, and Wharton's cavalry on McCown's left. McCown advanced first, and it was his troops that first struck Willich. By arrangement with General Withers, during the battle he commanded my two right brigades, and I commanded his two left brigades. You can rely upon the positions as given on the map as being correct. My headquarters were on the left of Coltart's brigade.

     Yours respectfully,
        B. F. CHEATHAM.

Now we are able to determine just how the attack was made. Anderson's and Chalmers's brigade of Withers's division, supported by Stewart's and Donelson's brigades of Cheatham's division, attacked Sheridan.

Coltart's and Manygault's brigades of Withers's division, supported by Vaughn's and Maney's brigades of Cheatham's division, attacked Davis.

Cleburne's four brigades attacked Kirk's brigade of my division, and McCown's four brigades attacked Willich's brigade, while Wharton's cavalry operated on Willich's flank.

The concentration of the force to attack my position was made during the night, and this movement on the part of the enemy was noticed by Lieutenant-Colonel Fielding Jones, the officer in charge of my picket-line, and he reported it to me. I reported to McCook, who at once made the fact known to General Rosecrans, who did not think it advisable to make any change in his programme; at least none was made. At three o'clock on the 31st I breakfasted, and had the transportation connected with my headquarters moved to the rear,—a movement the teamsters did not stop until they had reached Nashville. The horses belonging to myself, staff, and orderlies were saddled and ready for immediate use. About six o'clock General Willich rode up to my headquarters, and while talking with me a shot was fired. I looked at my watch, and it was just twenty-two minutes after six o'clock. At once Willich started at full speed to join his command, and in his haste ran through his line; his horse was killed, and he was captured by the enemy and his valuable services were lost to us. Onward advanced the countless legions of the enemy. The color of their uniforms blending with the gray of the morning rendered their movements discernible only by the terrific fire of artillery and musketry, which mowed deep and broad furrows in our ranks. The muzzles of a hundred cannon belched forth fire, shot, and shell, and the earth and the air were tremulous with the terrific vibration.

The atmosphere was heavy with sulphurous smoke from these countless engines of war. At times dense clouds would envelop the combatants, and then lift themselves up like feathery fringes and be carried away, revealing the advancing but depleted columns of the enemy. McCook was everywhere urging the men to deeds of noble daring, and proved himself a hero worthy of the honored name he bore. General Kirk was seriously wounded about the first fire, and had to leave the field. These two casualties necessitated the change of brigade commanders in the face of an outnumbering foe. Colonel W. H. Gibson succeeded Willich, and Colonel J. B. Dodge succeeded Kirk. Under these gallant commanders the brave men of these brigades were rallied, and did efficient service during the day. Now, any one can see the utter absurdity of two brigades, outnumbered more than four to one, holding their ground against such odds. That they fell back in disorder was not to their discredit. No equal number of troops could have done better.

As soon as Willich started from my headquarters, I mounted and started down after him at full speed. Soon I heard a soldier say, "Don't go there, general, or you will be captured." Turning at once to the right, I joined Baldwin's reserve brigade, and had him deploy along a fence, in front of which was an open field over which the enemy had to pass. While they were marching over that field the fire of this brigade told with fearful effect; but it, too, had to fall back. In a short time my division was reformed on the Nashville pike, and assisted in checking the enemy in his victorious march. The dead of both armies, which were strewn on the field passed over by my command, showed very conclusively that it did most excellent service. The first fire in the morning killed or crippled nearly all the horses in Edgarton's battery; and he, badly wounded, with his guns, fell into the hands of the enemy. It has been said many times that the reason this battery was lost was due to the fact that the horses had been taken away for water, and some have censured me for not having them harnessed and hitched. Now, is it not reasonably certain that if the horses had been taken away to water they would have been taken to some pool or stream in the rear? If taken to the rear, would they have been captured? If the guns had been without horses our loss would have been the guns only; but few, if any, of the horses were ever seen alive after that battle. If away to water, how can we account for the seventy-five dead horses around where the battery stood?

Admitting that they were taken to water, would it be expected that a division commander would have to tell a brigade commander to see that his artillery horses were harnessed and hitched, when he had already told him that a battle was to be fought on the following morning? I should think such precaution as unnecessary as to instruct him to have his guns loaded when he went into battle, or to tell each man to press on the trigger of his gun when he wished to discharge it at an enemy.

But, unfortunately for those who raised that point, it was untrue. General Kirk was a gallant man, a good soldier, and a careful commander, who died from the wound received in this battle, thus sealing his devotion to his country with his life's blood. A braver man never went to battle than E. N. Kirk, and the members of his family have every reason to be proud of the splendid record for courage and devotion to duty which he has left them.

But this matter of sending the horses to water in the face of the enemy is one of the errors which time does not seem to correct.

The curtain of night fell upon the scene, and the tired and jaded soldiers lay down upon the battlefield to rest, in order to be prepared for a renewal of the contest on the following morning. Morning came, but the enemy had withdrawn during the night from our immediate front. On the 2d day of January a large body of Confederates attacked with great fierceness General Crittenden's command on our left. One of my brigades, under Colonel W. H. Gibson, was sent to reinforce him. The enemy was severely punished, and fell back confused and demoralized. Murfreesboro' was evacuated on the 3d, and our army took possession of the town. General Rosecrans, in his telegraphic report to the general-in-chief, stated, in substance, that the battle would have been a complete success on the first day had it not been for a "partial surprise" on our right. Time has not corrected this error. It was sent off hastily on the wings of lightning, penetrating every portion of the country, and to-day there are thousands who believe that our right was attacked while in bed. How absurd to suppose that the ever-vigilant McCook, always on the alert, should permit any troops under his command to be surprised! He belongs to a race of soldiers, and his courage has been tested in contests as fierce as ever shook the earth or crimsoned the battle-field.

How absurd to suppose that troops who had been up and breakfasted hours before the battle began could be taken by surprise! After the battle I rode over the field with General Rosecrans and others, and showed him my position and explained to him with what I had to contend, and he expressed himself as well satisfied with what I had done with my command, and said that no two brigades could stand up against such fearful odds. Yet the error first committed has passed into history, and will probably outlive all the participants in that terrible struggle.

After the war I was stationed in Murfreesboro', where I became acquainted with several returned Confederates of high rank who had participated in the battle at Stone River. By them I was assured that not less than twenty-five thousand men attacked my position. When my line was repulsed, I suppose this force in part fell on Davis's line, and then on Sheridan's. The casualties in my division in this battle were: killed, two hundred and sixty; wounded, ten hundred and five; missing, twelve hundred and eighty. Of the missing it was subsequently ascertained that some had been killed, others wounded and captured, while some, becoming separated from their companies and regiments, did not find them for several days.

Our provision train having returned to Nashville, my command subsisted on parched corn until the evacuation of Murfreesboro', when supplies were brought forward.

Willich, Kirk, and Baldwin, my three original brigade commanders, are dead. Two were killed in battle, and one has died since the war. Braver officers or better commanders never drew swords nor commanded more gallant men than those composing my division at the battle of Stone River.

In this battle the field-officers of the Seventy-ninth Pennsylvania Volunteers were killed or wounded, and Captain Thomas E. Rose assumed command of the regiment. His courage and skill were so conspicuous that I asked that he might be promoted to the rank of colonel. The request was complied with, and he ever proved an able commander. He was captured subsequently and confined in Libby prison. There he conceived the idea of escaping through a tunnel under the wall. His plans were carried out, and, after weeks of suffering, he reached the Federal lines in safety. At the close of the war he was appointed in the regular army, and is at this time a captain in the Sixteenth Infantry and brevet lieutenant-colonel United States army.

CHAPTER XVIII.

Murfreesboro'—Fortifications—A Spy—Two Spies at Franklin—
Onward March—Liberty Gap—Chickamauga—Sunday's Work—
Fall Back to Rossville—Sabbath Evening.

MURFREESBORO', before the war, was a beautiful little town of about five thousand inhabitants, situated in one of the most picturesque and fertile regions of the State. The people were educated and refined, and many of them men of wealth. From the town radiated in all directions splendid pikes, enabling the farmers to bring their produce more easily to this market than to Nashville. The town itself is situated on high, commanding ground, and as soon as the experienced eye of General Rosecrans scanned it he determined on fortifying and establishing a depot for supplies. At once men were detailed to report to the chief-engineer, who designated the points to be fortified and the character of the works to be constructed at each point. Many of the men so employed had never before used picks and spades, but nearly every one in the army learned before the close of the war that these implements were as necessary for successful warfare as rifles, muskets, and cannon. In addition to this work, drills were resumed, and, between drills and work on the fortifications, there was little time for other enjoyments. One day I rode out through my command, and, seeing a large crowd of men assembled, rode up to ascertain the cause of the assemblage. I found that a Yankee singing-master was entertaining them with patriotic songs, and all seemed to enjoy the music and cheer the sentiments they expressed. I passed on, but subsequently some one suspected that he might be a spy. At all events it would be no harm to examine him closely. On removing one of his shoes a complete map of our fortifications was discovered clumsily concealed under a false sole.

He was taken to the guard-house, and would have been tried and executed; but he, knowing that his only chance for life was in making his escape, broke through the guard. However, an unerring shot of the sentinel passed through his heart, and he fell dead.

He proved to be a regular spy, and had he not been arrested it is probable that the Confederate commander would have had a complete drawing of our defences in a few days.

We had an outpost at Franklin, Tennessee, consisting of a brigade under the command of Colonel Baird. He had a singular experience with two spies, the facts of which are as follows:

On the afternoon of June 8, 1863, two men rode into the Federal camp at Franklin, Tennessee, and proceeded at once to the tent of Colonel Baird, the commanding officer, to whom they introduced themselves as Colonel Orton and Major Dunlap, both of the inspector-general's department of the United States army. Colonel Orton presented an order from the Secretary of War instructing him, in company with Major Dunlap, to proceed to make a critical inspection of the army at that time in the State of Tennessee, and also an order from General Rosecrans, then at Murfreesboro', to all officers commanding outposts and detachments to afford the inspectors every facility for the discharge of the responsible duties imposed upon them by the War Department. The papers seemed genuine,—in fact, there was no suspicion in regard to them,—and the commanding officer at Franklin proceeded at once with them to make a minute examination of the defences of the place, sanitary condition of the camp, etc. After the inspection the inspectors expressed satisfaction at the admirable police regulations established in the camp, and, after partaking of a bounteous lunch prepared for them, and borrowing fifty dollars from Colonel Baird, they mounted their steeds, saying that they were going to Nashville, and actually started on the main pike for that city. They were scarcely out of sight before the idea flashed across Colonel Baird's mind that they might be spies. He ordered Colonel Watkins, Sixth Kentucky Cavalry, to take a small detachment, pursue, arrest, and bring them back to his headquarters. There was no time to be lost, for it was now quite dark, and the two men were well on their way. Watkins, calling to his orderly to mount and follow him, started in hot pursuit. He instructed the orderly to carry his carbine in readiness for service, and when they overtook them, if he noticed any suspicious motions on the part of either, to fire on them without further orders. After an exciting chase of a few miles, they were overtaken, and informed that Colonel Baird wanted to make further inquiries, and requested them to return. This they politely consented to do, after some remonstrance on account of the late-ness of the hour and the distance they had to travel. Colonel Watkins led them to his tent, where he placed them under a strong guard. At once they began to manifest great uneasiness, and pretended great indignation at being thus treated. Colonel Baird told them frankly that he had his suspicions in regard to their true character, but if they were really what they represented themselves, surely they could not object to necessary caution on his part, as the safety of his command would be in jeopardy if they were really not what they professed to be. It was a very difficult matter to satisfy them, so the commander told them that no indignation on their part would deter him from doing his duty, and then informed them that they were under guard, and would be held as prisoners until he was satisfied that they were what they represented themselves to be. He telegraphed to General Rosecrans, and received a reply stating that he knew nothing of any such men, that there were no such men in his employ or travelling under a pass from his headquarters. Long before this despatch was received, however, every one who had an opportunity to hear their conversations were satisfied that they were spies. Shrewd as they were, they gave frequent and distinct evidences of duplicity. On receipt of General Rosecrans's despatch, which was about midnight, a search of their persons was ordered. To this the major readily assented, but the colonel protested against it as an indignity and outrage to an officer of his rank; but resistance was useless, and both submitted. When the major's sword was drawn from the scabbard there was found etched upon it these words: "Lt. W. G. Peter, C. S. A."

They then confessed the whole matter, and upon further search various papers showing their guilt were discovered on their persons. On removing the white flannel havelock from the cap of the major, it was discovered to be a uniform cap of the Southern army. All these facts were telegraphed General Rosecrans, whereupon he sent a despatch to Colonel Baird, directing him to try them by a drum-head court-martial, and if found guilty, "hang them immediately."

The court was convened, and before daylight the case was decided, and the prisoners were informed that they must prepare for immediate death by hanging. Workmen were ordered to erect a scaffold. One of the chaplains visited the prisoners, and at their request administered the sacrament to them. They wrote some letters and deposited their jewelry for transmission to their friends. The gallows was erected near the depot and in a very public place. Two ropes hung dangling from the beam. About nine o'clock the garrison was paraded to witness the execution. Two coarse, rough coffins were lying a few feet away. At twenty minutes after nine o'clock the guards conducted the prisoners to the scaffold, and they walked firmly and steadily as if unmindful of the terrible experience through which they were soon to pass. On their arrival at the place of execution they stepped upon the platform of the cart and took their respective places. Handkerchiefs were tied over their faces and the ropes adjusted.

They then asked the privilege of bidding each other a last farewell, which being granted they tenderly and lovingly embraced each other.

The cart moved from under them and they hung in the air. What a fearful penalty! What a sad end for two men of such rare and varied accomplishments! When life was pronounced extinct they were cut down and encoffined in their full dress. The colonel was buried with a gold locket and chain around his neck. The locket contained the picture and a lock of hair of his intended wife. In his vest pocket he had her photograph, and all these things were, at his request, buried with him. Both were buried in one grave,— companions in life and crime, and now companions in the cold embrace of death. When they learned that they were to be hanged, they requested a commutation of the sentence to being shot to death with musketry.

The elder and leader of these unfortunate men was said to have been formerly an officer in the regular army of the United States. He left the Federal service and joined the Confederate army under the assumed name of Lawrence W. Orton. At the time of his execution he was inspector-general on the staff of General Bragg.

The other victim of this delusive and reckless daring was Walter E. Peter. He was a tall, handsome young man about twenty-five years old, and was a man of education and refinement. History fails to furnish a parallel in the character and standing of the parties, the boldness and daring of the enterprise, and the swiftness with which discovery and punishment were visited upon them. They entered the Federal camp, went through it, minutely inspecting our position, fortifications, and troops, and the boldness of their conduct made their flimsy subterfuges almost successful. To the very last they denied being spies, but the proofs were too clear, and when called upon to pay the penalty of their rashness, met death with a coolness and courage worthy of an honorable cause.

While the troops were strengthening our defences at Murfreesboro', Rosecrans was busily occupied in ascertaining the location of Bragg's forces. Through his efficient spies he learned that Polk's corps was at Shelbyville. Hardee joined him on the right, and occupied Belle Buckle, Liberty Gap, and Hoover's Gap, and the effective force combined numbered about forty thousand. His base of supplies was at Chattanooga, with a temporary base at Tallahoma, in the rear of the centre of the Confederate line. Rosecrans's second campaign was to drive the Confederates out of the State of Tennessee. The plan of the campaign was to threaten the enemy's left and centre with a large force of infantry and cavalry, and, under cover of these demonstrations, to turn their right and force a battle on our own ground or compel a retreat over the mountains by a circuitous and dangerous route.

On the 24th day of June our movement began. McCook's corps was to march by Old Millersburg and drive the enemy from Liberty Gap. This is a narrow passage between two high ranges of mountains, which, if resolutely defended by a thousand men, could be held against ten times the number. Our troops moved gallantly forward and drove the enemy through and beyond the Gap, and encamped therein during the night. On the following morning the enemy was reinforced by Cleburne's division, and again offered battle, which was accepted. The fighting the day before was by my division, but on the second day Carlin's brigade of Davis's division was sent to support me. For a short time the battle raged furiously, but finally the enemy was repulsed. On the first day General John F. Miller was shot in the eye while gallantly leading his brigade. I visited him after dark, and never expected to see him again alive, but was pleased to renew my acquaintance recently in Washington. Miller was a senator from California, and one of the wealthy men of the Pacific slope, but died in Washington, March 8, 1886.

During the conflict at Liberty Gap, Thomas was pushing the enemy at Hoover's Gap. Their defeat at the former place caused a general retreat of the Confederate army to Tallahoma. For miles around this place the country is level. The forests approached the village on all sides. Bragg had the trees felled for a distance of two miles in all directions, in order to give his artillery an opportunity to do effective work upon our advancing columns, but before we got within range of his guns he and his army fell back. Chattanooga was the next place occupied by Bragg, but when we began to draw our lines around that place it was abandoned also. General Rosecrans then ordered his army to cross the Tennessee River at four or five different points, and the various columns moved so as to increase the distance between them. On the 16th of September the right and left were fully fifty miles apart. Bragg, who had been reinforced by Longstreet and had his army well in hand, could not have known the position of Rosecrans's forces, otherwise he would have attacked him before he could have concentrated. Rosecrans, learning the position of the enemy, ordered his army to close to the left and prepare for battle. McCook, who was in command of the extreme right and always ready to take a hand in battle, was not slow in moving his column; but long before he could close in on our left the roar of artillery and musketry told too plainly that Thomas had been attacked. The firing was so heavy that the men, forgetting fatigue, hastened to the conflict. My division was in advance, and at Crawfish Springs, Rosecrans ordered me to move my division at "double-quick" to Thomas and report to him in person. The other two divisions of McCook's corps were attacked in flank before they could be brought in line, and some confusion prevailed until the division commanders succeeded in rallying them, which was soon done. At sundown on the 19th the Confederate lines had been forced back at least a mile and a half.

Colonel J. B. Dodge, who commanded one of the brigades in my division, got in advance of his command and between the two lines. To move either way would surely draw the fire of some sharp-shooter. Not knowing what to do, he sat down at the root of a tree to calmly consider the uncertainty of life and possibly to pass in review his shortcomings from boyhood. In this position he was in full view of a Confederate battery. Three of the gunners, observing him and supposing that he was badly wounded, came to his assistance. The artillerymen had no arms, and, as their mission was one of mercy, did not think they would need any. As they raised Dodge up one of them remarked, "Let us see if the Yank has any arms." Quick as thought Dodge observed that they were unarmed, and, drawing his pistol, presented it and demanded their surrender. Seeing their helplessness, they surrendered, and Dodge marched his captives into the Federal camp. I do not know what became of the prisoners, but have always hoped that they fell into kind hands.

A short time after dark the enemy made a fierce assault upon us, but were finally repulsed and driven back.

Our lines were adjusted and preparations made for a renewal of the battle on the following morning (September 20).

I had a cup of black coffee at one o'clock on the morning of the 19th, and, as my servant failed to find me, I retired without dinner or supper, and in fact neither myself nor any member of my staff had anything to eat until Sunday night, when I accidentally discovered a supply train in camp at Rossville. From this train we got hard bread and bacon, cutting the bacon into thin slices and broiling it on the coals. I never enjoyed anything so much in my life.

When I reached Thomas, in accordance with the order of General Rosecrans, he indicated where my command should form, and then ordered me to move forward. Soon I came up to some troops lying down, which I learned was General W. B. Hazen's brigade, which had done gallant service, having expended their ammunition. My division passed on, and we had not gone far before our skirmish line became engaged with the enemy's, which was driven in, and soon my main line came in contact with the main line of the rebel army. My division drove the enemy at least a mile and a half and captured seven pieces of artillery.

In the report of that gallant soldier, General Thomas L. Crittenden, I find this reference to my division. The report is to General Rosecrans, and he says,—

> At 4.45 P.M. I received your note of 3.10 P.M., stating that Johnson was driving the rebels handsomely in the centre, that he had taken many prisoners, and expected to drive the enemy across Chickamauga to-night.

General McCook, the commander of the corps to which I was attached, said in his official report,—

> On the 19th, General Johnson's division fought near the extreme left of the line. It fought gloriously, driving the enemy for more than a mile, capturing seven of the enemy's guns and a large number of prisoners.

The attack made on my division on the night of the 19th was a fearful assault,—in fact, a hand-to-hand conflict when it was so dark we could not recognize friend from foe. But my glorious old division acquitted itself with great credit, and its honorable part in this battle was the cause of many compliments from almost every general officer in that battle. As soon as the fighting for the day was over, myself and staff retired for the night, without bedding beyond our saddles and saddle-blankets. Long before it was light I was up and moving around among my men, who seemed to sleep sweetly and soundly. All nature seemed to be wrapped in awful silence awaiting the coming of some important event. Some of the men near me would ere the sun went down on the 20th sleep the long sleep of death. Suddenly there darted up innumerable rays of light, like so many silver threads; these changed to gold, and their reddening glare first touched the hill-top, then, descending along the slope into the valley, they flooded the world as with liquid fire and warmed all nature into life. How softly and gently Aurora lifts the curtain to awake the slumbering hours to their daily rounds!

Broad, open daylight was upon us, and no sign of an attacking enemy. It was the Sabbath day,—a day that is dear to every one who loves his Lord. It is the day upon which we are accustomed to listen to the bells that summon worshippers to the house of God. There were no bells and few worshippers on that beautiful Sabbath day. The stillness of the morning was broken in upon by the sound of the axe used in felling timber for temporary breastworks. General Polk, who was Bishop of Tennessee, commanded in my front, and possibly he delayed his advance until he could go over the beautiful service of his church; but while he was doing this we were preparing to give him a warm and cordial reception.

The position of our line of battle was about as follows, beginning on our right and passing to the left: Lytle's brigade, Sheridan's division, Davis's division, Wood's division, Brannan's division, Reynolds's division, Palmer's division, Johnson's division, Baird's division, Bently's brigade. The cavalry on the flanks. The left was the vital point; and we were that day to fight for the existence of the army and the occupation of Chattanooga. Defeat here would have been the most terrible blow to our cause, for the Union army would have been compelled to cross the Tennessee River and yield up all that had been gained by the summer's campaign.

The field of battle was a vast forest, whose dense foliage prevented us from seeing fifty yards distant. No one commander could see the flanks of his regiment even, and so division commanders could only learn how the battle progressed through their orderlies, staff officers, and occasional wounded men brought from the various parts of the line. I remember seeing Captain E. C. Ellis, of the Ninety-third Ohio Volunteers, who was seriously wounded, and I feared mortally; but when I asked him how it was going in his front, with a smile on his face he replied, "General, our boys are giving them Hail Columbia in our front." This satisfied me in regard to the battle in front of the Ninety-third.

About nine o'clock the enemy moved up to attack. Our men held their fire until the front line was within a hundred yards, and then opened up with a volley which staggered the enemy. His second line was pushed on and met a similar fate. Their lines fell back, reformed, and tried it again. Five or six times this was gone through with. The loss was heavy on the part of the enemy, while ours was insignificant compared to the brave work done. Baird and Bently fought bravely against an outnumbering foe. The fighting was terrible in front of Baird, and had his command been driven from the field the day would have been lost, for the enemy would have struck me in flank, and the remainder of our line would have been taken in the same way. In fact, I felt uneasy on both flanks. If the divisions on my right failed to hold their places, I could not know it until the enemy was upon me. In the course of the afternoon the firing was very heavy to our right and rear, and Palmer suggested that we send our reserve brigades to that point, which we did; and I am sure these reinforcements helped to save the day. Had we been driven at that point our army would have been sadly defeated. But Thomas, who was there, was as firm as the rock of Gibraltar, and drove the enemy from the field. Long before this I had learned to confide in Thomas. Wherever he was, victory crowned our banners. Defeat was unknown to him. About six o'clock we fell back to Rossville and encamped for the night. It was the Sabbath evening, and I recalled, as I watched the silent stars that night, the beautiful lines by George D. Prentice:

SABBATH EVENING.

How calmly sinks the parting sun!
   Yet twilight lingers still;
And beautiful as dreams of Heaven
   It slumbers on the hill;
Earth sleeps, with all her glorious things,
Beneath the Holy Spirit's wings,
    And, rendering back the hues above,
    Seems resting in a trance of love.

Round yonder rocks the forest trees
   In shadowy groups recline,
Like saints at evening, bowed in prayer
   Around their holy shrine;

And through their leaves the night-winds blow
So calm and still, their music, low,
   Seems the mysterious voice of prayer,
   Soft echoed on the evening air.

And yonder western throng of clouds,
   Retiring from the sky,
So calmly move, so softly glow,
   They seem to Fancy's eye
Bright creatures of a better sphere,
Come down at noon to worship here,
   And from their sacrifice of love
   Returning to their home above.

The blue isles of the golden sea,
   The night-arch floating high,
The flowers that gaze upon the heavens,
   The bright streams leaping by,
Are living with religion; deep
On earth and sea its glories sleep,
   And mingle with the starlight rays,
   Like the soft light of parted days.

The spirit of the holy eve
   Comes through the silent air
To feeling's hidden spring, and wakes
   A gush of music there!
And the far depths of ether beam
So passing fair we almost dream
   That we can rise, and wander through
   Their open paths of trackless blue.

Each soul is filled with glorious dreams,
   Each pulse is beating wild;
And thought is soaring to the shrine
   Of glory undefiled!
And holy aspirations start,
Like blessed angels, from the heart,
   And bind—for earth's dark ties are riven—
   Our spirits to the gates of Heaven.

CHAPTER XIX.

Chattanooga—Short Rations—Scarcity of Forage—Edward Davis, A.D.C., appointed Cadet—Captain E. A. Otis off on Sick-Leave for a Few Weeks—Return, and assigned to First Division, Fourteenth Corps—King, Carlin, and Starkweather Brigade Commanders—Generals W. F. Smith and W. B. Hazen perform a Gallant Act—General Sherman Arrives—Then General Grant—Battle of Mission Ridge.

THEN back through the bitter night we filed and pitched our camps at Chattanooga, and there for long, woful weeks our army held its position in the face of the beleaguering enemy without, and griping famine and mortal disease, grim and unsparing, in its very midst. But, in the language of General Thomas, we proposed "to hold the place till we starved." The enemy was around us and on the river below, making it necessary for us to haul all supplies used over a rough, rocky, mountainous country. No forage could be brought, for, with all the transportation we had, a full supply of provisions for the men could not be procured. At first we were reduced to half rations, then to one-third, then to one-fourth, and finally, the man who got a piece of hard bread imagined that he fared quite sumptuously. It was strange that through all this I never heard a murmur. Each man knew that Pap Thomas was doing all in his power for them, and nothing more could be done. I had my horse subsisted on tender cane cut from the river bottom, but daily I could see his flesh departing and his bones becoming more prominent. Poor fellow! I had no rations to divide with him. Afterwards, in the battle of Missionary Ridge, I attempted to ride him up the slope, but he was too weak to carry me, and getting down on his knees, as if begging humbly for mercy, I dismounted and led him up. A boat arrived that same evening, and the devoted animal had a "good square meal" on oats on that night. Soon he recuperated and was as gay as ever.

While the army was cooped up in Chattanooga, Mr. Davis came out, bringing with him a number of ladies. They visited Lookout, and the officer in charge of the rebel battery on the top of the mountain endeavored to entertain them by firing at the Yankees. The guns could not be depressed enough to fire directly at us, but he would cut his fuse so that the shells might explode and the pieces fly into our tents or houses. I was quartered in a house occupying a prominent eminence, and that seemed to be his target, but his shells either fell short or passed beyond; still it was embarrassing to be made the subject of such marked attention.

While on the march one day I saw a young soldier in the ranks of the Twenty-ninth Indiana. His handsome, girl-like face attracted my attention. I directed him to report to me on his arrival at camp. I found his name to be Frank N. Sheets, and that he was a bright, intelligent young fellow, about seventeen years old. General John W. Finnell, adjutant-general of Kentucky, was at my headquarters when he reported, and I requested him to issue a commission to Sheets as a lieutenant in one of the Kentucky cavalry regiments. He made out the commission at once, and Lieutenant Frank N. Sheets was announced as aide-de-camp on my staff. Although a boy, his judgment was well matured for one so young. He was brave, intelligent, and faithful, and made a most efficient staff officer. His handsome face, his pleasing manners, and his general intelligence made him a great favorite in the division.

I remember having sent him with a message to General George H. Thomas, who afterwards said to me, "That is a very intelligent aide you have. He delivered your message as correctly as if it had been written down, and he seemed to have an intelligent, comprehensive view of your position, as well as the character and size of the force opposed to you. I was impressed with his manliness and self-possession."

In the battle of Chickamauga he was killed by a shot of grape and canister. He was on horseback at the time, and both he and his horse were instantly killed. He was so devoted to me, and so anxious to serve and please me, that my affection for him was like that of a father for his son. His death was a great loss to me, officially and socially, for in life he was always with me. Another aide was Lieutenant Edward Davis, a son of my friend, Mrs. B. O. Davis, of Louisville, Kentucky.

General Rosecrans was authorized to designate eight young men to represent the Southern States as cadets at West Point, and he allowed me to designate one of them. I suggested young Davis, on account of his intelligence, soldierly bearing, and his established courage. He was appointed, and entered the class of 1863, after the battle of Chickamauga. In June, 1867, he was graduated and assigned to the Third Regiment of Artillery, of which regiment he is still a member. These young officers were very efficient and always ready for any service required of them.

While I was at Murfreesboro' I ordered a general court-martial, and Lieutenant E. T. Wells, Eighty-ninth Illinois Volunteers, was designated as judge advocate. The business of the court was conducted so regularly and the record was so neat and business-like that I had him detailed as judge advocate of the division. Subsequently, at my request, he was appointed assistant adjutant-general, with the rank of captain, and assigned to duty on my staff. He was one of the very best officers I ever met, and ought to have commanded a brigade, for which he was eminently fitted. I soon found that all routine matters could be safely intrusted to him, and this relieved me from an immense amount of troublesome details. At the battle of Peach Tree Creek he was severely wounded, but recovered and served until the end of the war, when he received the appointment of United States judge for the Territory of Colorado. On the admission of that Territory to Statehood he was elected Chief-Justice of the Supreme Court of the State, which position he resigned in order to enter upon the practice of the law. He now resides in Denver, is a man of undoubted integrity, and an able and successful practitioner.

One of the first officers I selected for duty as aide-de-camp was Lieutenant E. A. Otis, of the Second

Minnesota Volunteers. A correspondent from that regiment to the *St. Paul Pioneer* said of him,—

> Lieutenant E. A. Otis, of Captain J. J. Noah's company, has just been appointed aide-de-camp to General R. W. Johnson. General Johnson is an old Minnesotean,—that is to say, he married a Minnesota wife. He was on our Northwest station for some years, and selected one of our officers on his staff because he felt himself identified with us somewhat in our past history and progress. We are not brigaded with him, and this separates from us an officer generally beloved and highly esteemed by all in our regiment.
>
> In parting with Lieutenant Otis, Captain Noah loses an officer endeared to him by the deepest and warmest ties of friendship and confidence, and the entire regiment, as well as his company, share alike in regretting the consummation which takes him from his beloved comrades in arms. He carries with him our best wishes for his success and happiness.

I found that I had really secured a grand prize in this young officer. He was brave, industrious, and faithful, and he soon stood in the estimation of the division just where he did in his own regiment. After the close of the war he was appointed by Governor Brownlow district judge in Tennessee. This position he soon gave up and removed to Chicago, where he stands high as an able and conscientious lawyer.

When the army first took possession of Chattanooga it was a beautiful place. Many fine residences with large grounds, beautifully laid out and studded with fruit, ornamental, and shade trees, gave it an aristocratic appearance; but the scarcity of firewood necessitated the levelling of these fine trees and the destruction of fences, and starving horses and mules played sad havoc with the tender shrubbery.

Chattanooga is surrounded on all sides by high

mountains which overlook the city. Above the town the Tennessee River winds its way along the base of the mountains like a silver thread; passing in front of the city, thence running directly toward the northern peak of Lookout Mountain, it strikes its base with all the force of the current; thence almost at right angles disappears from view through its mountain passes. It was a place of some importance before the war, and at this time the manufacturing interests are such as to attract capital and labor, which will in time make it a large city.

In relation to my division at Chickamauga, General George H. Thomas said in his official report,—

> Johnson's division of McCook's corps opportunely arrived and reported to me. It was deployed and engaged the enemy, and after a desperate struggle drove him handsomely for a mile or more, capturing seven pieces of artillery.

After our arrival in Chattanooga I issued the following:

SOLDIERS OF THE SECOND DIVISION:

> I must congratulate you on your brilliant achievements on the 19th and 20th. Seven pieces of artillery, two battle-flags, and a large number of prisoners are among your trophies. Your division commander expected much of you, and he is happy to say that his most sanguine expectation has been more than realized. Although you lost many of your comrades, yet you will remember Chickamauga with pleasure, as it was, so far as you were concerned, a glorious victory. You defeated the enemy on five different occasions. Soldiers, I thank and congratulate you.

For some weeks preceding the battle of Chickamauga I was really too unwell to be in the field, but under the circumstances I could not ask to be absent; but after the battle I took a short sick-leave, and during my absence the entire army was reorganized by discontinuing the Twentieth and Twenty-first Corps, consolidating the troops, and forming the Fourth Corps under the command of Major-General Gordon Granger. Such divisions as were not transferred to this new organization in a body were divided up and distributed to other brigades and divisions.

My division was so divided because I was not present to protest against such rank injustice. It was a measure I deeply regretted. For two years the command had been together, and the most enduring friendships had been formed. Together these troops had marched and countermarched; together they had fought, and all in common had endured hardships and privations. An order easily given at once destroyed these associations and scattered us broadcast throughout the army to form other acquaintances and associations. The noble men of this division, whose glorious record was the pride and boast of each one, were assigned to new commands, strange and untried to them. But men who had so well established their reputations for courage and devotion could not fail to prove themselves heroes when the occasion presented itself, no matter to what corps or division they belonged. If the command had behaved badly or taken an insignificant part in the battle of Chickamauga there might have been some excuse for destroying the organization, but the contrary was true. It neither flinched nor faltered nor lost ground during the engagement, and was the only command to capture any pieces of artillery. Its commander was complimented for their heroic conduct by nearly every general officer in the army. Such a command deserved to perpetuate its organization, and had I been present my protest would have been so earnest that I think General Rosecrans would have let it remain intact.

On my return I found my command wiped out and a new one made up for me. It was the First Division of the Fourteenth Army Corps, General John M. Palmer commanding. This was a fine body of men, made up as follows:

First Brigade: Brigadier-General William P. Carlin, commanding.—One Hundred and Fourth Illinois; Thirty-eighth, Forty-second, and Eighty-eighth Indiana; Fifteenth Kentucky; Second, Thirty-third, and Ninety-fourth Ohio, and Tenth Wisconsin.

Second Brigade: Brigadier-General John H. King, commanding.—Nineteenth Illinois; Eleventh Michigan; Eighteenth and Sixty-ninth Ohio; Fifteenth, Sixteenth, Eighteenth, and Nineteenth United States.

Third Brigade: Brigadier-General John C. Starkweather, commanding.—Twenty-fourth Illinois; Thirty-seventh Indiana; Twenty-first and Seventy-fourth Ohio; Seventy-eighth and Seventy-ninth Pennsylvania; First and Twenty-first Wisconsin.

Artillery: Battery C, First Illinois; A, First Michigan; Battery H, Fifth United States.

One of the disagreeable features of this assignment was my being placed over General John H. King, who was an old captain in the First Infantry when I joined the regiment as a second lieutenant. Through no fault of his I was appointed a brigadier-general before he was, and hence in the volunteer service I was his senior and entitled to command over him. I called on him at once and expressed my regret that we were brought together under such circumstances, and his reply gave me unbounded pleasure and satisfaction. It it due to him to say that he regarded the final triumph of our arms of much more importance than any question of rank, and he was willing and glad to serve in any capacity where he could be of service to his country. His loyalty to the cause was such that he raised no question as to previous rank. His ready compliance with all instructions from division headquarters, and the gallant and skilful management of his command showed him to be a true soldier in every sense of the term. So the fear I had of the possibility of a lukewarm support on his part proved unfounded, and our official intercourse was as pleasant as our social intercourse had been in years gone by. This service with King is one of the pleasant memories of the war.

I had known General W. P. Carlin since we were boys together at West Point, where I was his senior by one year. His courage, skill, and ability had been tested on other fields, and I confidently relied upon his cordial co-operation and support, and through all and over all I found him prompt to obey orders and always ready for any service however dangerous or disagreeable. Wherever he was ordered he went without question, and when he led his gallant brigade into action, he did so intelligently and fearlessly. Subsequently he commanded the division and earned for himself the reputation of being one of the very best division commanders in the army.

I find in my scrap-book the following notice of

General Carlin, by an army correspondent in 1864, which I reproduce:

"General William P. Carlin, in 1861, accepted the colonelcy of the Thirty-eighth Illinois. After the battle of Stone River he received his commission as brigadier-general. His campaign against General Jeff Thompson, in Southwest Missouri, was brilliant and successful, and totally destroyed rebel sway in that State. During the terrible struggle at Stone River, General Carlin's command played the part of 'Stonewall' Jackson, and stood like a mountain against the sudden and powerful onslaught of the rebel columns. General Carlin, in personal appearance, has much of the poet about him, and the keenest phrenologist or physiologist can see nothing in that fair, white countenance to indicate the dash, earnestness, and bravery which characterizes him. He is quite delicate looking, about five feet eight inches high, and slight build. A finely-formed and good-sized head, covered with a profusion of rich, brown hair, a high forehead, and grayish eyes, indicating determination, with an intellectual and refined expression of countenance, gives you a picture of General W. P. Carlin."

General Starkweather was soon detached and placed in command of Pulaski, Tennessee, and Colonel B. F. Scribner, Colonel M. T. Moore, and Colonel Anson G. McCook served as brigade commanders. Justice was never meted out to Scribner. He should have been a general officer from the beginning of the rebellion, as he was an experienced soldier of the Mexican war and a brave man, strict in the performance of duty, attentive to the wants of his men, and in every way worthy and qualified for a higher position. Colonel Moore was a self-possessed, reliable soldier, brave in battle and safe in council.

Colonel A. G. McCook belonged to that fighting McCook family, took great pride in his command, and maintained splendid discipline. When his brigade went into action he was always in the forefront, where his gallantry and cool courage were ever conspicuous.

Besieged as we were and on short rations, our cause was becoming more and more hopeless each day, and the necessity of striking a blow with an iron hand to remove the rebel obstructions to the navigation of the Tennessee became more evident every hour. The army had at Bridgeport a large supply of provisions, and the steamboats to transport them, but the rebels held the river at several points. General Thomas directed General Hooker to cross his force at Bridgeport, and move along the line of the railroad in the direction of Chattanooga. Other troops were sent down the river on the north side to cross and reinforce him. Two thousand men, under General W. F. Smith and General W. B. Hazen, were detailed to man a number of pontoon boats, float down the river some eight miles, land, and capture the rebel guard at that point. This fleet cut loose from its moorings on a dark, rainy night, descended the river, passing under the frowning brow of Lookout, whose summit was occupied by the unsuspecting enemy. Not a word was spoken, not an oar moved. Gently and noiselessly this expedition passed down unobserved. At a suitable place the boats landed, and with the rapidity of the thunder-bolt the men rushed on shore, surprised and captured the whole rebel force, not one of whom escaped to tell the story. Before the silver gray of morning appeared a pontoon bridge spanned the river at that point, and the gallant two thousand were so reinforced that they could not be dislodged. This gave us uninterrupted navigation to within eight miles, and soon the haversacks of our starving men were partially filled with good, wholesome food, and happiness and contentment once more reigned in Chattanooga among the rank and file. Not so, however, with those high in command. The driving back of the defiant enemy from the immediate front was a necessity which became more glaring every day.

The Army of the Cumberland was reinforced by General Sherman and his army, and General Grant arrived and assumed command of all the forces. He visited the various camps, conversed with the officers, found all in good spirits and anxious to be led against the insolent enemy by which they were surrounded. With such a state of feeling that he found to exist, he felt sure of victory when his arrangements were all perfected. Troops were placed in position, weak points were strengthened, ammunition issued, and the general plan of the impending battle discussed among the army and corps commanders.

On the 23d day of November the movement against the enemy on Mission Ridge began. Thomas's command rushed out of the temporary works by which they had been sheltered, and drove the enemy beyond Orchard Knob, which was seized and fortified during the night. On the following morning he pushed Howard's corps along the south bank of Citico Creek, where he reported to General Sherman, under whose command he served during the continuance of the battle and the subsequent march to East Tennessee for the relief of beleaguered Knoxville.

Under Thomas's supervision, Hooker scaled the western slope of Lookout Mountain during the evening, driving the enemy from his rifle-pits on the northern extremity and slope of the mountain, aided by General W. P. Carlin's brigade of my division, which was temporarily detached for this particular service. During the advance of Hooker's command up the rugged slope of old Lookout, the thin, misty clouds which had enveloped the crest of the mountain lowered so as to obscure his entire force from the view of the main army in the plain below. The rattle and roar of musketry was terrific and deafening; and as there was no way by which it could be ascertained how the conflict was going, the anxiety was intense, and all eyes were turned in the direction of Hooker. Suddenly, as if to relieve the army from the painful suspense, a friendly breeze lifted the clouds, revealing the Federal line moving steadily onward and upward. The sight was grand beyond description,—a battle in the clouds and a victory for the Union forces.

On the following day our army rushed from its rifle-pits, and with a yell and a shout scaled the side of Mission Ridge, driving the rebel army in great confusion from the strong position it had held for months. No longer the rebel battery on the top of Lookout obstructed the free navigation of the river. The day's work was complete. Every stain of defeat had been wiped away from our shredded and riven banners, and the cloud-capped brows of Lookout and Mission Ridge had been crested with a halo of triumph. This was one of the prettiest battles I ever witnessed. In the absence, to a great extent, of timber, the movement of the entire army as it ascended the slope could be seen. General Grant and General Thomas both said in their reports that the crest was carried simultaneously at all points, and that accords with my own observation. Certainly a period of a few moments only could have elapsed between the first and last arrival on the crest of the ridge.

CHAPTER XX.

The Killing of General Nelson by General Davis—General J. B. Fry—Death of Nelson Serious Loss to Buell—Part taken by Governor Morton.

AFTER General Buell fell back to Louisville a terrible tragedy was enacted in the Galt House by two prominent officers, one shooting and killing the other. Both of these officers had warm friends, and the circumstance at one time threatened a very serious outbreak. General James B. Fry, who was in the hotel at the time and who became conversant with all the facts, has recently written and published a very interesting account of this lamentable affair, and from it I take the following, believing it to be substantially correct. I was in the city at the time, and the facts as given by General Fry are as I then understood them. The death of General Nelson, necessitating a reorganization of the army on the eve of battle, unquestionably had a material bearing on the success of our arms at Perryville. Had General Buell had the benefit of his services in that memorable battle, it is clear to my mind that the result would have been different. General Fry says,—

"*General Davis has just shot General Nelson!*" said John J. Crittenden, as he walked rapidly up to his son, General T. L. Crittenden, at the Galt House breakfast-table, on the 29th of September, 1862. This announcement, in the clear and impressive voice peculiar to the great Kentucky orator and statesman, sent a thrill of horror through all who heard it. Men hurried to witness or hear of the death-scene in the tragedy. Nelson, shot through the heart, lay at full length upon the floor. General Crittenden kneeled, took his hand, and said, "Nelson, are you seriously hurt?" "Tom, I am murdered," was the reply.

When the Army of the Ohio, under Buell, was moving on Chattanooga, in the summer of 1862, the line of railroad, some three hundred miles long, from Louisville, Kentucky, upon which the troops were dependent for supplies, was so frequently broken by the enemy that Buell detached Nelson, in whom he had great confidence, and sent him to Kentucky, with orders to take command there and re-establish and protect the line of supply. Upon reaching his destination, Nelson found himself second to General H. G. Wright, whom the President, without Buell's knowledge, had placed in command of a military department embracing the State of Kentucky. Wright's troops, under the immediate command of Nelson, and the Confederate forces, under Kirby Smith, fought a battle at Richmond, Kentucky, on the 30th of August, in which the former were defeated, and Nelson was wounded. The Confederates took possession of Lexington and Frankfort, held the "Blue-grass" region, and threatened Cincinnati and Louisville. Wright himself looked to Cincinnati, his headquarters being there, and intrusted the defence of Louisville to Nelson. Louisville, threatened by both Bragg and Kirby Smith, was in great peril. Nelson—able, energetic, arbitrary—was straining every nerve for the defence of the city. Davis, who was then on sick-leave in Indiana, appreciating the condition of affairs in Kentucky, and hearing that general officers were needed there, volunteered his services, and was directed by Wright to report to Nelson, which he did, and was charged with the duty of organizing and arming the citizens of Louisville. Nelson's quarters and offices were in the Galt House, at the north end of the west corridor, on the first or main floor. His adjutant-general's office was in room No. 12, and his medical director's office in room No. 10. After Davis had been for a day or two on the duty to which he had been assigned, he called in the afternoon at headquarters, and Nelson said, "Well, Davis, how are you getting along with your command?" Davis replied, "I don't know." Nelson asked, "How many regiments have you organized?" Davis again replied, "I don't know." Then Nelson said, "How many companies have you?" To which Davis responded in a seemingly careless tone, "I don't know." Nelson then said, testily, "But you should know," adding, as he rose from his seat, "I am disappointed in you, General Davis. I selected you for this duty because you are an officer of the regular army, but I find I made a mistake." Davis arose, and remarked, in a cool, deliberate manner, "General Nelson, I am a regular soldier, and I demand the treatment due to me as a general officer." Davis then stepped across to the door of the medical director's room, both doors being open, as the weather was very warm, and said, "Dr. Irwin, I wish you to be a witness to this conversation." At the same time Nelson said, "Yes, doctor, I want you to remember this." Davis then said to Nelson, "I demand from you the courtesy due to my rank." Nelson replied, "I will treat you as you deserve. You have disappointed me; you have been unfaithful to the trust which I reposed in you, and I shall relieve you at once;" adding, "You are relieved from duty here, and you will proceed to Cincinnati and report to General Wright." Davis said, "You have no authority to order me." Nelson turned toward the adjutant-general, and said, "Captain, if General Davis does not leave the city by nine o'clock to-night, give instructions to the provost-marshal to see that he shall be put across the Ohio."* Upon such occasions Nelson was overbearing, and his manner was peculiarly offensive. Highly incensed by the treatment he had received, Davis withdrew; and that night went to Cincinnati and reported to Wright, who assigned him to command in front of Covington and Newport, Kentucky. A few days thereafter (September 25) Buell reached Louisville, and superseded Nelson in command, and Wright ordered Davis to return to Louisville and report to Buell. In pursuance of Wright's order, Davis, on the morning of September 29, 1862, appeared at the Galt House, Louisville, the headquarters at that time of both Buell and Nelson. When Nelson entered the grand hall, or office, of the hotel, just after breakfast, there were many men there, among them Davis and Governor O. P. Morton, of Indiana. Nelson went to

---

* As given by Dr. Irwin, now surgeon, with rank of major and brevet colonel, United States army.

the clerk's office, asked if General Buell had breakfasted, and then turned, leaned his back against the counter, faced the assembled people, and glanced over the hall with his clear black eye. In the prime of life, in perfect health, six feet two inches in height, weighing three hundred pounds, his great body covered by a capacious white vest, his coat open and thrown back, he was the one conspicuous feature of the grand hall. Davis, a small, sallow, blue-eyed, dyspeptic-looking man, less than five feet nine inches high, and weighing only about one hundred and twenty-five pounds, approached, charged Nelson with having insulted him at their last meeting, and said he must have satisfaction. Nelson told him abruptly to go away. Davis, however, who was accompanied by Morton, pressed his demand till Nelson said, "Go away, you d——d puppy, I don't want anything to do with you!" Davis had taken from the box on the counter one of the visiting-cards kept there for common use, and, in the excitement of the interview, had squeezed it into a small ball, which, upon hearing the insulting words just quoted, he flipped into Nelson's face with his forefinger and thumb, as boys shoot marbles. Thereupon, Nelson, with the back of his hand, slapped Davis in the face. He then turned to Morton, and said, "Did you come here, sir, to see me insulted?" "No, sir," replied Morton; and Nelson walked away towards his room, which, it will be remembered, was on the office floor, and at the north end of the hall or corridor, which extends along the west side of the building. A door-way connects this corridor with the grand or office hall, and near that door-way starts a staircase, which leads from the hall to the floor above. After the slap, Davis turned to Captain ——, an old Mexican-war friend from Indiana, and asked for a pistol. Captain —— did not have a pistol, but he immediately obtained one from Thomas W. Gibson, and gave it to Davis. Gibson was a friend of Davis, and was from Indiana, but at the time of this occurrence he was a practising lawyer in Louisville. In the mean time Nelson had passed from the office hall into the corridor which led to his room, had walked towards his room, then turned back, and was near the foot of the staircase and in front of the door-way leading to the office hall, when Davis reached the threshold from the office. They were face to face and about a yard apart, the one with pistol in hand, the other entirely unarmed.

Davis fired, and Nelson walked on up-stairs. Buell, at the time, was in his room, which was near the head of the stairs on the second floor. It is believed that Nelson was on his way to report to Buell what had occurred, when he was confronted and shot by Davis. Be that as it may, he walked up stairs after he was shot, and fell in the hall between the head of the stairs and Buell's apartment. Those who had gathered around carried him into the room nearest the spot where he fell, and laid him on the floor. He said to Silas F. Miller, proprietor of the hotel, who had rushed to the scene when he heard the pistol, "Send for a clergyman; I wish to be baptized. I have been basely murdered." The Rev. J. Talbot, an Episcopal minister, was called. All the medical aid available was summoned. Surgeon Robert Murray, Buell's medical director at the time (now surgeon-general of the army), says, "I was summoned from the Louisville Hotel to the Galt House when he was shot. I found him on the floor of his room, insensible, with stertorous breathing, and evidently dying from hemorrhage. The ball—a small one—entered just over the heart, had passed through that organ or the large vessels connected with it. I am quite sure that he did not utter an intelligible word after I saw him." Before Surgeon Murray arrived, however, a number of persons went into the room, among them General Crittenden, mentioned in the opening of this narrative, the Rev. J. Talbot, and myself.

At half-past 8 A.M., within less than an hour from the time Nelson was shot, he was dead.

I was in the grand hall of the Galt House when the encounter took place, but I did not know Davis was there; nor had I heard of the difficulty that had occurred some days before between him and Nelson. They were both my warm friends. Davis had been second lieutenant in the company of which I was first lieutenant, and part of the time commander. We had been companions and messmates. Upon hearing the sound of the pistol I ascertained what had happened and made my way through the crowd that had gathered around Davis, put my hand upon his shoulder, and told him that I placed him in arrest by order of General Buell. I was at that time Buell's chief of staff. Davis, though greatly agitated, showed no signs of rage. He was glad to be taken from his surroundings and placed in formal military custody by a friend and fully-empowered military official. I took his arm, and we immediately went together to his room on an upper floor of the Galt House. No policeman had anything to do with his arrest; nor did one appear so far as I know. When we entered the room and closed the door, Davis said he wanted to tell me the facts in the case while they were fresh. He then gave me details of the affair, including the decisive incident of flipping the paper wad into Nelson's face. I remained with Davis but a few minutes. I am satisfied that he had not anticipated the fatal ending to the encounter he had just closed with Nelson. He sought the interview unarmed, and so far as known none of his friends were armed except Gibson, and it is not probable that he had provided himself for this occasion with the small pistol which was passed from him to Davis. It seemed to be Davis's purpose to confront Nelson in a public place, demand satisfaction for the wrong done him a few days before, and, if he received no apology, to insult Nelson openly, and then leave him to seek satisfaction in any way, personally or officially, that he saw fit. It was to fasten upon Nelson the insult of a blow that the paper wad was flipped into his face. Nelson, no doubt, had that offensive act in mind when he said to Morton just after it was committed, "Did you come here, sir, to see me insulted?" But, instead of waiting to send a challenge or take official action, if he had been inclined to do either, for the insult he had received through the paper wad, Nelson avenged himself on the spot by returning the blow. Davis then carried on the fight, and it reached an end he had not designed. Nelson (as well as Davis) had many devoted friends about the Galt House at the time, and there were mutterings of vengeance among them. But wiser counsels prevailed. Generals Jackson and Terrill were the most difficult to appease. They both found soldiers' graves a few days later upon the battle-field of Perryville.

Buell regarded Davis's action not only as a high crime, but as a gross violation of military discipline. He felt that the case called for prompt and vigorous treatment; but he could not administer it. The campaign was beginning. A new commander was found for Nelson's corps, and the army marched the second day after his death. Buell could neither spare from his forces the high officers necessary to constitute a proper court-martial, nor could he give the necessary attention to preparing the case for trial in Louisville, where it was best, if not necessary, to try it. He therefore reported by telegraph as follows:

FLOYD'S FORK, KY.,
Via LOUISVILLE, October 3, 1862. (Received 6.20 P.M.)

GENERAL H. W. HALLECK:

Brigadier-General Davis is under arrest at Louisville for the killing of General Nelson. His trial by a court-martial or military commission should take place immediately, but I can't spare officers from the army now in motion to compose a court. It can perhaps better be done from Washington.

The circumstances are, that on a previous occasion Nelson censured Davis for what he considered neglect of duty, ordered him to report to General Wright at Cincinnati, Ohio. Davis said with reference to that matter that if he could not get satisfaction or justice he would take the law into his own hands. On the occasion of the killing he approached Nelson in a large company and introduced the subject. Harsh or violent words ensued, and Nelson slapped Davis in the face and walked off. Davis followed him, having procured a pistol from some person in the party, and met Nelson in the hall of the hotel. Davis fired. The ball entered the right breast, inflicting a mortal wound, and causing death in a few minutes.

D. C. BUELL,
Major-General.

The military authorities did not institute the proceedings suggested in the foregoing report from Buell to Halleck; nor was Davis taken from military custody by the civil authorities; but in a few days he was at large. Wright, the general commanding the military department in which the offence was committed, explains Davis's release as follows: "The period during which an officer could be continued in arrest without charges (none had been preferred) having expired, and General Buell being then in the field, Davis appealed to me, and I notified him that he should no longer consider himself in arrest." Wright adds, "I was satisfied that Davis acted purely on the defensive in the unfortunate affair, and I presume that Buell held very similar views, as he took no action in the matter after placing him in arrest." I do not know upon what Wright based his opinion that Davis acted purely on the defensive, but I am sure he is in error as to Buell's views in the matter. Davis's course in taking the law into his own hands, and the failure to bring him to trial, both met with Buell's unqualified disapprobation.

The case is without a parallel. A brigadier-general in the highly-disciplined army of a law-abiding people, reaching the headquarters just as the forces were ready to march to the battle-field, instead of reporting for duty against the common enemy, as he was under orders to do, sought out a major-general commanding a corps of the army to which both belonged, killed him on the spot, and then went to duty without punishment, trial, or rebuke. Though officially reported, as already shown, no military trial was instituted.

It appears from the records of the Jefferson Circuit Court, Louisville, Kentucky, that on the 27th of October (1862) Davis was indicted by the grand jury for "manslaughter," and admitted to bail in the sum of five thousand dollars. T. W. Gibson, who furnished the pistol with which Davis killed Nelson, and W. P. Thomasson were sureties on his bond. The case was continued from time to time until the 24th of May, 1864, when it "was stricken from the docket, with leave to reinstate," and nothing more was heard of it in the halls of justice.

It has been said that Davis was pardoned by the Governor of Kentucky; but the Secretary of State of the Commonwealth contradicts this in a letter dated April 8, 1885, saying, "There is nothing on the Executive Journal to indicate that Governor Robinson or Governor Bramlette issued a pardon to General Jeff. C. Davis for the killing of General Nelson."

There is good reason for the belief that Morton's influence was exerted to prevent proceedings against Davis. An able and influential lawyer, James Speed, Esq., of Louisville, who was afterwards appointed attorney-general in President Lincoln's Cabinet, was retained as Davis's counsel, and succeeded in saving his client from both civil and military prosecution.

* * * * * * * *

The summary of services and character made in Buell's order issued upon the occasion of Nelson's death is enough for the purpose of this article. The order says,—

"The general commanding announces with inexpressible regret the death of Major-General William Nelson, which occurred in this city at half-past eight o'clock this morning. The deceased was bred a sailor, and was an officer of the navy while holding a commission in the military service. History will honor him as one of the first to organize by his individual exertion a military force in Kentucky, his native State, to rescue her from the vortex of rebellion toward which she was drifting.

"He was a man of extensive information, comprehensive views, and great energy and force of character. By his nature he was intolerant of disobedience or neglect of public duty, but no man was more prompt to recognize and foster merit in his inferiors, and in his own conduct he set an example of vigilance, industry, and prompt attention to duty which he exacted from others. In battle his example was equally marked. On more than one field—at Shiloh, Richmond, and Ivy Mountain—he was conspicuous for his gallant bearing."

Nelson's remains were buried at Cave Hill Cemetery, Louisville, October 2, 1862. On the 21st of August, 1863, they were transferred to Camp Dick Robinson, and interred there with appropriate honors, but were subsequently removed by his relatives to his native place, Maysville, Kentucky, where they now rest.

Erroneous versions of the encounter between Nelson and Davis, unfavorable to the former, were scattered broadcast at the time. Nelson's habitual violence of character was exaggerated; the idea of retribution supplanted the demands of justice, and public attention became fixed upon Nelson's alleged violent conduct toward men generally, and not upon Davis's specific act of violence in shooting Nelson. Though Davis was aggrieved, it is difficult to see now, even if it was not then, how he can be justified in provoking the final quarrel and committing the foul deed of death. The facts will not sustain the theory of self-defence, and the military law, as he well knew, offered prompt and ample redress for all the wrong Nelson had done him at their first meeting. But he made no appeal to law. On the contrary, he deliberately took all law into his own hands. Whether he proceeded solely upon his own judgment or was advised and incited by others is not positively known, but I do not doubt that Morton, and perhaps others, without designing or foreseeing the fatal consequences, encouraged Davis to insult Nelson publicly for wrong done in an official interview. One step led to another in the attempt to place and fix the insult, until the end was Nelson's violent death.

It was a cruel fate that brought about a collision between these two rash men. General officers whose country needed them,—great soldiers, brother soldiers,—the one bearing an unhealed wound received in battle for the cause to which both had pledged their lives, was slain by the other; the Union arms, at a critical juncture, lost services of incalculable value, and the result of a great campaign was very different from what it would have been if these men had not prevented each other from performing their proper parts in it.

I have given all the facts in the case, in justice to both of these distinguished officers. I knew Nelson well. He was a man of energy, nerve, and ability, and his loss was a severe blow to our army, as true and tried men were scarce in the bleak, dark days of the rebellion. To one not well acquainted with him his manner appeared brusque, not to say rude; but within that rough exterior which he affected was a heart as warm and generous as ever pulsated in the bosom of man.

Governor Morton, who was in Louisville at the time, declared that Nelson's conduct towards Davis was an insult to Indiana; and I have no doubt whatever that it was the repetition of this remark that decided Davis to take the extreme course he did. Both were brave men, and neither would permit himself to be insulted; but both were too good soldiers, if left to themselves, to settle disputes in the way Davis settled this one.

The result of all this was the loss of a valuable officer and the clouding of the life of another. Once I was at Davis's headquarters, and he seemed gloomy and sad. I asked him the cause, and he replied, "Johnson, you have never had the cross to bear which has weighed me down." To what else could he have referred?

Although General Davis was never tried by either a civil or military court, and was never pardoned, yet the killing of Nelson did not seem to lessen his standing as an officer or interfere with his military advancement. He was soon in the command of a division, and, on the recommendation of General Sherman, advanced to the position of corps commander. At the close of the war he was appointed colonel of a new regiment.

At Nelson's funeral I was one of the pall-bearers, and opposite to me was General James S. Jackson. As we passed out of the church, he said, "Dick, who will be the next one?" Just one week from that day I acted in the same capacity for him, he having fallen while gallantly leading his men in the battle of Perryville.

CHAPTER XXI.

Graysville—Feeding the Destitute—Squabs—Feed your Enemies—Heavy Fall of Snow—Peach Crop—"In Search of his Rights"—Life in the Swamps of Georgia—Reconnoissance to Buzzard Roost Gap—Capture of Lieutenant Ayers—Occupying Tunnel Hill—Character of Country between Ringgold and Dalton—Major-General Thomas—Snake Creek Gap—Cost of Loyalty—Killing Domestic Animals Prohibited.

AFTER the battle of Mission Ridge, the Fourteenth Corps in common with the entire army followed up the retreating enemy. General Palmer was with my division after dark, when we came suddenly upon General A. P. Stewart's division, then in camp. The surprise was complete, and we captured four pieces of artillery, two caissons, and many prisoners. The pursuit was kept up for several days, when we returned and encamped near Chattanooga, first at Tyner's Station, and then at Graysville.

The staff of my division was as follows:

Captain E. T. Wells, assistant adjutant-general.

Lieutenant H. P. Schuyler, First Wisconsin Volunteers, A.D.C.

Captain L. H. Drury, Third Wisconsin Battery, chief of artillery.

Captain C. F. Trowbridge, Sixteenth United States Infantry, provost marshal.

Captain E. F. Deaton, C. S. Volunteers, commissary.

Lieutenant John Bohan, Thirty-ninth Indiana Volunteers, quartermaster.

Captain J. E. Edwards, Ninety-fourth Ohio Volunteers, inspector.

Captain A. Metzner, Thirty-second Indiana Volunteers, topographical officer.

Lieutenant L. T. Morris, Nineteenth United States Infantry, commissary of musters.

Lieutenant W. R. Lowe, Nineteenth United States Infantry, ordnance officer.

Surgeon S. Marks, Tenth Wisconsin Volunteers, medical director.

Lieutenant W. R. Maize, Seventy-eighth Pennsylvania Volunteers, ambulance director.

The above staff officers were selected because of the fitness of each one for the duties required of him.

I was often complimented on the perfect hospital arrangements of my division. The compliments should have been bestowed on Surgeon Marks, who had exclusive and complete control of that department. He was attentive to his duties and skilful in the treatment of diseases and of wounds. At the close of the war he returned to Milwaukee, Wisconsin, his former home, where he now resides and has a large and lucrative practice.

Graysville was a little town built around a railroad station, with no resources and completely overshadowed by Chattanooga, only a few miles away.

The male inhabitants of the place capable of bearing arms were absent in the rebel army, and the wives of such, if pecuniarily able to get away, had gone with or followed them. The people we found there were the old and the poor, and very few of the former. One old gentleman came to my head-quarters, after I had been encamped about a month in Graysville, to ask for some flour and meat. He asked me if I was not very fond of squabs. I told him that I had never eaten one in my life. "Why," said he, "there has been a soldier at my house every day for a month to get a pair of squabs for your dinner." Some man who thought that a request of the general would be considered equivalent to an order had imposed upon the old man and been able to live sumptuously upon the delicate flesh of squabs, while his commander was "roughing it" on bacon and hard bread.

Here we had to feed the people. The rebel army had consumed all the supplies for miles in its rear, and the few remaining people were left in utter destitution. Hence it was absolutely necessary for us to issue rations to them to prevent suffering. We are commanded to feed our enemies, and the people in that neighborhood were entitled to rations on that score.

Once while on the march we were about to halt for the night near a neat-looking farm-house, at which I expected to get a good "square meal." I sent a member of the escort to see the lady of the house to ascertain if she would prepare dinner for myself and staff and send it to us at the spring. He was instructed to say to her that she would be fully compensated. She replied, "We must feed our enemies, and God knows I am yours." In due time a splendid dinner was prepared for us, which we enjoyed very much, but the good woman refused to accept any compensation whatever.

In the month of February, 1864, the peach-trees were in full bloom and everything indicated an early spring, when we should embark on a long campaign through Georgia. About this time snow fell to the depth of nine inches, an unusual fall for that latitude. I supposed that the peach crop would be a failure, but it was not injured, and fine peaches were enjoyed by our army as we moved south that summer. In fact, fruit was about all that was left on the line of march upon which a human being could subsist. A brother of mine, Dr. John M. Johnson,* now of Atlanta, Georgia, left the State of Kentucky "in search of his rights." For a long time he was a surgeon in the Confederate army. At one time he and his family were in danger of capture by a raiding party under General L. H. Rousseau. To avoid capture he took his family and a fine cow and started for the swamps, where he remained until the danger passed. During his concealment all he had upon which to subsist was the milk from the cow, and he says, "As long as I live I will remember old 'Blossom' with great kindness, not to say affection." About this time, I suppose, he found in the dismal swamps of Georgia all of the rights of which he thought he had been so cruelly deprived.

On February 22, 1864, a reconnoissance in force, under the command of Major-General Palmer, was made in the direction of Dalton. King's brigade of my division was in advance, supported by the other brigades. At the end of the first day we encamped near Ringgold. Heavy pickets were thrown out,

---

* Died May 18, 1886.

which occasionally varied the monotony by advancing upon each other and firing with some animation. On the second day, Carlin's brigade was in the advance. Lieutenant Ayers, Nineteenth United States Infantry, ventured out too far and was captured by the enemy. Ayers had married, a short time before, the daughter of Benny Havens, and although my acquaintance with his father-in-law was quite limited, yet I had heard of him so frequently while at West Point that even his son-in-law seemed near to me, and I was sorry that he had determined on taking a trip through Georgia in advance of the main army. Carlin placed the Thirty-ninth Indiana Mounted Infantry in advance. This regiment, one of the best in the army, was commanded by Colonel Thomas J. Harrison. Just before reaching Tunnel Hill the enemy's cavalry, about three hundred strong, dismounted and erected a hasty barricade of rails on either side of the road.

The Thirty-ninth charged up the road and drove the enemy behind the barricades. Carlin advanced gallantly with his brigade, and for some moments the firing was quite brisk. The commander of this brigade, fearless and cool as ever, was in the advance, constantly under fire, but fortunately escaped uninjured. This engagement ended in the dislodgement and retreat of the enemy in great confusion.

The country between Ringgold and Dalton lies well for defence. It is a valley, through which the railroad passes, with chains of commanding ridges on either side, and innumerable knobs here and there along the valley, from which artillery could do fearful execution. At 4 o'clock P.M. on the 27th, King and Carlin's brigades entered the town, driving the enemy before them. Captain E. T. Wells and Captain A. Metzner of my staff were nearly all day under fire, and displayed their gallantry under circumstances calculated to put men's courage to the test. It was in this reconnoissance that I had the pleasure of witnessing the gallantry of Major Hotchkiss and his Minnesota battery. It was admirably handled, and did fine execution. Finally we reached Buzzard Roost, and the gap in the mountains known as Buzzard Roost Gap was plainly visible. The railroad passes through this gap, and the town of Dalton lies only a few miles south of it. This place was so fortified that its passage by an army, if properly defended, would be an impossibility. The day was one long to be remembered. Brave men, who in the morning were gay and hopeful, slept that night in the cold embrace of death, while others suffered from severe and ghastly wounds received while boldly advancing upon the foe. King and Hambright's brigades held the front line. Major-General Thomas arrived on the scene to take part in the fighting, but it was too late for anything more to be done on that day. About midnight an assault was made on Hambright's line, which was handsomely repulsed. On the following morning General Thomas took a general survey of the defences of Buzzard Roost Gap, and made up his mind that the enemy could not be successfully attacked at that point.

The object of the movement having been accomplished, the troops returned to their old camps.

Through this chain of mountains, and about eighteen miles from Buzzard Roost, is another gap or pass-way, known as Snake Creek Gap, which, strange to say, the enemy had not fortified. It was Thomas's plan, when the general movement began, to demonstrate in force against Buzzard Roost Gap, and send the main body of his army through Snake Creek Gap to strike the railroad in rear of Dalton, and thus prevent the retreat of the rebel army from that point by rail, but General Sherman succeeded him and adopted a plan of his own.

During the war it was not an unusual thing to meet with loyal men of the South, who invariably impressed upon their hearers what it had cost them to be loyal. Nearly all of them had lost their thousands, and, in many cases, it was an easy matter to see that some of them never had as many cents to lose. Once I fell in with one of these fellows, and his figure was thirty thousand dollars,—that is, thirty thousand dollars measured his loyalty. Being sure that he never had anything like that amount to lose, and becoming wearied with hearing it so often, I said to him that I had lost two hundred thousand dollars in gold by my loyalty to the government. Of course he asked me how it happened I had lost so heavily, and I said to him that it was in not having money to buy hogs to eat acorns and make pork for sale to the army. I never again heard of his losses.

The acorn was the badge of the Fourteenth Corps. General Palmer gave orders that no domestic animals belonging to the citizens should be killed. One day he discovered one of the men with a pig on his shoulder. It had evidently died from the effects of a gunshot wound, and the soldier was carrying it tenderly into camp expecting to feast upon it unknown to his officers. General Palmer said to him, "Have you not heard of my order about killing domestic animals?" Laying the pig down, the soldier said, "General, this brute eats our badge, and nothing shall live that shows any disrespect to the badge of the Fourteenth Corps." It is needless to say that the soldier carried his meat into camp, and who knows but that a choice cut was served on the table of his commander?

CHAPTER XXII.

Loyalty in Kentucky in 1861—Arming Loyal Men—Sherman advanced to Muldraugh's Hill—Home Guards again—Captain John M. Harlan takes Ammunition to Sherman—Sherman as a Smoker—Dry Tortugas—Pistol wanted Twenty Years after the War.

IN a previous chapter reference was made to the Home Guards of Louisville, Kentucky, which patriotically rallied to the defence of that city.

The fall of 1861 was a memorable period in the history of Kentucky. The attack on Sumter and the call for volunteers made it necessary that the State should at some time take a definite position in reference to the struggle for the preservation of the Union against armed rebellion. Those who adhered to the government recognized the extraordinary difficulties that lay in the way of placing the people of the State in line with those who believed that the national existence should be maintained at every cost of blood and treasure. All the officers of the State, without exception, sympathized with the rebellion, and the State guard was intensely disloyal. All arms and ammunition belonging to the State were in the possession or under the control of those who intended to ally Kentucky with the Southern Confederacy when they could safely undertake the task.

The State was in that condition when the true policy was to postpone active co-operation with the Union forces until the loyal men could be organized and armed. Mr. Lincoln approved that course, and hence did not at the outset occupy the State with the military forces of the government. Believing that the mass of the people were thoroughly devoted to the Union, he gave the friends of the government an opportunity to educate the public mind by discussion as to the danger and wickedness of secession. He avoided giving the rebels the excuse for saying that he was unwilling to give the people an opportunity to decide the pending question for themselves, unintimidated by armed forces. The Union men entered vigorously upon the canvass for members of the Lower House of Congress, in the summer of 1861, upon the single issue whether Kentucky should withdraw from the Union. Upon that issue every district was carried by the Unionists. That election fixed the popular mind against the rebel cause and held the State firmly in the loyal ranks.

The next step was to arm the Union men of the State. To effect that result, General William Nelson was given full authority by President Lincoln. He entered into correspondence with Hon. James Harlan, James Guthrie, and other leading Union men, and made every possible effort to introduce arms into the State. He shipped a large number of arm-chests by the Kentucky Central Railroad from Covington for Camp Dick Robinson, which had been established only a few days before. The rebels at Cynthiana got wind of this shipment and stopped the train at that place, and the arms were returned to Cincinnati. From that city, following the suggestion of prominent Union men in Louisville, he shipped the arms by boat to that place. The boat reached Louisville in the night-time, and, under the direction of Joshua F. Bullitt, John M. Harlan, and others, they were transferred before daylight to the Louisville and Lexington Railroad and forwarded to Lexington, where, in accordance with previous understanding, they were to be received by Ethalbert Dudley's Union company. As soon as the Confederate company of that city heard of the arrival of the guns they rallied under John Morgan and then proceeded to the depot to seize them; but the arrival, "just in the nick of time," of Bramlette from Camp Dick Robinson, at the head of several hundred mounted men, prevented such seizure and secured the guns for the Union cause.

Throughout the State at that time there was imminent danger of conflicts between individual citizens and organizations, on account of their differences in reference to the pending struggle.

At last the rebel forces occupied the extreme southwestern part of Kentucky, under General Polk, and shortly afterwards followed Buckner's invasion from Nashville. Then the Union troops from the West, fully armed and equipped, poured into the State for the purpose of resisting the advancing forces of the enemy. General Anderson, of Sumter fame, was ordered to the State, and he was soon succeeded by General Sherman and General Thomas, and a number of general officers were ordered to report to him. Then it was that the Union men set about to organize and meet the responsibilities of the hour. Rumors came to Louisville, thick and fast, of an advance upon that city by Buckner at the head of a large Confederate force. Sherman determined to occupy Muldraugh's Hill, beyond Lebanon Junction, with such forces as he could hurriedly collect together. It was in this neighborhood, and only about forty miles apart, that Mr. Lincoln and Mr. Davis were born.

Sherman requested the assistance of the Louisville Home Guards, one of which—"The Crittenden Union Zouaves"—was under the command of Captain John M. Harlan; and this company constituted the guard at General Sherman's headquarters, which were established in the hotel at Lebanon Junction. Sherman's watchful eye was never closed. After some few days' delay he determined to advance as far as Elizabethtown and occupy Muldraugh's Hill with the few soldiers at his command. It was here that he called the prominent officers of his command around him and informed them that he expected to fight a battle, and that "each man must understand that he is to stand and fight down to the stubbs."

When he moved from Lebanon Junction he left me in command, with only Captain Harlan's company. Late in the evening of the day upon which he occupied Muldraugh's Hill he sent me a note, in which he stated that he would probably have a fight, and that he wanted me to send him five thousand rounds of ammunition. I ordered Captain Harlan to comply with the order with all possible despatch. The railroad bridge beyond was down, and how he was to get that quantity of ammunition to Sherman across the Rolling Fork was a question of much importance, and one not easily solved. He went back that night some two miles along the railroad and aroused a farmer, and told him to hitch up his wagon, with body on, and prepare for a movement into the enemy's country. The farmer demurred, but, seeing that resistance was useless, he got up and harnessed his team. Then he was required to drive to the Junction, where there was a hand-car. This hand-car was placed on top and across the wagon body, and around it were placed the boxes of ammunition. About this time it was broad daylight, and Harlan started with the team for the crossing of the Rolling Fork. The stream was "belly deep" to the horses, but the Rubicon was safely crossed. In order to direct the team, Harlan mounted the leader without saddle or equipments. On reaching the south bank the hand-car was placed on the railroad track, the ammunition loaded thereon, and then pushed to the top of the hill, thence down grade to Sherman's headquarters.

As Harlan was about to enter the stream, mounted on the leader, a special artist of some Eastern illustrated paper was on hand to make a sketch of the perilous undertaking. This sketch would have been much more interesting if it had been known that the saddleless outrider was destined to act a prominent part in the great war and finally become a member of the Supreme Court of the United States.

While at the Junction, Sherman was walking on the platform in front of the hotel, with a cigar in his mouth, nearly smoked up and unlighted. Observing a soldier smoking, he asked him for a light. The soldier handed him his fresh-lighted cigar. Sherman lighted his stump, put the soldier's good cigar in his own mouth, threw his stump away, thanked the soldier for his courtesy, and walked on, not realizing what he had done. The soldier good-naturedly laughed, and remarked in an undertone, "That's cool, isn't it?"

It is not at all surprising that old Tecumseh was at that time forgetful of many things. All was confusion around him. Much was expected, yet he had very little with which to do anything. I remember to have often heard him, while at Lebanon Junction, declare that neither the authorities in Washington nor the people at large had any conception of the vast work before them in conquering the rebellion; that the war would last for several years before the rebels would be overthrown and the Union restored. His genius for war was evidence to the politicians that he lacked mental balance. But subsequent events showed that he was wiser than all who were around him.

While at the Junction the pickets arrested a young man by the name of Payne. He was well mounted, fully armed, and on his way to join the rebel army at Bowling Green. He was disarmed and brought to my headquarters for examination and final orders in his case. He was candid in his answers to all questions I asked him, and was free to confess his object and intentions.

For some time I held him in suspense, and at last, becoming impatient, he asked me what I was going to do with him. Pausing for a few moments to prolong his agony, I said, "I shall send you to the Dry Tortugas to remain during the war." This was a place of which he had never heard; so I explained its geographical location, character, etc. I saw he was not pleased, and directly he said to me that if I would pardon his offence he would return to his home, and remain during the war a true and loyal citizen. So I ordered his release. A few years since I had a letter from his father, asking me to send him his son's pistol.

On another occasion the guard brought in two citizens who had just arrived from the enemy's lines and were on their way to Louisville. Their names were given to me as Bob Bell and O. W. Thomas, of Louisville. Bell I had known from boyhood; in fact, we were boys together. When he was told that he would have to go to the headquarters of Colonel Johnson, he was not aware that his old-time friend was the Colonel Johnson into whose presence he was soon to appear.

When my door was opened and these two men were ushered in, they were too mad to look at me, but kept their eyes on the floor. I said, "Well, Bob Bell, what are you doing here?" He looked up, and, recognizing me, he said, "Dick Johnson, I was never so glad to see you in all my life; give me your hand, old fellow." Then he introduced me to Mr. Thomas. I learned that they had been South to collect some outstanding debts, and that they were then *en route* to their homes in Louisville. I ordered their release, and two very happy men went on their way rejoicing. From that time to the present I have always numbered Thomas among my friends, and whenever I see him he invariably refers to his first introduction to me.

On another occasion a lady was arrested. She was on her way to Louisville, and had a ponderous trunk in her possession. It was but right that the contents of the trunk should be examined. Not wishing to overhaul a female's wardrobe, of which I knew so little, and learning that her brother, Major Nicholas, was in my command, I had him examine her baggage, and, as he reported finding nothing "contraband of war," I permitted her to pass on to her home. On the following day I received a large basket of choice fruit, in recognition of my "kindness and consideration for her."

CHAPTER XXIII.

During Winter of 1863-64 Preparations made for a Grand Campaign—Duplicate Bridges prepared—Buzzard Roost Gap moved upon—General John A. Logan—Resaca—Singular Death Wounds—Captain Henry M. Stinson, of General Howard's Staff—General King—Wounded by Shot fired from Captain Howell's Battery—Captain Dilger—McPherson Fell—Chief of Cavalry.

DURING the winter of 1863-64 the preparations were made for a grand campaign. All the troops that could be spared from other points were concentrated under Sherman near Chattanooga. Grant in the East and Sherman in the West were too far apart to be of any assistance to each other, except by indirection. If Grant pushed the enemy closely no troops could be spared to operate against Sherman, and *vice versa*.

General Grant designated the 2d day of May for the advance of both armies, but finally the 5th was agreed upon, and the same was announced in orders. On the 2d, Davis's and Baird's divisions joined at Ringgold, and on the following day my division closed upon the other two, and thus we had our entire corps concentrated under the command of Major-General John M. Palmer.

Sherman had an army not less than one hundred thousand strong, composed of as fine troops as were ever assembled together. The Union forces exceeded the rebels, but this preponderance was overbalanced by the nature of the campaign. General Johnston, the commander of the Confederate army, was acting on the defensive, and when he fell back he had no detached positions to be held by which his main army was depleted. As the Federal army advanced, Sherman was compelled to protect his line of communication, and this implied a constant depletion of the main army. Every bridge and tunnel had to be guarded, and protection had to be furnished to trains and supply depots, so the army did not advance far before the strength—I mean the fighting strength—of both armies was about equal.

Some of General Sherman's staff officers ascertained the length of every bridge and culvert from Chattanooga to Atlanta. Duplicates of the most important ones were made in anticipation of the possible destruction of the originals by the enemy, and these duplicates were hurried forward as soon as needed. It was a mystery to the enemy how little our army was delayed by destroyed bridges. A captured rebel once said that it was generally believed in the South that Sherman not only moved with duplicate bridges but also duplicate tunnels, as the destruction of either failed to delay the onward march of his grand army. At Tunnel Hill our corps met with determined resistance, but on the arrival of General Howard with his corps the enemy fell back to Buzzard Roost.

It was Sherman's plan to make a demonstration in force at Buzzard Roost to convey the impression that it was his main point of attack, and while this demonstration was progressing, McPherson, with his corps, was to pass through Snake Creek Gap, strike, and destroy the railroad in rear of the Confederates. Had this plan been successful, Johnston would have been compelled to retreat independent of the railroad, and could have been pursued and destroyed in a very short time. After a few days spent demonstrating at Buzzard Roost, the greater portion of our army was ordered to move to the right and pass through Snake Creek Gap. The enemy got wind of our movement, and fell back, destroying the bridge over the Oostanaula River, after a sharp conflict with the Union forces in the vicinity of Resaca. McPherson found, on his approach to Resaca, that it was fortified and manned so heavily that he could not hope to dislodge the enemy, and so he encamped near the south end of Snake Creek Gap. I passed through this narrow gorge after dusk, and seeing my corps commander, I rode up to him, and was then and there introduced to General John A. Logan, the first and last time I ever saw him. I remember I was impressed with the idea that something had gone wrong with him, and that he was out of humor in consequence. Conscious that I was not the offending party, I bade him good-evening and joined my command. I confess that I have always been curious to know just the cause of his displeasure.

After the retreat of the enemy from Resaca, I passed over the battle-field and noticed the peculiar manner in which one of the enemy's sharp-shooters had been killed. He had been lying on the ground behind an old, decayed log. His head was raised, and he was in the act of firing when a cannon-ball struck the log, passing through it, striking him just below the chin, and passing through him on a line parallel to his backbone. On another occasion I was with General King. A halt had been made for some reason, and one of the regular soldiers lay down, with his head against an old, badly-decayed log, to take a short sleep. When the order was given to fall in, he did not move, and, on examination, he was found to be dead. An ordinary bullet had passed through the log and entered his skull, producing instant death.

On another occasion a soldier was asleep, when a shell from the enemy's line, in passing over him, cast off a sharp, rusty scale, which, striking him in the jugular vein, produced almost instant death.

It is astonishing what severe wounds some men can receive and yet recover, while others die from injuries apparently of the slightest character. Gunshot wounds which cause men to fall to the ground at once are mortal nine times out of ten. While on the Atlanta campaign, General O. O. Howard invited me to ride out with him in front and to the left of our lines. Arriving near the edge of a large field, we left our staff officers and orderlies in a sheltered position and stepped near the edge of the field. Howard, with his field-glass, looked across the clearing and discovered men throwing up breastworks on the elevated ground beyond. He passed the glass to me and I observed the same thing. Just at this time Captain Harry M. Stinson, of General Howard's staff, stepped in between us and took the glass, and was sweeping the woods beyond the field, when suddenly I heard two distinct reports, as if two objects had been struck at almost the same instant. Young Stinson reeled and fell. The ball passed through him and buried itself in an oak-tree in his rear. It was the striking of the tree which made the second report. We got the young man to the rear and examined his wounds. I supposed that he could not possibly survive many hours, and General Howard thought so likewise, for he began to question him as to his faith and hope. Even away off in that dangerous locality the Christian soldier breathed words of encouragement in the ears of that young man. In a short time he was able to go back to East Tennessee, where, in Cleveland, he was for several months tenderly and lovingly cared for. When sufficiently strong he rejoined General Howard. One day when riding around my lines I met him, and was surprised, for I had supposed him dead and buried months before. He continued on duty, and was in Florida at the surrender of the troops in that State, where, by over-exertion, he died from internal hemorrhage on February 22, 1866. General Howard says of this young officer, "He was a nephew of James G. Blaine. First went out as a private in the Fifth Maine; was taken prisoner at Bull Run while caring for his brother, who was mortally wounded. After he was exchanged he was promoted to the rank of lieutenant, and was ever after that on my staff."

On the night of the day upon which this young man was wounded we had a heavy battle. After the firing ceased both armies rested on their arms for the night. Our wagons could not find us, and hence we had nothing to eat and no blankets upon which to sleep. General King and myself bivouacked together, sleeping on a saddle-blanket and covering ourselves with an India-rubber blanket which some unselfish soldier let us have for the night. Our pillow was a stone which we found against the root of a large tree. Of course we could sleep only for a few moments at a time, but we managed to get through the night. The following morning a dense, heavy fog hung over and around us, and it seemed that daylight would never again appear. Finally my cook came up and informed me that if permitted to make a fire he could soon have some coffee prepared. I pointed out to him a low place in the dry bed of a wet-weather stream, and soon he had a fire under headway. Others, seeing him, made fires, and soon a heavy column of smoke ascended above the tops of the trees, revealing our exact whereabouts. At this time King and myself were sitting on the stone which we had used for a pillow, with our faces buried in our hands and our hands on our knees. Suddenly the enemy opened with one or more batteries upon our position. I straightened myself up in time to see the effect of the first shot, which was to cut a soldier into two pieces; the second shot carried away the arm of Colonel Niebling, of Ohio; the third shot grazed the talma of King and struck me just over the liver and disabled me. I was taken back to a safe place and King assumed command of the division. If he had had the same amount of curiosity that I exhibited he would have received the twelve-pound shell instead of myself.

In a few days I went North, and was absent from the army until after the battle of Kenesaw Mountain. I returned July 18, 1864, and assumed command of my division the day before it crossed the Chattahoochie.

When on a visit recently to Atlanta I was invited to dine with a number of gentlemen at the house of Mr. A. W. Hill. I was seated by the side of Captain Howell, one of the able editors of the *Atlanta Con-*

stitution. I was explaining to him when and how I was wounded, and he remarked, "It was my battery that fired the shot, but I am glad it did not kill you." I asked him if he would like to have the shell, and he replied, "No, indeed; I hope I shall never see another twelve-pound shell as long as I live."

On the morning of the 20th day of July I met General Mackay, of General Thomas's staff. I had known him years before in Texas, and he knew Hood very well when he was a lieutenant in my regiment. He said, "We are going to have a hard battle to-day." I asked him why he thought so, and he replied, "I have just seen an Atlanta paper which contains an order placing Hood in command and relieving Johnston; and," said Mackay, "a man who will bet a thousand dollars without having a pair in his hand will fight when he has the troops with which to do it."

Sure enough, about three o'clock that same afternoon Hood moved his army out, as if forming on parade, and when all was in readiness he sprang upon us. The main portion of his army was thrown against the left of ours, his extreme right being opposite to my left brigade, which was commanded by Colonel A. G. McCook. My other brigades and Davis's and Baird's divisions were to the right, and were not engaged. The assault was a desperate one, and the casualties great on both sides. Hooker's corps, immediately on the left of my command, suffered most heavily. Hood was finally repulsed, and fell back on his intrenchments.

I had attached to my division an Illinois battery, commanded by Captain Dilger, an officer in the Prussian army. It was said that he, in company with another young officer of the Prussian service, came to this country to witness the war, and that it was decided, on their arrival in New York, that one should join the Federals and the other the Confederates. It fell to Dilger's lot to join the Federal army. Through some instrumentality he secured Battery C, of Illinois artillery. Dilger dressed in buckskin clothing, and was known throughout the army as "Leather Breeches." He was a gallant fellow, and when an engagement took place generally rushed his battery out to the skirmish line. I was always fearful that the enemy would charge upon him suddenly and capture his entire outfit, and so I had him instructed not to leave the main line unless ordered forward. In the battle of the 20th, regardless of my orders, he moved forward to the front line and had several of his cannoneers killed by the enemy's sharp-shooters. After the battle I said to him that he had violated my orders in going too far to the front, and in doing so had lost several men. "No, no, general, I did not lose any men." I told him that it had been reported to me that several of his men had been picked off by the enemy's sharp-shooters. "Oh, yes, with dem leetle balls; none by artillery." Belonging to the artillery, he did not count a man killed unless he was killed by a cannon ball or shell. He was a fearless fellow and had a splendid battery, and was never so happy as when engaged with the enemy. He did not again return to his native country. While General Palmer was Governor of Illinois, I think "Leather Breeches" was his adjutant-general. I believe he still resides in that State.

On July 22, Hood made another sortie, this time striking our extreme left. Again the losses were heavy. It was here that the gallant McPherson fell; and as soon as his death was known, General John A. Logan took command, and by his good management showed himself to be a splendid soldier and an able commander. General O. O. Howard succeeded to the command of McPherson a few days after this battle. Sherman decided on the movement of his army to the right, and to effect this he ordered Howard to move in rear of our line and take position on our right. It seems that this movement was not known to Hood. One day I heard one of our pickets call to the rebel picket, saying, "Johnnie, how many men have you got left?" He replied, "Enough for one or two more killings." On the 28th, Hood moved out on the Lick Skillet road to attack our right. Here he found the same troops he had encountered on the 22d, and with about the same result. This was Howard's first battle with his new command, and so well did he handle it that his army was convinced that the gallant McPherson had a worthy successor. If there had been any silent opposition to him before, it was forever silenced after this engagement.

General Hood telegraphed to Richmond that he had been compelled to fight a hard battle on the Lick Skillet road; "but," said he, "we hold the road." That was true, but the part of it that his army held was inside of the city of Atlanta.

General Palmer was relieved of the command of the Fourteenth Corps at his own request, and by virtue of seniority I commanded it until a successor was designated. General Jeff. C. Davis was appointed major-general by brevet and assigned to duty according to his brevet rank and placed in command of the corps. I was really unfitted for active service, and General Sherman assigned me to duty as chief of cavalry, and ordered me to take post at Nashville and superintend the equipping and forwarding of all cavalry reaching that city.

I have hurriedly passed over this campaign simply for the reason that I did not wish to weary the general reader with details which can be procured in the many excellent histories of the war already published. The march from Chattanooga to Atlanta was one general battle. It might almost be said, during those long months of combat which culminated in the capture of Atlanta and Northern Georgia, that, like the Israelites of old, we followed a cloud by day and a pillar of fire by night. For in that time Dalton, Resaca, Kenesaw, New Hope Church, Picket's Mill, Peach Tree Creek, Jonesboro', and Altoona, and all those other crimson names of battle, had been traced bloodily into the history of our grand army. Every day had the smoke-cloud of battle kissed the heavens, and each night had flamed and flashed with the lambent lights of our blazing guns, and we had followed that smoke-cloud and those blazing guns over a hundred fields of strife until the old flag floated in exultation over the great "Gate City" of the South.

At Atlanta our legions separated, many of them never to meet again this side of the dark valley of death. The Fourteenth and Twentieth Corps, with most of the cavalry of the command, joined Sherman in that eagle swoop of his which served in so great a measure to stamp out the expiring embers of the rebellion, and participated in that storied "march down to the sea."

This command went the whole "grand rounds" through Georgia and the Carolinas, and graced with the blazonry of its presence the supreme crisis of that proud triumph when the second great military stay of the rebellion succumbed to the logic of war and the point of the bayonet in North Carolina. It also joined in that gala day of glory, when two hundred thousand soldiers, in all the splendid pomp and glittering pageantry of their magnificent equipment, tramped up the avenues of the capital city of the land, and the pæans of the great jubilee of the nation's deliverance rang in deep thankfulness from ocean to ocean.

CHAPTER XXIV.

Sherman starts South—Hood starts North—The Race for Nashville—Battle at Franklin—Battle of Nashville—Pursuit of Hood—Crossing the Harpeth—Smith's Artillery—Entrance into Franklin—Our Wounded—Mr. Lincoln's Estimate of the Number of the Enemy—Battle of Nashville—Reported Dead—Was Hood justified in making a Campaign to Tennessee?—An Enlisted Man on Battle of Nashville.

WHEN Sherman started for the sea, Hood concluded to operate in his rear, and if he could seize Nashville he was perfectly willing that Sherman should have a triumphal march to the sea. To provide against this contingency, Sherman left Thomas, with the Fourth and Twenty-third Corps, to look after the safety of his rear. After some days of preparation, Hood marched for Florence, Alabama, intending to cross the Tennessee at that point and march directly upon Nashville. With all possible despatch Thomas moved his troops to Pulaski, Tennessee. He remained in Nashville to collect all the available troops and have them organized and ready for service on Hood's arrival in front of the city. The advance was in command of General John M. Schofield, who was ably assisted by General D. S. Stanley, the commander of the Fourth Corps. Schofield fell back to Columbia and then to Franklin, Tennessee. Having practically nothing to do, I reported to General Thomas and asked to be assigned to any command where I could be of any service, and he gave me a division of cavalry, command of which I assumed at Pulaski, being under the immediate command of General J. H. Wilson, the commander of all Federal cavalry in the South. When Schofield fell back to Franklin our cavalry was on the flank on the Harpeth, about two miles from the town. Temporary breastworks were thrown up by Schofield in front of Franklin, and Hood rashly marched his command against them. A terrible battle resulted, in which there were seven Confederate general officers killed. One of these, General John Adams, formerly of the regular army, was killed and fell upon our intrenchments. Such marked bravery was never before shown on any battlefield. At one time there was a break in our line, and had it not been for the presence and gallantry of General Stanley and General Opdyke it is probable that our entire line would have been driven back. But Stanley, placing himself at the head of a brigade, charged the enemy and drove him back, thus reestablishing our line. About nine o'clock at night General Schofield sent a despatch to General Wilson announcing the result of the battle, which was the first intimation we had that a severe battle had been fought. The sound of cannon and musketry failed to reach us, although we were within less than three miles of the battle-field. Stanley had a horse killed under him and was himself wounded. Few officers in the war did more faithful service than Stanley, who has only received, within a year, his well-earned promotion to a brigadiership. I think of all the generals I met during the war Schofield was the coolest and most self-possessed. I never saw him excited; he was always ready for any emergency, and had many points in common with General George H. Thomas, "the rock of Chickamauga," my beau ideal of a thorough soldier. When he fell back from Franklin to Nashville he coolly marched through the enemy's camp, and some of his soldiers lighted their pipes at the Confederate camp-fires, at least such is claimed by a part of his command.

At last our entire army was concentrated at Nashville, with the exception of Rousseau's division, which was left in the fortifications at Murfreesboro'. Soon Hood appeared and encamped around the city and in full view of our fortifications. Thomas did not wish to offer battle until his arrangements were completed, and the passiveness of Hood was just what he most desired. He was strongly urged from Washington to attack at once, but his uniform reply was, "You can relieve me if you wish, but I will not offer battle till I am ready. I am doing all in my power, and I hope to be able to move by a certain date." That day arrived, but the ground was covered with ice. The horses were smooth-shod, and it was impossible to move the cavalry or the artillery. On the 14th day of December, 1864, the ice had disappeared, and Thomas ordered a movement against the enemy on the following morning. At the appointed time the army swept out of its fortifications and actually and utterly annihilated the veteran ranks of the enemy. Not, perhaps, in all the history of authentic war is there another case where the besieged, gathered, as was this command, on the spur of the occasion from every direction,—detachments, raw recruits, drafted men, new regiments, with the Fourth and Twenty-third Corps as the nucleus of organization,—throwing down every barrier and laying aside every artificial defence, rushed out upon an outnumbering foe, versed in all the strategy of war, and beat him face to face and front to front in fair and open contest. Never was victory more complete or defeat more crushing and overwhelming. Hood's army was literally and actually broken up and destroyed, and its usefulness as an effective military organization ruined effectually and forever. Sennacherib's host scarcely melted away more completely.

The battle of Nashville was the last staggering blow at the failing Confederacy, and contributed in a large degree to the success of military operations in the East. Had the termination been different the rebellion would have received a new lease of life, and other and bloody campaigns would have been the legitimate consequences. Richmond would have been reinforced and the rear of Sherman's army would have been endangered, while but a flimsy line of posts would have intervened between the rich cities of the Northwest and the sack and pillage of Hood's needy and desperate squadrons.

In this battle my cavalry division occupied the extreme right of our army, and succeeded during the first day in driving the enemy about eight miles. At night I occupied, with my staff, the house of a Mrs. Bass. She said she had no forage for our horses, having been deprived of all corn and oats by the Confederate army. While sitting with the family, after supper, in front of a fine open fire, a little urchin thrust his head through the door-way and said, "Mamma, we have got all the corn into the cellar."

I pretended not to hear him, for the poor woman had but little, and I thought it would be cruel to take that little from her.

As soon as it was light enough to see, my command was again in motion. We soon engaged the enemy, and constantly pressed him back. At night I occupied the best house I could find. There was only one room, and of this the owner, his wife, children, and dogs were tenants in common; however, we all crowded together in that one room. It had rained all day and we were wet to the skin, and when the odors natural to the house were combined with those of wet horse-blankets, wet dogs, and other mal-odors I could not dream of the sweet and rich perfumes of Arabia. I never prayed more earnestly in my life for the coming of the light of another day, whatever might be its issues. Here I received an order from General Thomas to push on, cross the Harpeth, and attack the enemy then in the town of Franklin. When we reached the Harpeth it was rising rapidly, owing to the incessant rains, and it was necessary to hasten the crossing before the depth of water would be too great to permit of the passage of the artillery. The battery was under the command of Lieutenant F. G. Smith, now brevet major, a splendid officer, a brave and thorough soldier. We finally succeeded in reaching the south bank, and marched up the stream in the direction of the town. Reaching the bluff overlooking the village, Smith brought his guns in position and fired a volley, the rebels fell back in great confusion, and my division moved at a rapid pace into the town, where we were greeted by all of our wounded in the battle previously fought near that place. They were greatly delighted at getting once more under the shadow of the stars and stripes.

While I believe that my command was the first to reoccupy the town of Franklin, yet I suppose there are a dozen divisions to claim the honor, so I will not raise the issue here, but simply say that we got into the town as soon as we could get there, and were soon joined by other commands, who were enabled to cross the bridge when Smith's volley compelled the rebels to retire. I have often supposed the rebels imagined that the greater part of our army was on the south side of the Harpeth, whereas I had only about two thousand men; and had it been known that we were completely cut off from our army by high water, they might have turned against us and made it very uncomfortable, even if they had failed to kill or capture the last one of the command. But I suppose the leader of the rebel forces imagined that he was outnumbered three to one.

It is astonishing how commanders are apt to overestimate the strength of their opponents in battle. A delegation of ministers of the gospel called to pay their respects to Mr. Lincoln, and in course of conversation one of them asked the President how many men Mr. Davis had under arms. Mr. Lincoln replied, "Three millions, sir." "Can that be possible?" queried the divine. "Oh, yes," said the President, "I have the figures for it. We have one million under arms, and all my generals report in every engagement that they are outnumbered three to one. Admitting this, it is clear that the rebel army must be three times as large as ours, and hence I assert positively that there are three millions of men under arms against the government of the United States."

For some days before the battle of Nashville my wife had been a guest at the St. Cloud Hotel, and she could hear the roar of artillery and the rattling of musketry as the battle progressed. As my command was on the right, and as my instructions were to move with my right on the bank of the river, I soon lost communication with the main army. Some time in the afternoon a local paper issued an extra, and among the items of news was the following:

"It is reported that General R. W. Johnson has been killed. He was an excellent officer, a clever gentleman, and in his death the service loses a worthy and indispensable leader." I was glad to read the item, not only because I knew it was not true as to my death, but from it I learned just what would have been said of me if I had died for my country.

The heavy rains, producing swollen streams, favored Hood's escape. When his army crossed a stream the bridge would be destroyed and we would have to delay until another was constructed. In this way the enemy crossed the Tennessee River and made good his escape. Hood was charged with great rashness in penetrating the State of Tennessee. Let us look at his campaign in the light of probable success. Sherman had started for the sea, taking with him the greater portion of his grand army which had been opposing Johnston and Hood all summer. Thomas was left with a small command, and everything seemed favorable for a successful invasion of Middle Tennessee, the capture of Nashville, and even the planting of the Confederate flag on the banks of the Ohio River. The Union cause would have been seriously damaged by the capture of Nashville, with its immense stores of provisions, camp and garrison equipage, to say nothing of the large quantity of artillery, small arms, and ammunition which would have fallen into the hands of the Confederates.

The chances of success were so much in Hood's favor, and, if successful, so fraught with advantages to the insurgents, that in my opinion he was warranted in taking the risk. Fortunately for the cause of the Union, Sherman had left behind him a man of energy and ability; a man in whom all had confidence; a man who had never known defeat. General George H. Thomas, "the greatest Roman of them all," was called upon to decide the fate of the State,—ah, of the nation itself! Hurriedly he gathered his forces together. His subordinate commanders were called around him, and each was told the part he had to take in the coming conflict. His order of battle was a full report of what was done; no word of explanation was necessary. He ordered; it was obeyed. At a given signal our entire line advanced, and with a whoop and a yell all the various parts of the army were engaged, from the cavalry on the right to the dusky sons of Mars, under Steadman, on our left.

The plan was without a flaw, and the general whose peerless wisdom projected it had the consummate skill to accomplish it in all its details, from the opening volleys of the left wing, where the colored troops bore the national flag up to the very intrenchments of the enemy, and breasted the hurtling storm of lead and flame and steel, to the awful tempest of death which rained in torrents of blood upon the quaking breast of Overton's Hill.

The victory was complete, and in a few days the last hostile rebel was driven from the State.

A short time since I received a very interesting letter from Mr. V. H. Harris, now of Litchfield, Minnesota, but formerly a member of the One Hundred and Eleventh Ohio Volunteers. From this letter I gather the views of an enlisted man in regard to the battle of Nashville. He says,—

"At the battle of Nashville the Army of the Ohio, commanded by General Schofield, had fought its way into position on the right, and lay on the morning of the 16th in line of battle facing to the east, at right angles with Smith's Sixteenth Corps, and parallel to the Granny White pike. From this position we were in full view of the Harpeth and Brentwood ranges of hills. We had prepared our frugal meal long before the dawn of day, and at sunrise could plainly see the rebels on the timber-covered slopes not far away. We were cautioned to remain concealed as much as possible, and not to fire under any circumstances. But our position was discovered, and a rebel battery opened upon us with shot and shell, which, passing over our line, caused a falling of trees and limbs almost as destructive as the iron missiles which whistled over us would have been, had they fallen and exploded in our ranks. When the whizzing sound of a shell was heard, the usual cry of 'Grab a root' ran through the line, the effect of which was to induce the braves to adopt the doctrine of 'squatter sovereignty' without question; and as time wore on each warrior loved his country more in fact, for they hugged it, embraced it, felt as if they wanted to get right down into it, at least far enough to shelter them from the fire of the enemy.

"About noon the firing of the cavalry on our right was music to our ears, for we knew enough of the country to know that our men were in possession of or very near to the pike on the south of the Brentwood hills. On the other side of the low ridge occupied by us was one still lower, upon which ran a slight elevation of earth, which may have been at some time a hedge. It was high enough to hide the form of a man on a level plain, and we were told that we were to occupy it as our next position. At a given signal the entire line moved rapidly and occupied it without firing a shot. Here we were concealed from the view of the rebels. As soon as this movement was accomplished our old position was occupied by thirty pieces of artillery, which opened up a most terrific cannonade upon the rebel works, not over three hundred yards distant. The shot and shell from our own guns tore the tops and limbs from the huge oaks in our front and rear. One large limb fell on our company and spread its whole length, the heavy end striking James Bemis and knocking him senseless; another came near killing James Carter, and the switch end struck me just below the cartridge-box, calling to mind my school-boy days. A charge of buckshot could not have pained me more than did the switching that limb gave me. The smoke of the cannon settled in the valley, completely enveloping us and concealing from our view both friends and foes. And now the rattle of musketry, like an unceasing hail-storm, kept time with the deafening roar of artillery. The earth and the mighty oaks trembled and shook again with the echo that came back from Brentwood's quivering crest. The Confederate works were levelled with solid shot, and their brave defenders lay crouched to earth. No rebel yell arose above the deafening din. The stars and bars were furled forever, and freedom's flag waved in triumph over the bloody field.

"The pass through the Brentwood Range, through which the Granny White pike was made, was in plain view. No field of battle ever presented a landscape so plain, so beautiful as this. Our artillery had not only ruined the defences of the enemy, but had dashed the timbers to splinters on the sides of the hill beyond. Shot, shell, and minie-balls had driven the teamsters and skulkers in the rebel rear to wild desperation. There was no escape for them except by the pike, and now, in a moment's lull, there came a living stream from east and west, and, meeting on the pike, broke pell-mell for the Southern Confederacy. This host was governed by no order, but there in view of friend and foe they lashed their jaded steeds in a furious race through the Brentwood Pass. As soon as this movement was discovered our artillery opened upon the fugitives, and in their rapid flight they so closed up that it was simply impossible for them to move. Many abandoned their wagons, mules, and horses and fled for safety to the hills. Bull Run never presented such utter demoralization as was visible in the rebel rear. The victorious Federals required no order to advance. With a yell that seemed to shake the foundations of the everlasting hills, ten thousand men from older fields than this rushed forward in pursuit of a beaten enemy. The war in the West was ended. So sudden was the change in the form of government in the eyes of our late foes that they laughed and clapped their hands, more pleased than we were over the situation. I heard one lean, lank, cadaverous prisoner say, 'You licked us at Franklin because you had more to eat than we had. Can't you give me a cracker?' We divided our rations. Why, bless your soul, we would have given them the coats off our backs. No shout of victory was raised over a surrendered foe. And now came a small campaign not laid down in 'Pap' Thomas's original plan of battle. Several hundred yards in front of what had been the rebel rear lay immense quantities of broken and abandoned war material of Hood's almost 'invincible legion,' for men were never braver than they. To get there was a duty fully recognized by every soldier. Thomas Barr, my chum and messmate, accompanied me. About one hundred yards from our line and on the left of the pike my eyes fell upon a picture—not painted—that I shall never forget. An old citizen appears to have entered the rebel lines for the purpose of selling milk. He was seated in an old-fashioned one-horse shay. The horse had been instantly killed by a cannon-ball. The old man was dead, and had fallen forward and hung over two large milk-cans, and in his hands he held the reins. I raised his face, but all was still. The milk was wasting through holes made by minié-balls and slowly dropping through the loose bottom of the vehicle. Barr laid his gun down and seemed indisposed to push his investigation any further, but soon realized the necessity of prompt action, and onward we journeyed. We were not long in reaching the point for which we started. Here we had a fair view of the horrors of war. Dead men were strewn upon the ground on a common level with dead horses and mules. There we saw horses and mules uninjured, but held in place by a dead or badly-wounded mate, and I could read despair in the eyes of these poor, dumb brutes. A short distance off I saw three rebels working like demons removing broken wagons and obstructions towards the left, while up close to them and near the fence rode a gray-coat with two horses drawing off a beautiful piece of artillery. It occurred to me that this was a good opportunity for me to earn my thirteen dollars a month, and I resolved then and there to capture that gun. I charged upon the lingering quartet and demanded their surrender in the usual pleasant army form. The three working heroes in front jumped over the fence and were soon out of sight. I rushed upon the man with the cannon and seized one of his horses by the rein and ordered him to dismount, which he declined to do, but proceeded to rap me over the head with the loose end of the reins, at the same time urging his team forward to break loose from a heavy wagon against which his wheel had caught. By this time Barr had arrived and stood near me, and I felt then extremely bold. The man making no demonstration calculated to convince me that he intended to dismount, I determined to use the whole power vested in me by the Constitution of the United States; accordingly I gave him a blow which sent him tumbling over between the horses. My gun not being loaded, he slipped out under the off-horse and started down the pike as fast as his feet could carry him. Neither Barr nor myself ever went on another side campaign without loading our guns. Back to camp we went with our captures, meeting on the way our colonel, Sherwood, who thanked us for what we had done and promised that our prowess should be suitably announced in orders; but as we did not occupy the same camp two successive nights for five months, there was no time for making out congratulatory orders. This battle closed the rebellion in the Southwest. And now, dear, brave old Pap Thomas, thy fame and name are written in the hearts of thy countrymen. Thy mould in bronze and marble shall yet stand on Brentwood's crest, and ages hence our people shall point in pride to you as the very embodiment of all that was good, pure, brave, noble, and patriotic."

CHAPTER XXV.

Condition of Things at Pulaski—Death of President Lincoln—Andrew Johnson's Loyalty—Judge-Advocate—Nashville at the Close of the War—Lawlessness—Hanging of Three Highwaymen for Murder—Cholera—General Thomas removes his Headquarters to Louisville—Status of Class at the close of Thirty-six Years.

GENERAL WILSON pushed on after the retreating enemy, while I was left at Pulaski to command the district known as Middle Tennessee. All was confusion. The people were idle; the schools and churches were closed. All branches of industry were suspended. All was doubt and uncertainty. We had the schoolhouse repaired, seats provided, and secured the services of an experienced teacher, and invited parents to send their children to school. In a few days the school was full. Next, worthy parties were authorized to open stores for the sale of dry goods, groceries, and clothing. The churches were opened on the Sabbath, and were well attended. In this way, little by little, the old order of things was restored. A military commission was instituted for the trial of bushwhackers and guerrillas. All persons convicted were sentenced to hard work in the penitentiary. In this way evil-doing soon ceased and law and order were restored.

On the 15th day of April, 1865, a despatch reached us announcing the assassination of President Lincoln. Of course the officers and soldiers were distressed beyond measure, for all had learned to love good

Abraham Lincoln; and his death seemed to distress the citizens, not so much that they cared for him, but they had an awful dread of falling into the hands of Andy Johnson, who up to that time had favored the hanging of all the prominent men engaged in the rebellion, to the end that "treason might' be made odious."

Johnson had risen to his prominence notwithstanding the opposition on the part of what he was pleased to call the aristocratic class. He hated aristocracy, and the aristocracy had an ineffable contempt for him; not that he was unworthy, but because he had risen from obscurity. The very thing for which he deserved the most credit— rising by individual effort, in the face of all opposition, from obscurity to a high place in the political world— was lost sight of. He was considered a plebeian, because he could not boast of a long line of distinguished ancestry. Such a man, they said, when accidentally placed over us will rule as with a rod of iron. The effect upon the people was very perceptible. They were willing to accept any terms if their lives were spared. It was not long before it became evident that Johnson wanted to secure the good will of this aristocratic element. We soon ceased to hear about making "treason odious," and again the rebel element became defiant. These same men, who only a few weeks before were the most quiet and docile of their race, became intolerant to their Union neighbors and persecuted them in every conceivable way. Instead of Union men taking the lead in reconstruction, these returned rebels claimed that right and maintained it. It is not my province to criticise Mr. Johnson's motives, but I can say that his elevation to the Presidency materially retarded the reconstruction of the rebellious States. We have no means of knowing what would have been the policy of Mr. Lincoln, but this much we can safely say,—that he would not have had a policy except one in accord with the views of Congress. Johnson was a stubborn man, and could not tolerate opposition even on the part of the Congress of the United States. It has been said that he designed at one time to recognize a Congress composed of Southern members, and thus defeat and set at naught all that had been achieved by the war. This I regard as the sheerest nonsense. Mr. Johnson was not an idiot, but knew full well that the American people would never sanction such a course on his part. In fact, had he attempted it he would have been disposed of in short order. This is simply my opinion, knowing him as well as I did. It may be that there are papers in existence to prove what has been asserted; but before I can believe Andrew Johnson to have been a traitor I shall have to see the evidence myself.

While in Pulaski I had my office and sleeping apartments at the house of a Mr. Jones. When I first took possession of part of the house, with the consent of Mrs. Jones, her husband was in the South, a member of Congress, I believe. He returned while I was in his house, and I found him an agreeable gentleman. Jones was a lawyer of fine reputation before the war, and, while he lived in town for convenience, he had a large farm in the neighborhood. It is said that on one occasion his foreman or overseer came to him for some money with which to purchase provisions for his slaves.

He gave him the amount asked for, and told him to say to the negroes that if they did not work more and get along better he would *stop practising law for them.* On his return he found himself relieved of that burden.

The headquarters of the district were transferred to Murfreesboro' by an order issued about July 1, and I arrived at that place on July 3. Here I remained until some time in the fall, when I was relieved by Major-General William B. Hazen. About this time, General J. G. Parkhurst, who had been for some time on the staff of General Thomas as provost-marshal-general, was mustered out of the service, and I was detailed to relieve him. My predecessor had managed the department so well, and had reduced everything to such a perfect system, that I found little difficulty in my new position. In a short time the necessity for such an officer ceased, and General Thomas detailed me as judge-advocate-general of the military division commanded by him. On the 15th day of January, 1866, in common with hundreds of other officers, I was mustered out of the volunteer service as brigadier-general, and fell back to my old position in the regular army, that of major of the Fourth Cavalry. Being incapacitated for active operations in the field, I asked to be placed on the retired list. I was ordered before the Retiring Board for examination, and was retired October 11, 1867.

And thus the story of the war is briefly told, and we all know how, when peace had been conquered to the land again, and the authority of the government had forced itself to be recognized through all the broad confines of the Republic, those massive armies resolved themselves once more into their constituent parts, and, with the exception of such as had adopted the profession of arms as a lifetime avocation, the hundreds of thousands of soldiers laid aside their warlike guise and turned themselves naturally and zealously to the arts of peace. The necessity that had made them soldiers of the Republic having passed away, they turned with eagerness and earnestness to the homes that had sent them forth, and, with true American enterprise and energy, entered into the thick avenues of trade and business.

They presented to the world the lofty spectacle of soldiers becoming again civilians, and their history since that time conclusively shows that the stern probation of war did not unfit them for the gentle and beneficent walks of peace.

The arts of peace are better than the arts of war. But the arts of peace can only attain their noblest fruition in a land where the arts of war are widely understood and comprehended. The one is the co-ordinate of the other. The one requires the moral and physical countenance of the other. A government with no high military traditions, no glorious legends, no lofty exemplars, no great national sentiment, no warm pulse of national honor, is like a huge body without the vitalizing presence of a brave and contented soul. A nation whose loyal sons are her soldiers—a nation where the people themselves are the bulwarks of military strength—may bid defiance to the march of time and the revolutions of change. External assault and internal revolts are alike powerless to shake its throne in the affections of its citizens. Enemies without and enemies within can never shatter it. Foreign war may exhaust its powers, and domestic treason may expend all the rebellious efforts of its hate upon that nation, and it will live and strengthen and succeed in spite of them all. That outburst of popular affection, that exhibition of patriotic resolution, that simple, patient, unfaltering adherence to principle and to purpose which vindicated the authority and assured the existence of the American Republic through the crimson years of the late rebellion is the surest pledge of American perpetuity.

Our dead have not all died in vain. Our living have not battled and suffered all for naught.

About the close of the war Nashville was about as disorderly a place as I ever resided in. It was absolutely unsafe to be on the streets after dark. Murders and thefts were committed with impunity, and the perpetrators generally escaped. A gentleman by the name of Heffernan, in company with his family, went out one evening to attend some school celebration, and on his return his carriage was stopped by four highwaymen. Drawing his pistol, he fired and wounded one severely, but not until he had received a fatal shot, from which he died the next day. The wounded highwayman could not make his escape, and was arrested. He gave the names of those associated with him, and they, too, were apprehended. General W. D. Whipple, in the absence of General Thomas, ordered a military commission for their trial. I was president, Colonel R. E. A. Crofton was a member, and Colonel Blackman judge-advocate. The facts were all proven, and the prisoners were sentenced to death by hanging, and the sentence was duly carried into effect. From that time onward lawlessness ceased.

From being a most lawless, disorderly city, Nashville became noted as being an orderly, law-abiding city. Citizens went about, day and night, with impunity, in perfect confidence that they would not be robbed or murdered.

In the summer of 1866, the cholera, in a most virulent form, visited the city. All who could get away fled to the Cumberland Mountains or elsewhere, but many had to remain. It was estimated at the time that the number of whites in the city did not exceed sixteen thousand. The greatest mortality any one day was one hundred and fifty. In many cases men in perfect health in the morning were dead and buried before sundown. The city had a large force engaged digging graves. A colored man dug one in the forenoon, and was buried in it himself about sundown of the same day. My wife and children were with me. I tried to prevail upon them to flee, but they would not go without me, and I could not go had I desired to do so. Fortunately, all escaped. When cholera is epidemic, the dangers and anxieties one experiences are greater than those incident to the battle-field. After the fearful disease abated, General Thomas removed his headquarters to Louisville.

Thirty-six years have elapsed since my class separated on the plain at West Point. Some of them I have never met. Nine only remain on the active list, four have been retired, eleven have resigned, and nineteen have passed through the "dim waters of death."

How short is the time separating mature manhood from old age! It seems but yesterday that we received our diplomas, yet we have all passed the meridian mile-post, and are wending our way down the western slope of our lives, guided by the flickering, uncertain light of our setting sun.

We are nearing the beach of that mighty ocean which rolls between Time and Eternity, and can almost hear the buffetings of the waves as they beat and break on the opposite shore. In a few years, at most, we shall join those who have gone before, and the class of 1849 will live only by the history it has made.

CHAPTER XXVI.

Recollections of Grant, Sherman, Thomas, Terry, Stanley, McCook, Carlin, Palmer, Baird, Howard, Jeff. C. Davis, Logan, Hazen, Gibson, Rousseau, Berry, T. L. Crittenden, John M. Harlan, James B. Steedman.

During the war I was thrown with many officers whose names shine on the pages of our national history. Some of these are well known, and about whom it is hardly necessary for me to give my impressions at any great length. General Grant and General Sherman, two of the most eminent men produced by the civil contest, and who were friends in war and in peace, were as unlike as day and night. Grant had no nerves, while Sherman was made up of nerves. Grant never gave himself any concern in regard to an enemy he could not see, while a concealed foe was more dreadful to Sherman than one in full view. Grant's strategy consisted in getting as near an enemy as possible, and then "moving on his works without delay." Sherman was more of a strategist, and believed in surprising his enemy by a masterly move by which he would attack him on the flank or in the rear. Grant reached Richmond by more fighting than strategy. Sherman reached Atlanta by more strategy than fighting, yet he gave us as much of the latter as we had any desire for. Grant was a blazing comet, Sherman a brilliant meteor. It has always been a wonder to me how two men so unlike in their general make-up could be such fast friends, yet there never was any disagreement between them of which the world knew anything. It was said that while Grant was President an attempt was made to get Sherman to antagonize some of his reconstruction ideas. "No," replied Sherman; "Grant stood by me when I was crazy, and I stood by him when he was drunk, and now we stand by each other."

Each gave to the other the credit for the success which had fallen to him, and in this way "honors were even," and a warm personal friendship was maintained between them. To Sheridan I have referred elsewhere.

MAJOR-GENERAL GEORGE H. THOMAS

was the old, reliable wheel-horse of the army. He was slow but sure. He never made a mistake and never lost a battle. When I first became acquainted with him he was a major in the regiment in which I was a captain. For thirteen years we were together, and I was as intimate with him as any one not of his own family. A truer or braver man never lived. Naturally reticent and of a stern exterior, there throbbed in his manly bosom a heart as soft and tender as ever beat within the breast of man. He was just and generous to all under his command, and if he ever wronged anyone it was under a misapprehension of the facts in the case.

Sherman's march to the sea reflected great credit upon its originator because of Thomas's grand battle at Nashville. Had he been defeated, and had Hood reached the Ohio River simultaneously with Sherman's reaching the ocean, the country would hardly have been satisfied with the exchange, and it is possible that the "march to the sea" would not have been rendered immortal in prose and verse. It is probable, however, that Sherman knew just what Thomas could, and would, do, and it may have been that he left him behind for that very purpose.

GENERAL DAVID S. STANLEY.

Few officers did more faithful service than General Stanley. When he commanded cavalry he was the eyes of the army and was ever on the alert. When in command of infantry he was always in the fore-front of battle, and no troops did more effective service than those under his leadership. At Franklin he was the hero of the occasion, and had it not been for his promptness and daring it is more than probable that our army would have been defeated. But fortunately he was on the ground when a portion of our army was driven back. Placing himself at the head of a brigade, he charged, drove the enemy back, and re-established our line.

GENERAL A. McD. McCOOK.

He belonged to the celebrated fighting family of that name, and on many hard-fought fields he showed himself worthy of his name. Wherever fighting was hardest there was he to be found. His keen eye enabled him to detect weak points in his line, and his quick mind always suggested a remedy in time to avert disaster. At Stone River his command was attacked by the entire army of the enemy, excepting

Breckenridge's division. At midnight before the battle he knew the position of the enemy's line of battle and so reported to General Rosecrans, who was so intent upon carrying out his original order that he did not change his plan, and the result of this was to leave McCook's corps to fight all of the army of the enemy excepting one division. The final issue of such an unequal contest could be readily divined. But through all, and over all, McCook bore himself gallantly and did good service, and deserves well of his country.

GENERAL WILLIAM P. CARLIN.

This officer I have known for more than forty years, during which time he rose by his own gallantry from a second lieutenant to brevet major-general. For some time he was under my command, and I had ample opportunity of witnessing his soldierly qualities in the discipline he enforced and the results achieved in battle, where he was a terror to his foe, without fear, and always at the post of danger. In social life, surrounded by his friends, he is as modest and as diffident as a woman.

GENERAL JOHN M. PALMER,

a lawyer by profession, entered the volunteer service as a colonel of an Illinois regiment. By his bravery and devotion to duty he rose to the rank of brigadier-general, and was subsequently promoted to the grade of major-general for gallantry on the field of battle. At the request of General Thomas he was assigned to the command of the Fourteenth army corps, and became my corps commander. In the exercise of this command he proved himself eminently fitted and qualified for it, and demonstrated to General Thomas that he had not made an improper estimate of him as a soldier and as a commander. After the war he was elected governor of his State. He resides in Springfield, Illinois, where he is engaged in the practice of law. It would not surprise me if the next National Democratic Convention should call upon him to step up higher. Should he ever occupy the presidential chair, an honest, incorruptible man will preside over our destinies so long as he holds the reins of government in his hands.

GENERAL ABSOLEM BAIRD

was a classmate of mine, and hence I know him well. He commanded a division in the same corps with me, and did effective service whenever and wherever he was called into action. He was a fine disciplinarian, and his command was well drilled and ever ready for service. Always cool and collected, he never lost control of himself in the heat of battle, but was at all times in the front personally directing the movements of his command. After a battle his first thought was for the wounded, and he gave himself no rest until he was satisfied that they were receiving the attention they deserved. Such a commander endears himself to his men, and hence it is not difficult to account for his popularity in the army, and particularly with those under his command.

GENERAL O. O. HOWARD

was the Havelock of the American army. He carried his religion with him on the march, in battle, or in camp, and yet he never allowed his Christian duties to interfere with the duties he owed the army he commanded. If his military duties required his services during the day, at night, in his tent, he was a true Christian soldier. He always handled his men with consummate skill, and his personal gallantry was always conspicuous.

I remember at Big Shanty, when, owing to the heavy rains, it was impossible to move a gun-carriage off a well-beaten road, Sherman turned to Howard and said, "Howard, is not this enough to try your Christian patience?" "No," replied Howard; "not in the least; our cause is just and we must triumph, regardless of the kind of weather God gives us." Sherman remarked, "I guess you are right, Howard, but I wish God would give us clear weather until we finish this picnic, after which I shall be content to take just such weather as He may desire to give us." Howard was a great favorite with General Sherman, for he knew that he could rely upon him in every emergency. He has been appointed major-general *vice* Pope retired.

GENERAL ALFRED H. TERRY.

My acquaintance with this officer was formed after the war, as he served in a different army. He was educated at Yale College, and subsequently studied law and was admitted to the bar in 1848. In 1861 he led the Second Regiment Connecticut Volunteers in the first Bull Run, and after the Federal army was defeated he brought up the rear in the retreat and saved large quantities of government property, which had been abandoned by the fleeing army. Subsequently he organized the Seventh Connecticut Regiment, which was attached to the expedition under General T. W. Sherman. At the head of the first division of the Twenty-fourth Corps, aided by the fleet of Commodore Porter, he carried Fort Fisher by assault, thus ending Confederate supremacy on the Cape Fear River. He was promoted to the rank of major-general of volunteers and brigadier-general United States army on the 15th day of January, 1865. During the period of reconstruction his knowledge of the law was of great service to him. Probably the first Southern State to be thoroughly reconstructed was Georgia, and this was due to the policy pursued by him. Every one in Atlanta, at which point he had his headquarters, speaks in the highest terms of him as a soldier and gentleman. While he carried out his views strictly, yet he did so considerately and so as to gain the good will of those over whom he ruled.

For some time he was in command of the Department of Dakota, where he had the respect and confidence of the army and the people. General Sherman, in speaking of him, says, "Terry is the very soul of honor," and all with whom he has had business or official intercourse will agree with Sherman. No officer of the army has a more brilliant record, and no officer of the army did more hard fighting during the war, nor more faithful service since its close. He is a tall, fine-looking gentleman, and would be readily selected out of a crowd as a distinguished man, and a brave and daring soldier. He was appointed major-general United States army to fill the vacancy occasioned by the death of Major-General W. S. Hancock. He now commands the Military Division of the Missouri, with headquarters at Chicago, Illinois.

GENERAL JEFFERSON C. DAVIS

was one of the officers in Fort Sumter at the time it was bombarded, and was soon thereafter appointed a brigadier-general in the volunteer service. He was a genial, clever fellow, a good soldier, and made a fine record for himself during the war, but I believe the unfortunate affair in which he shot and killed General William Nelson, cast a gloom over him which he was never able to throw off. On the "March to the Sea" he commanded the Fourteenth Corps, and was highly commended by General Sherman for the able and gallant manner in which he, at all times, handled his troops.

GENERAL JOHN A. LOGAN

was an able corps commander, and after the death of McPherson, on July 22, 1864, was the senior officer with the Army of the Tennessee. He assumed command, and under his guidance and direction this command fought one of the most desperate battles of the war. The Army of the Tennessee was unanimous in desiring Logan's permanent assignment to this command, but for some reason unknown, General Sherman designated Howard for that position. This created a good deal of dissatisfaction, not so much with Logan as with those under him, for he was too good a soldier to object to serving in any capacity to which he was assigned. However, all soon became reconciled to the change, and Logan continued to command his corps as he had previously done, satisfactorily to his superiors, and profitably to the cause which was uppermost in every patriot's heart.

GENERAL WILLIAM B. HAZEN

was in the regular army at the breaking out of the war. I had known him in Texas, where he was recognized as a successful Indian fighter, having had several severe combats with them. In one of these he was severely wounded, and commended for his gallantry in general orders. He entered the volunteer service as colonel of an Ohio regiment, and rose to the rank of major-general. He was a gallant soldier, a good disciplinarian, and thoroughly conversant with his duties. He made a good record, and at the close of the war was appointed colonel of one of the new regiments, and subsequently appointed chief signal officer of the army, with the rank of brigadier-general, a position which he now holds.

There has been some controversy in regard to the failure of the first expedition sent out for the relief of the Greely Arctic expedition. According to my understanding of the case, Lieutenant E. A. Garlington, a young, energetic officer of the Seventh Cavalry, was despatched with supplies for Greely's party. His expedition proved a failure; not, however, because of any neglect on his part, or from any cause that he could foresee. On his return he was anxious to be fitted out at once and permitted to make a second effort. Hazen approved of it, but no relief expedition was sent out until the following spring. If these are the facts, and such I understand them to be, I am clearly of the opinion that so far Hazen was right and should not be held responsible for the loss of valuable lives which would have been, in all probability, saved had Lieutenant Garlington been permitted to return and make another effort to reach the exploring party. That any of Lieutenant Greely's party was rescued, alive, is almost a miracle. It is pretty clear that all would have perished within a few days had not relief reached them. For this some one was to blame, but in all fairness I cannot see that any blame should attach to General Hazen, who, from the first return of Lieutenant Garlington, was anxious to make a second trial. Knowing the reputation of Lieutenant Garlington for activity and enterprise, and with his acquired experience in the Arctic seas, I believe that he would have succeeded in reaching Lieutenant Greely before the setting in of winter, and thus saved the lives of many of the daring adventurers.

GENERAL W. H. GIBSON

entered the service as colonel of the Forty-ninth Ohio, and was attached to the first brigade which I commanded. A fine soldier, a clever gentleman, and one of the best stump speakers I ever heard. If any dissatisfaction outcropped in his regiment, he would usually mount a barrel or stump, and with a ready flow of wit, clothed in the most beautiful language and expressed only as an orator could give it utterance, he would soon have the men in a good humor, and all satisfied. After the battle of Stone River we were for a few days without rations. Some of his men complained to him. He proposed to accompany them to my headquarters and ask me to share my stores with his famished men, knowing that I fared just as they did. When he and those with him reached my camp-fire they found me parching corn, and thus preparing my daily food. As soon as the men saw that they fared no worse than their division commander, they became satisfied, and no further complaint was heard.

Gibson was a brave soldier, a valuable officer, and a gentleman in every sense of the term.

GENERAL LOVELL H. ROUSSEAU.

No man in Kentucky did more for the Union cause than Rousseau. He was for the Union first, last, and all the time. He was the first to organize troops for the Federal service. For a long time his regiment was known as the Louisville Legion, and no troops did more service than those organized by him in the early days of the war. He was a brave, adventurous man, always ready to embark in any enterprise which suggested hardship and danger. At one time, on the Atlanta campaign, he said to me, "I do wish this cruel war was over." I asked him why he desired it brought to an end, and he replied, "I am afraid I shall be killed." I said to him, "General, God has covered your head in the day of battle and preserved you thus far; can you not trust Him longer?" "Yes," said Rousseau, "that may be all true, but I do not wish to impose upon Him too long. He might get tired of looking after me."

After the war he was elected to Congress, and, while a member, engaged in an altercation with a fellow-member by the name of Grinnell. For this he was called before the bar of the House and reprimanded. Smarting under the humiliation, he resigned and returned to his people, and asked for a unanimous re-election. In the mean time the return of the Confederates had changed the political complexion of his district, and threats were made that an opponent would be named against him. It was in this perplexed state of mind that I met him, and he said, "Johnson, have you ever had anything to do with politics?" I replied, "No; never voted in my life." "Well," said he, "never touch him; he is an infernal scoundrel." From Congress he passed to the grade of brigadier-general United States army, but soon thereafter died while in command of the Department of Louisiana.

COLONEL WILLIAM W. BERRY

entered the service with the Louisville Legion, of which he subsequently became the colonel. His loyalty to the cause dated from the firing on Fort Sumter, and continued as long as there was an armed rebel on the soil of our country. He was a splendid soldier, and was ably assisted by his officers, all of whom knew what it cost to be loyal. His men were thoroughly disciplined, and better or more determined fighters could not be found in our army. Berry, who always led his regiment, was wounded several times.

I have always been at a loss to know why he was not appointed a general officer, for, although a colonel, he generally had the command of a brigade, and always handled it with marked skill and ability.

GENERAL THOMAS L. CRITTENDEN

was one of Kentucky's favorite sons. Following his distinguished father, he early proclaimed in favor of the war for the suppression of the rebellion, let it cost what it might. His influence did much to restrain the hot-headed secessionists of his native State; and while he talked neutrality to them, he was engaged in getting the Union men armed so that they could protect themselves until assistance could be furnished by the United States. Sitting in the Galt House on a certain occasion conversing with the father of General Crittenden, I remarked that I could not see why any one could for one moment believe that a State could be neutral under such circumstances. He replied, in an undertone, " Of course it is absurd, but it will do to occupy the people until we can get ready to assert and maintain our authority." This remark let a flood of light in upon me. From that time forth I understood what neutrality signified when used by a loyal man. General Crittenden was soon assigned to the command of a division, and on the reorganization of the army under Buell he became commander of the left wing of the Fourteenth Army Corps, which was subsequently designated as the Twenty-first Army Corps. His gallantry was conspicuous in every engagement. A more earnest, attentive, and faithful corps commander was not to be found in our army, and a braver man never drew a sword. His brilliant feat at Stone River was of itself sufficient to immortalize his name.

GENERAL JOHN M. HARLAN

I first met as the enterprising captain of one of the home guards at Lebanon Junction. Soon after this he raised a regiment and became one of our most distinguished officers. His name, too, was a potent factor in Kentucky politics, and had great weight in determining many men for the Union in opposition to the turbulent faction which seemed determined on forcing the State into a position of antagonism to the general government. General Harlan is now one of the justices of the Supreme Court, and one of the most laborious and painstaking members of that august tribunal.

GENERAL JAMES B. STEEDMAN

was born in Northumberland County, Pennsylvania, July 30, 1818. He removed to Ohio in 1837, where he was engaged in the construction of the Wabash and Erie Canal. In 1843 he was elected to the legislature, and became distinguished as a clear, sound thinker and an able speaker. In 1849 he went to California as a gold hunter, but returned in 1850. In 1861 he organized the Fourth Ohio Volunteers, of which he was appointed colonel, and served in Western Virginia, being engaged in the battle of Philippi. Soon after this he was ordered to report to General Buell, in Kentucky. On the 17th July, 1862, he was appointed brigadier-general. He participated in the battles of Perryville and Chickamauga, in both of which his gallantry was conspicuous, and for his valuable services in the latter was promoted to the rank of major-general. General Steedman was a conspicuous figure in the Atlanta campaign. When Sherman marched to the sea he joined General Thomas, and was greatly distinguished in the battle of Nashville, having command of the left of the Federal army. His bravery and his ability brought him to the notice of General Thomas, who never let an opportunity pass to speak of him in the highest terms of praise. The war of the rebellion developed no one superior to him in true courage, and few equal to him in all that went to make up the thorough soldier and gentleman. He died a short time since in Toledo, Ohio, regretted by all classes of people. His ear was ever open to the cry of the destitute, and no one ever appealed to him for aid and went away empty-handed. He was indeed an honor to his country.

I would like to refer to many of the subordinate officers who served with me, but cannot do so at this time. I remember them all as good officers and worthy men, who reflected credit upon the States which sent them forth. I cannot recall a single exception, and with each and all my official and personal intercourse was of the most pleasant character. Their gallant and faithful services, their cheerful obedience, willing co-operation, and bravery on the battle-field will ever be among my dearest memories.

CHAPTER XXVII.

Abraham Lincoln—His Assassination—Fate of the Assassins—Other Conspirators—The Course of England—Mason and Slidell—Earl Russell, etc.

DURING the war I met President Lincoln several times, and on every occasion he seemed to be in good spirits and ready for a joke. That he could be, apparently, so light-hearted all the time surprised me, for the weight of the great responsibilities resting upon him would have crushed any ordinary man. With the cares of office upon him he was stricken down with varioloid. On one occasion, when visited by his physician, he said, "Doctor, tell any office-seekers you see to come on, for I have something to give to each one."

While he was ever ready with a witty story, the weighty affairs of his office were never neglected. In fact, he was the leading spirit of his administration, and gave his attention not only to civil matters, but also to those relating to the most unimportant military operations. In conversation with him during the first year of the war, he remarked, "What we really need is a military railroad from Louisville, Kentucky, through Cumberland Gap to Knoxville, Tennessee. Whenever we reach that point we will be between the enemy and his hog and hominy, and under such circumstances he will have to give up the contest."

The road was not constructed, but it is a fact that when Knoxville fell into our possession the "bottom dropped out" of the Confederacy. Mr. Lincoln was a statesman and a soldier; a great and a good man, who waged war only because it was the surest way to a lasting peace.

I now desire to refer to the conspiracy which culminated in his assassination.

The rebellion, in aid of which this conspiracy was formed, was itself nothing less than a criminal conspiracy, the like of which was unknown before. And if all that was agreed upon, and attempted, by the conspirators had been accomplished, the combination of atrocities would have been without a parallel in the annals of history. In order to understand more fully the animus of those who planned, and attempted to execute, the deep-laid scheme of murder, desolation, and ruin that would result therefrom, I invite attention to the laws then in force, to show how narrowly we escaped the destruction which was planned by our would-be destroyers.

The Constitution of the United States provides, in case of the death, resignation, or inability of the President to discharge the duties of President, the office devolves on the Vice-President, and that Congress shall declare what officer shall be President until the disabilities are removed or President elected. Under the laws in force at that time, "in case of the removal, death, resignation, or inability of both the President and Vice-President, the President of the Senate, or if none, the Speaker of the House to act until the disability is removed or President elected." When the offices of President and Vice-President both became vacant, the Secretary of State was to notify the Governors of the several States, and an election was then to be held for President and Vice-President to fill the unexpired term of those two officers.

President Lincoln had been inaugurated for his second term on the 4th day of March, 1865, and was assassinated on the night of the 14th day of April following. The usual executive session of the Senate, called on such occasions, after transacting such business as came before it, and electing a President *pro tempore* of the Senate, adjourned about the 1st day of April.

The two Houses of Congress having adjourned *sine die* on the 3d day of March of that year, there was, consequently, no Speaker of the House at that time. It will thus be seen that if there were neither President, Vice-President, nor Speaker of the House in existence, there was no one to hold the office of President until an election could be had as contemplated under the provisions of the Constitution and laws then in force. And, still worse, if the office of Secretary of State was vacant, there was no other officer who could give the requisite notice of another or new election for President and Vice-President. So it will be seen that if the conspirators had accomplished their purpose, and had murdered the President, Vice-President, and Secretary of State, the work of destroying the government would have been complete. The interregnum would have continued until the time of holding the next regular election came around for electing those officers.

The anarchy, bloodshed, and destruction that would have followed in the train of such a dire calamity can scarcely be imagined, much less described or realized.

The testimony elicited on the trial of the conspirators made it appear beyond a reasonable doubt that John Wilkes Booth, John H. Surratt, Harold, Atzerodt, Payne, O'Laughlin, Spangler, Arnold, Mary E. Surratt, and Samuel A Mudd, in aid of the rebellion, and in combination and confederation with Jeff. Davis, George N. Sanders, B. Tucker, Jacob Thompson, W. C. Cleary, C. C. Clay, Harper, Young, and others unknown, intended to murder President Lincoln, Vice-President Johnson, Secretary of State Seward, and Lieutenant-General Grant, then in command of the armies of the United States; and Jeff. Davis was the instigator and procurer, through accredited agents in Canada, Great Britain, and elsewhere, of this treasonable conspiracy. It is not intended by this statement to limit the number of those aiding and assisting in this infamous crime to the names above given. The guilt reaches far higher than the ignorant, infatuated individuals whose lives paid the penalty for crimes invoked and set on foot by wiser heads and more honorable names than theirs.

It may be of interest to the readers of this volume to recall the part acted and taken by each of the foregoing persons in the murderous conspiracy in which they were engaged.

J. Wilkes Booth was perhaps the most conspicuous and intelligent of those immediately connected with the plot in Washington City. He was the central figure of the group, and the accredited leader of the others around about him, and to whom attaches the unenviable infamy of firing the fatal shot that ended the life of one of the most gifted and pure of American statesmen.

This occurred late at night in Ford's Theatre in Washington City.

Almost instantly after the commission of the deed, Booth made his escape from the city, in company with his co-conspirator Harold, and was afterwards captured and killed in a barn on the farm of Mr. Garrett, in Caroline County, Virginia, only a few days after the assassination.

David E. Harold, who was captured in company with Booth, was then about twenty-three years old. It was said by those well acquainted with him that he was a light, trifling young man, easily persuaded and led more than is usually the case with young men of his age. He was tried and convicted, with others, before a military commission, and executed under military orders.

Lewis Payne, another of the conspirators, went to the house of Secretary Seward, on the night of the 14th day of April, with a little package in his hand, and said it was medicine for Mr. Seward from Dr. Verdi, and he was sent by the doctor to direct Mr. Seward how to take it. When told that he could not see Mr. Seward, he commenced an attack upon Major Seward and wounded him very seriously, and then rushed into the room where Secretary Seward was in bed, cutting and stabbing him in several places, inflicting ghastly and dangerous wounds. This man was captured in a short time after he left Mr. Seward's house, and was one of those convicted before the military commission, and executed, with others, on July 7, 1865.

The plea of insanity was set up in his behalf, but it

was unavailing as a defence, and he was convicted notwithstanding.

Michael O'Laughlin was a school-mate of J. Wilkes Booth, and his mother was the tenant of Mrs. Booth, the mother of J. Wilkes Booth, and the families were quite intimate. He was proven to be in frequent private conferences with Booth and Arnold; had been in the Southern army, and had received a telegram from Booth which implicated him as one of the conspirators, and as he was seen at, and about, the residence of Secretary Stanton, it was believed that he was the one selected to make way with, or murder, the Secretary of War. He was convicted before the commission and sentenced to confinement for life at the Dry Tortugas.

George A. Atzerodt was the individual to whom was assigned the work of killing Vice-President Johnson, at the Kirkwood House, in Washington.

Atzerodt took a room at this house on the morning of the 14th of April, and late that evening was making inquiries for the Vice-President, and would have, without doubt, accomplished his fell purpose; but the Vice-President was either in company with others during the evening, or absent from his hotel, so that an opportunity to kill him did not offer until after Booth had killed the President, and the whole city was aroused with excitement and alarm.

Atzerodt then sneaked out of the city, and tried to make his escape, but was soon captured, tried, condemned, and executed. The evidences of his complicity in the assassination plot are so overwhelming as to leave no room to doubt the justness of his sentence.

Samuel Arnold was a resident of Maryland; had been in the rebel army up to a short time before the assassination. He was arrested because of letters and other evidences of his guilt found in the trunk of J. Wilkes Booth. He was convicted partly on his own statement of a guilty knowledge of the conspiracy, in which he was to take part, but claimed to have abandoned any active participation in it. He was at Fortress Monroe when arrested. The sentence in his case was life confinement at the Dry Tortugas.

Mrs. Mary E. Surratt was the mother of John H. Surratt, and her house seems to have been the rendezvous of all the conspirators in and about Washington. She and her son John H. were actively and zealously engaged in all of the schemes and plots that preceded and attended the final consummation of the fatal drama. These operations extended from Richmond through Washington and Baltimore to Canada, and embraced an extensive correspondence and associations with Confederate officials and their *confrères* in Canada, and extended through several months of the winter and spring of 1865. In Mrs. Surratt's house after the assassination were found *cartes de visite* of Jefferson Davis, Beauregard, Stephens, etc., and behind a picture-frame a photograph of J. Wilkes Booth.

Mrs. Surratt was executed under the sentence of the military commission before mentioned. Whilst none can claim that she was guiltless, it is much to be regretted that she was made to suffer this severe penalty, whilst those who instigated these horrible crimes were permitted to go unpunished.

John H. Surratt, after the murder of President Lincoln, made his way to Canada, and thereby made his escape, but was subsequently captured in Italy and returned to the United States.

Edward Spangler was an employé at Ford's theatre, and was present at the time the President was shot. He was convicted upon the testimony of witnesses, by whom it was proven that he held the horse on which Booth made his escape, and aided him in his flight and tried to prevent his capture.

He was a man of little intelligence or learning, and was sentenced to the Dry Tortugas.

Dr. Samuel A. Mudd was arraigned and tried with the others and sentenced to the Dry Tortugas. The principal testimony against him was that connecting him with harboring and concealing Booth after the assassination. He was, if guilty of anything, merely an accessory after the fact.

I have attempted to briefly outline the acts and deeds of the sub-agents—the minor tools engaged in this unholy conspiracy—and the fearfully ignominious end to which they were brought therefor. This, however, leaves the sickening story less than half told. We must look elsewhere to find vengeful malice that instigated the scheme, and the guiding heads and hands that gave it life and power. When it is remembered that these ignorant, misguided, and infatuated people were but the dupes of the monster conspirators behind the scenes, we are led rather to pity than condemn them. This thought, however, only heightens and intensifies the guilt of the men who incited and urged them on in their bloody task. A brief review of other diabolical schemes and plots of kindred character, concocted and attempted by officers and agents of the Southern Confederacy prior to this time, leaves no room to doubt their readiness to commit any crime, however malignant, in order to accomplish their unhallowed purpose. Notably among them may be classed the introduction of pestilence into the States by infected clothing, poisoning of the Croton reservoir near New York, the St. Albans raid, rebel commissions for raiders, Knights of the Golden Circle, the plot to destroy vessels on many streams and buildings in divers places, City Point explosions, plot to burn New York City, starvation of prisoners in Southern prisons, mining of Libby prison by torpedoes, all endorsed and acquiesced in by Jefferson Davis, and in most instances known to and approved by the rebel chiefs and leaders, Jacob Thompson, Sanders, Clay, Cleary, Tucker, Holcombe, etc., all accredited agents of the rebel government, congregated in Canada, and in daily communication with their co-conspirators in Richmond.

That President Davis was in complicity with these, connected with, or assisting in one way or another in these plots and conspiracies, can scarcely be doubted. When advised of Mr. Lincoln's assassination he is reported as saying, "If it were to be done at all, it were better it were well done; and if the same had been done to Andy Johnson, the beast, and to Secretary Stanton, the job would then be complete."

Mr. Jacob Thompson kept a bank account, in the Ontario Bank, as financial agent of the Confederate States, of six hundred and forty-nine thousand dollars. A draft from this fund was found on the body of J. Wilkes Booth after he was killed, in April, 1865.

It is by no means the purpose of these recitals to revive the animosities and acerbities that were engendered during the war, but simply to fix the responsibility and guilt where it properly belongs.

It is now a conceded fact that the great mass of the Southern people were opposed to, the war, but were inveigled and dragged into it by their leaders, and the consequences resulting therefrom are properly chargeable to those who inaugurated and carried on the rebellion.

It must not be forgotten that there are rules, usages, and laws of war as imperative and obligatory as the statute laws of the State in which we reside.

These laws of war form a part of our international code that is recognized and respected by civilians and warriors in all the civilized nations of the earth.

Now, whatever may be said in justification of the Southern rebellion, and those engaged in the effort to overturn our government and set up another, it will be the universal judgment of the impartial historian that many of the acts hereinbefore referred to are without the pale of civilized, Christian warfare, and becloud the names and darken the escutcheons of many of the champions of the Southern cause.

I wish it to be distinctly understood that I do not place the shame and dishonor of this vile conspiracy at the door of every Southern man. There were hosts of honest, Christian people in the South who believed their cause to be just, but who would scorn the attempt to carry it to a successful issue by means so revolting as those resorted to by the leaders, and of which they stand convicted before the bar of public opinion.

The review of the times and scenes referred to in the foregoing pages would be incomplete without a reference to the part taken and enacted by the people and government of Great Britain in the stirring events transpiring in the United States.

The malevolence, duplicity, and ill-concealed hostility of that government to the people and government of the United States were never more strikingly illustrated than in the course pursued towards us during the days of our peril and struggle for a national existence.

England has, for more than a century, cherished the most envious bitterness toward her disobedient cousins on this side of the sea, and when we were engaged in a hand-to-hand struggle for life, she deemed the time and the occasion opportune to wreak her pent-up malice in aiding our overthrow. Notwithstanding all her vaunted opposition to human slavery and its propagation, she early espoused the cause of the South and gave the rebel cause her active sympathy and support. At the earliest moment she accorded the insurgents belligerent rights, and her known desire to acknowledge the independence of the Southern Confederacy was apparent on all occasions. Her love for "cotton" far exceeded her love for the freedom of the "slave." The South was supplied from her shores with all that was needed of munitions of war and supplies of all kinds. Her government workshops fitted out all the rebel cruisers that were needed to destroy our commerce and impair our navy.

On the day preceding the night of the assassination of Mr. Lincoln, Earl Russell was inveighing against the government of the United States for retaking from on board the "Trent" the rebel commissioners, Mason and Slidell, who were on their way to treat with the British authorities looking to the recognition of the independence of the Southern government. The intensity of English feeling against the Northern government was manifested in the Parliament, then in session, by the prolonged cheering of Earl Russell on the conclusion of his speech.

The deep significance of all this will be apparent when all of the circumstances are considered. If the government of the United States was destroyed or paralyzed for the want of an official head with which to treat, then, as the rebel government would be the only one in existence either *de facto* or *de jure*, the right and power to recognize it as the existing government in the United States would have been justified, and thereafter the United States government, the old rival of England, would have been a thing of the past.

The further we pursue this subject the more apparent becomes the extent and magnitude of the conspiracy, the chief leaders of which have escaped punishment for the great crimes they originated and did so much to carry out. The brutal murder of Abraham Lincoln makes a dark, dark page in our national history, from which I cheerfully turn.

CHAPTER XXVIII.

The Cavalry—General Sheridan and his Lieutenants—General J. H. Wilson and his Cavalry—J. E. B. Stuart, Fitzhugh Lee, Jos. Wheeler, and Forrest as Cavalry Leaders—The Staff of the Army—General M. C. Meigs as Quartermaster-General—Subsistence, Ordnance, Medical, and Pay Departments—General W. G. Le Duc as Chief Quartermaster and Pilot on the Tennessee River.

THE cavalry arm of the service in the early years of the war was not brought to a very high state of efficiency, owing to the peculiar character of the duties imposed upon it. In many cases regiments were practically broken up and the companies assigned to escort or courier duty. In this way little opportunity was offered regimental commanders to drill and discipline their commands. In 1864, General Sheridan was placed in command of the cavalry of the Army of the Potomac. Every one knew that he would not be willing to command a force of which no fighting was expected. Accordingly, he consolidated the companies into regiments, which he formed into brigades and divisions, placing these organizations under such active, enterprising leaders as Averill, Merritt, Custer, Wilson, and others, and he soon had a body of cavalry that was seen and felt in every engagement. I am inclined to doubt if there ever was a cavalry command superior to Sheridan's, under the gallant leaders such as I have named.

In the West the wants of the cavalry were neglected.

In many cases the men were poorly mounted and badly armed and equipped, and yet it is astonishing what good service it did under Stanley, Stoneman, Mitchell, Eli Long, Hatch, Elliot, Garrard, Grierson, Knipe, Kilpatrick, Minty, Otis, and others. Seeing the great improvement of this arm of service in the Army of the Potomac, General J. H. Wilson was ordered West to assume command of all the cavalry operating under the command of General Sherman. He was young, active, and ambitious, and soon did for our cavalry what Sheridan had done for the cavalry in the East. The battle of Nashville and the retreat of Hood gave Wilson a fair opportunity to show what could be done by cavalry when properly handled, and it was generally acknowledged that a very perceptible improvement in the fighting qualities was observable.

The war terminated so soon thereafter that little time was allowed Wilson to perfect the discipline of his command.

I watched the services of the rebel cavalry and its leaders. It is probable that J. E. B. Stuart was the leading cavalryman of the army of General R. E. Lee, and next to him, undoubtedly, stood Fitzhugh Lee. In the South, Wheeler and Forrest were the cavalry leaders who for dash and enterprise were far in advance of any of their associates. Wheeler, with his cavalry, was ever on our flanks and rear, and had to be closely watched to keep him away from our baggage-trains and prevent him from destroying the bridges in our rear.

Had the war continued several years longer the cavalry on both sides would have been brought to a much higher state of efficiency and acted a much more prominent part in every campaign.

I desire to speak of the staff departments of our army, and, for the information of the unprofessional reader, it may be well to say that these consisted of the Adjutant-General's Department, Quartermaster's Department, Subsistence Department, Corps of Engineers, Ordnance Corps, Medical Corps, Pay Department.

On the breaking out of the late war many of the heads of these various departments were unfitted for active, vigorous service on account of the infirmities of age. These had to be disposed of in some way, and to this end Congress passed a law authorizing the President to retire from active service such as were incapacitated from any cause whatever.

General Joseph E. Johnston resigned his position as quartermaster-general to enable him to accept service in the rebel army. His place had to be supplied, and as the success of our army depended in a great measure upon the efficient workings of the quartermaster's department, care had to be taken to secure the right man. The subject was thoroughly canvassed by the proper authorities, and finally it was agreed to appoint Captain Montgomery C. Meigs, of the corps of engineers, chief of the department. Captain Meigs was universally recognized as an able engineer, but there were some who doubted the wisdom of appointing him to a position the duties of which he had never performed. However, he entered upon the duties devolving upon him in his new position, and his subsequent administration of the affairs of the quartermaster's department demonstrated very thoroughly that his selection was a most happy one.

All of the staff corps and departments were reorganized by eliminating the old and feeble and supplying their places by young, active men, and when this was done we had a most efficient staff. No army ever went to the field with one equal to it. All through the war its faithful work was manifest, but it has never received the credit to which it was fairly entitled. The success of every campaign depended, more or less, upon one or more of these staff departments, and it is sufficient to say that no campaign ever failed on account of the inefficiency of either. It is an easy matter for a commander to order the movement of troops from one point to another and to direct the "subsistence department to furnish the rations and the quartermaster's department the necessary transportation," but few persons stop to think of the amount of labor required on the part of these departments to carry out such orders.

Our engineers were ever ready to direct the construction of all classes of defences and to perform such duties as devolved upon them, while our medical staff was perfect in all of the details for caring for the sick and disabled. It was astonishing to see how soon the wounded were taken from the field of battle to receive the attention of our faithful, efficient surgeons. These devoted men have never received the proper credit for the noble part they took in the great war of the rebellion. Night and day they labored with our sick and wounded, and not a complaint was heard from a single one of them. The adjutant-general's department was a most important one. Often the chief of staff would have to be up all night to superintend the distribution of orders for the following day, and in many instances they were called on, in the absence of their chiefs, to give orders involving great responsibility. In fact, in some cases the staff officer was in every way superior to his commander, but when the time came around for the awarding of credit the adjutant was ignored. This department of the staff failed to receive the credit to which it was fairly entitled by the gallantry, devotion, and hard service of its members.

Then the ordnance department was a power of strength in itself. There was always an abundance of ammunition, and the very best arms to be had were in the hands of our troops. Last, although not least, I come to the pay department. These faithful disbursers of Uncle Sam's greenbacks were always in the forefront and ready with crisp government bills to pay the gallant soldiers their monthly stipend. It is true that the currency was depreciated, but that was not their fault. It was the best the country could do, and those who braved the dangers on the battle-field were satisfied to accept the same in full for services rendered.

At one time it took two hundred and eighty cents in greenbacks to make one hundred cents in gold. The price of living—in fact, the price of everything—was regulated on a gold basis, and when a soldier converted his greenbacks into gold he had a very small sum of money to compensate him for facing the cannon's mouth on the bloody field of battle.

Some of our very best generals were furnished by some of the staff corps. Notably among these I recall H. G. Wright, Godfrey Weitzel, John Newton, Z. B. Tower, Jesse L. Reno, and many others. I served with one of these,—John Newton,—who commanded a division in the Atlanta campaign and proved himself to be a skilful and gallant commander. At present he is the chief engineer of the army, a position for which he is admirably qualified. His name will ever be associated with the great improvement in New York harbor, in the removal of obstructions at Hell Gate. He was a brave commander, and is to-day at the very head of American engineers. While the army was besieged at Chattanooga, General William G. Le Duc, the chief quartermaster on the staff of General Hooker, was at Bridgeport, on the Tennessee. He had in store at that place abundance of provisions for transportation to Chattanooga, but no means to send them forward except by mule-teams over rough, mountainous roads. If he relied upon that mode of transportation, he readily saw that starvation of the troops was only a question of a very short time. He determined on a more expeditious method. We held the river at Kelly's Ferry, and if he could procure a fleet of boats large quantities of rations might be sent to that point, from whence they could be much more easily conveyed to the troops, as the distance to be hauled by teams would be greatly diminished. Le Duc was an energetic man of great resources, and he determined on building one or more small stern-wheel steamers. It was astonishing how soon he had a boat ready for the service. When finished he loaded it with provisions, but he had no pilot. No one knew anything about the river, and he could find no man willing to engage in such a hazardous enterprise. Having previously owned and operated a steam ferry from Hastings, Minnesota, to Prescott, Wisconsin, and having occasionally acted as pilot, he concluded to see what he could do in the way of navigating the unknown waters of the Tennessee. Taking his position in the pilot-house, he ordered the cable drawn in, and away steamed the little craft up the river, destined for Kelly's Ferry. All went well until overtaken by night. He had a man on board who had been a lake pilot, and he called on him to stand at the wheel for a while until he could rest himself. The lake pilot said that he could do nothing after dark without a compass, which Le Duc thought unnecessary in a tortuous stream like the Tennessee. However, the old tar would not risk his life and reputation without a compass, and so the chief quartermaster had to remain on duty. Suddenly two lights appeared, one on either side of the river. The boat was steered to the north shore, as that light was supposed to be in a camp of our own soldiers. As soon as the vessel got within hailing distance, Le Duc asked, "What troops are those?" The reply came back, "The Ninth Tennessee." This caused a cold chill to creep up his spinal column, as the number indicated a rebel organization; but as quick as possible the question was asked, "Who is your colonel?" and when the reply came back, "Colonel Stokes," it brought relief, for Stokes was known to be a loyal Tennesseean, who had raised a regiment for the Union army. Le Duc then asked,

"What light is that on the other side?" and when informed that it was Kelly's Ferry he felt greatly relieved, and at once steered for it, and when his boat was fastened to the shore he and his daring crew were received with open arms by our half-starved men, to whom rations were at once issued, and a happy set of fellows slept that night on the wooded banks of the Tennessee River.

Who will ever say that proper credit has been awarded this enterprising, active quartermaster? And yet this is only one instance of his valuable service in the war.

CHAPTER XXIX.

Professor of Military Science in University of Missouri and University of Minnesota—Troops furnished by the State of Minnesota—Names of Colonels and Battery Commanders—Names of Commanders of Independent Cavalry Commands.

THE injuries I received in the war incapacitated me for active service, and I applied to be placed on the retired list. In due time I was ordered to appear before the Retiring Board in New York City, and having been examined was declared unfit for active duty, and was accordingly placed on the retired list on October 11, 1867.

During the following year the president of the University of Missouri asked me to accept the position of military professor in that institution. I consented, and General John M. Schofield, then Secretary of War, directed an order to be issued placing me on that duty.

The University is located at Columbia, Boone County, a place represented to me as one of the loveliest spots on the face of the earth. Without going to examine into the probable desirability of Columbia as a place of residence, I removed at once so as to be on hand at the opening of the fall term. I arrived with my family after dark, and was conducted to the best hotel in town. Soon supper was announced, and we filed into the dark, dingy dining-room, the atmosphere of which was not at all pleasant, and seated ourselves around the table. As soon as seated, a dirty, greasy little negro placed his mouth to my ear and called out loud enough to be heard throughout the house, "Squirrel or mackerel?" Indifferent bread, poor coffee, squirrel, and mackerel made up the bill of fare. When I was a lad at school I boarded in a family with six other young fellows. For supper we invariably had mackerel, which the good man of the house always divided into six equal parts by measurement. My place at the table was on his right. In serving he always began with the one on his left, to whom he gave the tail, the sixth and last piece was mine, which was always the head. For long, weary months I lived on mackerel heads, and I then and there made a solemn promise never to look a mackerel in the face again. So, at Columbia, I asked to be served with squirrel. I left the table with an unsatisfied appetite, and soon asked to be shown to our rooms. Up-stairs we went into a dingy back room, in which there were two beds, neither of which was supplied with springs. The mattresses, only about two inches in thickness, rested on slats. I tried to sleep but could not. The odors were not agreeable, and suggested many unpleasant thoughts as to lodgers in that room that paid no board bills. It was the longest night I ever passed, but finally morning came. It was a gloomy morning, and I could hear the pelting of the rain on the roof above. Everything seemed damp and sticky. The marks on my body, made by the bed-slats, caused me to look as if I had reposed during the night on a large-sized gridiron. Mentally I resolved to leave the town, but my wife laughed good-naturedly, and suggested better things when we went to housekeeping. However, our room was changed the next day, and we fared much better.

There was only one vacant house in the town, and that was an old rattle-trap, really unfitted for occupancy, and for it a rent was demanded which would have secured a first-class house in St. Louis or New York. We took possession of it and made ourselves as comfortable as possible under the circumstances.

We were not long in making the acquaintance of the people, and soon found that we were in an educated, refined community. Columbia was the home of Hon. J. H. Rollins, a former member of Congress and a stanch Union man from first to last. I also met Hon. R. L. Todd and his charming family, whose kind hospitality we often enjoyed, and who did much to make our stay pleasant and enjoyable, and I can say the same of the families of Mr. Stephens, Hon. W. F. Switzler, Mrs. Royall, the mother of Colonel W. B. Royall, of the army, the professors and their families, and many others. We were not long in finding out that our first impressions were erroneous, and that we were really domiciled in the midst of an agreeable community. And now, in looking back, the only unpleasant memory of Columbia is connected with their poorly-kept hotel. For the credit of the place, I hope they have better hotel accommodations.

On a Sabbath morning, meeting Colonel Pat. Donan, now of Dakota, at church, and finding him an agreeable gentleman, and knowing that the accommodations of the hotel were not such as he was accustomed to, I invited him to stay with us while in the town.

He accepted my invitation, and we enjoyed his society very much. After he left us I received a newspaper in which there was an article from his pen in which he said,—

"General R. W. Johnson called and gave me a cordial invitation to become his guest during the remainder of my stay. Expecting to leave next morning, I promptly accepted. And I was glad I did. For to few occasions of my life do I look back with more satisfaction than to the night spent beneath his hospitable roof. It is a rare and real treat to meet with entertainers so kind, so courteous as he and his charming lady." And I can truthfully say that I never met with a more intelligent man or better conversationalist in my entire life.

The friends of the University desired to accept what was known as the "Agricultural Land Grant." To do this the law required that military science should be included in the curriculum, and hence I was wanted, not so much to teach the science of war as to make good their claim to this large grant of land. The only time allowed me for drill was the forenoon of every Saturday. In fact, the whole thing was a perfect farce as carried on under the President of the University. In the month of June, 1869, I severed my connection with that institution and removed to St. Paul, the home of my adoption. On my arrival in Minnesota I was elected professor of military science in our State University. Here I remained a year and a half, being allowed twenty minutes each day for military exercises. In addition to my appropriate duties I instructed classes in mathematics, history, etc.

This I did at the earnest request of President Folwell, for whom I entertained a high regard, and for whom I was willing to do anything in my power that he might request.

The art of teaching is a gift which kind nature never gave me, and no one knew it so well as I did myself. It was absolutely distasteful, and so I resigned my position and took up my residence in St. Paul. The valuable time passed at these institutions of learning I regard as absolutely lost. The attempt to teach military drills and manœuvres to young men in the colleges of the land can never be successful, unless they are quartered near the institution or within hearing of the bugle call, and certain punishments can be inflicted for absence from military duties.

Once more settled in St. Paul, I determined on making it my home for life, and every year I have resided here has made me more grateful to that Providence which guided my footsteps in early life to this land of blue skies and pure air.

I have always felt that Minnesota was my home. I was here at the birth of the Territory, watched it in the days of its infancy, and now, in the maturity of Statehood, I feel as proud of it as a father does of a son whom he sees developing into useful and honorable manhood.

Few States, if any, furnished as many troops for the suppression of the rebellion, in proportion to population, as did the State of Minnesota. The thrilling scenes of that eventful period in our country's history are now so far back in the past that our young, active business men know nothing about them, except what they derive from history or are told by the old, grizzly participants in that terrible and bloody struggle.

Minnesota furnished twenty-five thousand men for the war, as follows: Eleven regiments of infantry, one regiment of cavalry, one regiment of mounted rangers, one regiment of heavy artillery, three light batteries, and two independent battalions of cavalry.

The First Minnesota Volunteers was originally organized with Willis A. Gorman as its colonel. He was promoted, and was succeeded by N. J. T. Dana. Dana's promotion soon followed, and Alfred Sully was appointed in his stead. Sully remained colonel only for a short time, when he, too, was appointed brigadier-general. Then came Colonel George N. Morgan, who resigned, and that gallant old soldier, Colonel William Colville, succeeded to the command of the regiment and remained with it to the close of the war.

H. P. VanCleve was appointed colonel of the Second Regiment, and on his promotion was succeeded by James George, who not veteranizing with the regiment, Judson W. Bishop was appointed colonel. This was the only regiment that served near me, and the only one of which I have any personal knowledge, and I can say of its officers and men that none braver were to be found anywhere in the grand army of the Union. VanCleve was a graduate of West Point of the class of 1831, and on the declaration of war raised a regiment. He was a faithful, gallant soldier, and his regiment was among the best in the volunteer service. General Judson W. Bishop, who was the last colonel of the regiment, originally held the rank of captain, and by true merit passed to the head of the Second Minnesota.

The Third Regiment had four colonels in the order named: H. C. Lester, C. W. Griggs, C. C. Andrews, and Hans Mattson. Lester surrendered his regiment at Murfreesboro', notwithstanding the earnest protest of Captains Griggs, Andrews, and Hoit. For this Lester was dismissed, and thereafter "disappeared from history." Then Griggs, a brave, gallant soldier, was appointed colonel, and had he remained in service would have worn one or more stars, but his private business imperatively demanded his attention and he reluctantly resigned. He was succeeded by C. C. Andrews, whose gallantry and soldierly qualities soon won for him a brigadier's commission, and Hans Mattson, a good soldier, succeeded him.

Colonel John B. Sanborn organized the Fourth, and he handled it so ably that he was soon called to the exercise of higher and more responsible duties. He was succeeded by John E. Tourtelotte.

The Fifth Regiment was at first commanded by Rudolph Borgesrode, but he soon resigned, and our present worthy chief executive, Lucius F. Hubbard, took command and made a most excellent regiment of it. This regiment did valiant service in the battles resulting in the capture of Mobile, where General Hubbard was greatly distinguished as a brave and able leader.

That thorough soldier and gentleman, William Crooks, trained at West Point, organized the Sixth Regiment, but as it was ordered to remain in Minnesota to fight the Indians, and as he wanted to serve on the battle-fields of the rebellion, he resigned; not, however, until he had performed gallant services in the campaigns against hostile Indians on the borders of the State. Crooks was succeeded by John T. Averill, a worthy successor to a worthy man. After the close of the war he represented the St. Paul district in Congress for four years, and was a valuable, faithful, laborious member.

Steven Miller was the first colonel of the Seventh Regiment; his successor was William R. Marshall, whose gallant conduct in the battle of Nashville brought him and his regiment prominently to the notice of that grand old hero, General George H. Thomas.

The Eighth Regiment was organized and commanded by Colonel M. T. Thomas, an accomplished soldier and gentleman, who received the brevet of brigadier-general for gallant conduct on the battle-field.

The Ninth Regiment was mustered into the service with Alexander Wilkin as colonel. I knew him well, and a braver man, a better officer, a more thorough gentleman never drew a sword or commanded a regiment of men. He was killed in the battle of Guntown, Mississippi.

The Tenth was commanded by James H. Baker.

The Eleventh Regiment was organized and commanded by James Gilfillan, the present able chief justice of the State of Minnesota. He had a fine body of men, and placed them in a thorough state of discipline, and did good service on all occasions.

R. N. McLaren commanded the cavalry regiment,

with which he performed good service, and was made a brigadier-general by brevet for gallantry and good conduct.

Samuel McPhail commanded the regiment of mounted rangers, a good body of men, which, under McPhail, did good service. The three light batteries were commanded by Hotchkiss, Jones, and Pfaender. Hotchkiss had a splendid battery, which served near me. "Old Hotch" was at all times ready to let loose his dogs of war upon the enemy, and no battle ever occurred near him that he did not have a hand in it. He was always to be found with his battery where the battle raged most furiously. Jones and Pfaender were splendid officers, and their batteries, in efficiency and soldierly deportment, were second to none in the entire army. The two independent battalions of cavalry were commanded by A. B. Brackett and E. A. C. Hatch. As Brackett is now a terror to all evil-doers, so he was then a terror to all rebel organizations with which he came in contact. He was a stranger to fear, active and enterprising. No service was too dangerous, no duty too disagreeable for him to perform. At some time during the war his battalion was consolidated with the Fifth Iowa Cavalry, but subsequently he commanded a battalion under General Sully, and received two commissions from the President of the United States—those of lieutenant-colonel and colonel —"for gallant and meritorious services."

Hatch, who commanded the other battalion, was full of energy and courage. He engaged in the war from patriotic reasons and from love of adventure and daring, and never let an opportunity pass when he could enjoy a hazardous dash upon an enemy. He has passed over to the other side, but has left behind him a spotless name, both as a soldier and citizen, of which his family may be justly proud.

Minnesota, through Governor Ramsey, has the honor of being the first State to tender troops to the President for the purpose of suppressing the rebellion, and also of being the first State to furnish a regiment for three years or during the war. When the news reached Washington of the bombardment of Fort Sumter, Governor Ramsey happened to be in that city, and at once proceeded to the war office and made a formal tender of one thousand men. He telegraphed his action to Lieutenant-Governor Donnelly, who notified the Pioneer Guards. This organization met on the same evening, and volunteers were called upon to enroll their names; and let it be said to the credit of Josias R. King, now inspector-general of the State, that he was the very first to sign his name and volunteer. This was on the 14th day of April, 1861, and the night before President Lincoln issued his proclamation calling out seventy-five thousand men. I believe that King was the first man in the United States to volunteer in 1861. From the beginning to the close of the war he was always in the forefront of the battle, rising by regular promotion from his place in the ranks to be a lieutenant-colonel, and this was on his merit alone, for he had no friends to push him forward.

The First Minnesota Volunteers, with which King began his service, by its gallantry, good discipline, and soldierly conduct earned for the State a reputation and fame which it would not have acquired in fifty years of peace. Its reputation was not confined to this country only, but its good name spread over Europe. The citizens of Brussels, in recognition of its discipline, gallantry, and bravery, sent to this country a "steel battery," complete, as a token of their esteem and admiration for its splendid achievements on the battle-field.

No regiment during the entire war had a brighter or more glorious record. None of its men were wounded in the back, for their faces were ever to the foe. Where great danger was to be encountered or important points were to be held, this regiment was always selected, and always met the expectation of its friends. It never faltered nor flinched in the discharge of its duty, but was always at the post of danger until the lurid fires of the most wicked and causeless rebellion ever concocted by the malice and machinations of treason burnt themselves out amid the black ashes of overthrow and defeat.

At Gettysburg, General Hancock assigned it to hold the crest of Cemetery Hill, the key to the Union position, saying to Colonel Colville that the safety of the day depended upon that position remaining in our possession until reinforcements could arrive. The rebel divisions of Garnett and Hill were in plain view, charging upon this point, determined on carrying it for its strategic importance. The regiment had been reduced by the casualties of war to three hundred and fifteen men, and two hundred and forty of these were killed or wounded on that dreadful occasion, but the glorious little band of heroes held the point around which the fortunes of that desperate day revolved.

What the First was to the Army of the Potomac, the Second was to the Army of the Cumberland. But on every field where Minnesota was represented by her troops, her name and fame was on every tongue. At home there was a frightful outbreak among the Indians, and had it not been for the good management of General H. H. Sibley, who was in command of the district of Minnesota, the loss of life would have been simply appalling. But by good management and the efficiency of his troops the incipient rebellion or outbreak was soon suppressed, and the most prominent leaders were brought to pay the penalty of their crimes by the forfeiture of their lives. When the war was over, our brave boys came marching home.

There are three persons of whom mention should be made, although neither went to the field of battle, yet their services were equally as valuable. I refer to Alexander Ramsey, Henry M. Rice, and Morton S. Wilkinson. The first named, as governor of the State, was untiring in his efforts to furnish troops for the war, and he was particularly fortunate in making his selections of regimental commanders. The great success of our troops was due, in a great measure, to the splendid officers in command of them, and much of the credit they won should be attributed to his wise and judicious selections of able, skilful commanders for the various commands organized by him. Mr. Rice and Mr. Wilkinson were United States Senators, and as such were in hearty sympathy with the friends of the government, uniting and co-operating with them in voting men and money to carry on the war to a successful conclusion.

What shall be said of the rank and file? I wish I could mention each one by name and speak of his deeds of noble daring. There is a warm place in my heart for the private soldier, who, for a mere pittance, faced the cannon's mouth, and through whose bravery and devotion to duty the monster rebellion was crushed and peace restored to all parts of our national domain. May God bless the surviving veterans of the late war!

CHAPTER XXX.

Hon. N. W. Kittson, General H. H. Sibley, Hon. H. M. Rice, R. P. Russell, Esq., Merchants, Bankers, Lawyers, Railroad Men, Steamboat Men—Character of Population—Politics of the State—Army Life, Civil Life, Promptness, Dissipation—An overwrought People—Unequal and Unjust Compensation of Men and Women—The Laborer worthy of his Hire.

SOME of the men who first located in this country are still with us, and have always been active in the development of the resources of the State. These men formed our laws and put the machinery of the Territory and State in motion.

At this date I believe the oldest living settler is Hon. Norman W. Kittson. He came here in 1830, under great difficulties, having to travel on foot from Canada. He was employed by the Great American Fur Company, and at first took station between the Fox and Wisconsin Rivers, but in 1832 removed to the head-waters of the Minnesota River, and soon thereafter was transferred to Red Cedar River, in Iowa. In 1834 he became connected with the sutler's department at Fort Snelling.

Man was not made to live alone, and the existence of one pale-face in this then remote region was noised abroad, and another enterprising young man by the name of Henry H. Sibley put in his appearance. He pitched his tepee at St. Peter, now Mendota, and there he remained until he constructed substantial houses in which to live and in which to store goods for sale to the Indians in exchange for furs.

Color, language, and business brought these two men into close personal relations, and it is a beautiful fact that they have lived together for more than a half-century, during which time not a word has been spoken by either to alienate the affections of the other. No two brothers were ever so warmly attached as these two old settlers. Such long, unbroken attachments are beautiful because so rare. Two more noble, generous men never walked the streets of St. Paul. Both have labored to advance the interests of this State. Both have been in the front rank in every good work. Both have been true friends of the poor, and no two men have given more of their substance to assist the destitute and needy.

To this happy pair was soon added Mr. Henry M. Rice, a man of enterprise and public spirit, who at once entered into business with all the energy for which his whole life has been distinguished. He has held many places of honor and trust, and has at all times acquitted himself with great credit. He has probably done more to build up St. Paul, and the State at large, than any other living man. To these three add Mr. R. P. Russell, of Minneapolis, and we have a complete list of the survivors of those who arrived here prior to 1840. These were the foundation-stones upon which the State has been erected. Through their agency men of capital were induced to come out and invest it in some way to benefit the State and themselves. The magnificent railroad systems were perfected by such men as Hon. E. F. Drake, who embarked in the St. Paul and Sioux City Railroad scheme, and never rested until he had completed the work. And his public-spirited enterprise did not cease with the completion of the road, but he has invested largely in valuable real estate, which he has improved. Other capitalists have done likewise, and thus have the affairs of the State prospered beyond precedent.

These railroad and landed interests required men well versed in the law, and they were not "backward in coming forward." Among those arriving here at an early period in the history of the State, and who are here at this time, we recall Horace R. Bigelow, Charles E. Flandrau, H. J. Horn, John B. Sanborn, Aaron Goodrich, George L. Otis, I. V. D. Heard, J. B. Brisbin, W. W. Erwin, H. L. Williams, Greenleaf Clark, W. P. Murray, Westcott Wilkin, E. G. Rogers, and many others of equal prominence. Then came the retail merchants, Nicols & Dean, A. L. Larpenteur, D. W. Ingersoll, J. L. Forepaugh, Mannheimer Brothers, Lindeke Brothers, A. H. Cathcart, Powers & Co., and many others. Then came the wholesale merchants, such as Beaupre & Keogh, Allen, Moon & Co., Griggs & Co., Auerbach, Finch & Van Slyke, William Lee, Powers, Durkee & Co., Hall & Paar, Pascal Smith, etc. Banks were organized by such men as E. S. Edgerton, Thompson Brothers, Dawson, Smith & Scheffer, H. P. Upham, Walter Mann, Willins Brothers, Peter Berkey, W. R. Merriam, and others.

Physicians, commission men, real estate agents, and, in fact, all professions and trades became represented, and thus was a city formed which for growth was never surpassed and only equalled by Minneapolis, where the same energy and enterprise characterized her people. There are now within a radius of ten miles not less than three hundred thousand people. Thirty-six years ago there were not fifteen hundred in the same area. In 1849, St. Paul had a population of four hundred; in 1880, forty-three thousand; in 1885, one hundred and eleven thousand.

It was not until 1864 that a railroad reached St. Paul, and now not less than fifteen roads centre in this place. In connection with the railroads, the names of Hon. Edmund Rice and Hon. W. L. Banning will ever be associated. These two men have labored long in the interest of St. Paul's railroad systems, and it may be asserted, truthfully, that no two men were ever more loyal to their city's best interest, and their loyalty and devotion is made manifest by the construction of several of the main lines radiating from St. Paul. It is not alone by these roads that the worth of such men is to be estimated. They have been leaders in every enterprise calculated to promote the interests of St. Paul and of the State. The steamboat lines from St. Louis to St. Paul are ably represented by Commodore W. F. Davidson and Captain Russell Blakely, although the latter long since quit the business. Both of these men, in early life, stood upon the deck and controlled the freighting business to and from St. Paul. Commodore Davidson still owns a line of boats, but has it operated by others, while he gives his personal attention to his large real estate interests. Captain Blakely occupies himself with the affairs of various stage-lines, which penetrate every portion of the West not reached by rail or boat.

In addition to the business which occupied most of the time of our merchants, bankers, lawyers, steamboat men, and others, each endeavored to induce others to come with their capital and energy to aid in building up this city and State. The population is made up of people from all the States in the Union and from all parts of the Old World. The thrifty Germans, the industrious Scandinavians, the good-natured Irishmen, the urbane Frenchmen are all represented in this great bee-hive of the Northwest.

The first governor of the State, General Henry H. Sibley, was a Democrat, but when he laid aside the robe of office the position was filled by Alexander Ramsey, a Republican, and that party has controlled the State ever since. The Republican majority is about forty-five thousand. The Democratic party has maintained its organization, and deserves a great deal of credit for so doing, when there has not been the slightest chance for success within the last twenty years.

What the future has in store for the party in this State no one knows. However, it is a comforting reflection that Minnesota has been well managed under Republican rule, and should it continue forever we shall be secure in " the blessings of liberty to ourselves and to our posterity."

During my active service I heard officers often speak of resigning, which they disliked to do because it was the severing of old associations and the forming of new ones which might not be so pleasant. I suppose if one resigned from the army and lived a life of supreme idleness, they would have ample opportunity to think of their old friends and little desire to make new ones. I could not be idle. My life had been an active one, and it was necessary for me to have something to do, so I entered fully into business, and have never regretted the step I took in 1867. It is true the life I had lived unfitted me somewhat for the walks of civil life. I had been trained to believe that promptness was necessary in all the details of life. That if an engagement was made for three o'clock, it meant that hour, not several hours later. I find in civil life a great want of punctuality,—not intentional, but from habit. Agree to meet at a given time and place with five gentlemen, the chances are that two will forget all about the appointment, two will be from a half-hour to an hour late, and the other will possibly be on time. Now, of course, this would never do in the army. An officer ordered to be with his command at a certain place at a certain time must be there, for his failure might jeopardize the safety of an army. I was always in the habit of attending reveille, and I became so confirmed in it that even now I am awake at daylight. It is said of an old English officer who was placed on the retired list, that he often employed a drummer and fifer to sound reveille under his window, so that he could turn over in bed and enjoy the luxury of not having to get up and dress himself preparatory to attending the roll-call of his company. I am awake at the proper time, and usually rise and begin the duties of the day.

The advice of one whose life has been prolonged

almost to threescore years, to the young men, is to cultivate promptness and punctuality in all engagements, and thus improve upon their sires.

Drunkenness among gentlemen is unpardonable, but the effect of late hours in retiring or in rising is almost identical with dissipation over the wine-cup. Either will break down the strongest constitution and bring on early decay.

Excepting the human family, the usual longevity is about five times the length of time it takes to mature. A horse is mature at five years old, and will, if taken care of, live to be twenty-five years old. A dog matures at two years, and lives to be ten years old; and man, who matures at twenty-five, should live to be one hundred and twenty-five, but he shortens his life by eating, drinking, smoking, and chewing to excess, and by not giving himself the proper length of time for sleep. I have seen lawyers in this city labor on their cases all day and go home at dark with an armful of books and papers, to continue their work after the lapse of a few moments passed in hurriedly taking their dinner or supper.

If we could all adopt the masonic division of time, —eight hours for labor, eight hours for doing good to others, and eight hours for rest and refreshment,—the world would be happier and better. But there are persons in this city who work night and day, including the Sabbath. They will amass large fortunes, but they will not live to good old age to enjoy the accumulations of a life of drudgery and hardship. Again, the habit of requiring clerks to work sixteen and eighteen hours out of every twenty-four is cruel. We have societies for the prevention of cruelty to animals. Why not one for prevention of cruelty to young men and young women who have to earn their daily bread in our stores, shops, and factories? Again, a woman who does a man's work should receive a man's pay. Our overtaxed women teachers in the public schools, many of whom are as efficient as their male associates, should be paid accordingly.

The cost of living, the duties and responsibilities, are the same in both cases, then why an illiberal, unjust discrimination against them in the matter of compensation?

There is an old proverb which has struggled down to us through the thick mist of ages and the changing phases of empire, to the effect that "The laborer is worthy of his hire." But in these latter days there are many who are disposed to dispute the truthfulness of the proverb, and it is perfectly astonishing to see how many converts they are making. We are very apt to place the seal of condemnation upon all labor "strikes" without stopping to inquire for the cause. Men who are well paid for their services rarely ever "strike."

In times of financial troubles, when men and moneyed institutions begin to fail, there is something within that tells us we must exercise greater economy. Where shall we begin the curtailment? In conversation once with a gentleman he remarked that, "owing to the stringency of the times he had to inaugurate a system of economy far more sweeping than ever before." Where do you suppose he applied the pruning-knife? By giving up his pew in church. A poor place to begin. Generally, however, the wages of those who have served long and faithfully are first reduced. Is it right to reduce the wages of your employés below a point at which they can live and support those dependent upon them for daily bread? Is it not better to lessen expenses by dispensing with some of the luxuries, and leaving the necessaries of life within the reach of the hard-working, faithful employé?

The "jay-hawking" manner in which much of the business of western cities is carried on is calculated to rob not only labor, but capital, of fair compensation. A gentleman desires to erect a house. He calls on a builder, who is anxious for a job in order to have his men employed. In his estimate he puts everything down to the very lowest limit. His figures are taken to some other builder equally anxious for work, and he agrees to do the job for five or ten per cent. less. These are shown to a third builder, who cuts in on the figures of the second, and so on until finally the contract is awarded to some one at less than a living rate, and in this way the builder and laborers are robbed of their just dues, and men are required "to work for nothing and board themselves." In this way labor is demoralized and the laborer impoverished by systematic larceny.

A gentleman desires to purchase lumber, and by a similar process he procures it for less than the unmanufactured material cost, thus robbing capital of its just reward.

We are living in the light of the fullest, freest, grandest civilization ever given by the centuries to mankind. We boast of our charities, of our churches, almshouses, the progress of religion, and the growth of every Christian virtue, but are we not retrograding in common honesty among ourselves? Are we not trying to make money, not "by the sweat of our brow," but by the sweat, blood, and muscle of others? The golden rule, "Do unto others as you would have others do unto you," will give labor and capital in every community a fair equivalent for their services and their use. A contrary course will drive both to seek other localities.

CHAPTER XXXI.

First Proclamation of Governor Alexander Ramsey—The First Legislature—Old Settlers' Association—The Seal of the Old Settlers' Association—Pioneers of Ramsey County—What these Men have Done—James J. Hill—Railroad Men—St. Paul's Railroad Systems—Wonderful Growth of St. Paul.

ON the first day of June, 1849, Governor Ramsey, Chief Justice Goodrich, Associate Justice David Cooper, with H. L. Moss as United States District Attorney, assembled in a small room in the old St. Paul House, and there, seated upon trunks and beds, drew up the proclamation announcing the Territorial government fully organized and the courts opened for the adjudication of all civil misdemeanors. There was no table in the room, so the wash-bowl and pitcher were placed upon the floor and the wash-stand was made to answer for a table. Amid such poverty and gloomy surroundings the Territory of Minnesota had its birth.

I remember seeing the first legislature which convened. The upper house consisted of nine and the lower of eighteen members. These men represented much land but few constituents, and were gathered in from the most remote corners of the vast Territory. Some came in on Red River carts, others on dog-trains, a few by boat, and some on foot. None of them had any previous experience in deliberate bodies, but all were earnest, laborious men. No legislature which has ever assembled since has been composed of better material than the one assembled to lay the corner-stone upon which to build this great and prosperous State. Years have passed since that legislature finished its work, but many of the laws it enacted are still upon our statute-book.

There is an organization in this State, incorporated under the laws and known as the Old Settlers' Association. All male persons twenty-one years old, or over, in the Territory on January 1, 1850, are eligible to membership. To join this association it is only necessary to pay over one dollar to the treasurer, prove age and actual residence, and at once the applicant becomes a member in good and regular standing. The anniversary of the day upon which Governor Ramsey issued his first proclamation is the day upon which the association meets to reunite the bonds of companionship and good-fellowship. It is astonishing how prompt these old fellows are in attendance. Their first and most important duty to perform is to attend the old settlers' meeting, and all business must yield on this occasion. In former years their habit was to meet at high noon on the 1st, pass the usual resolutions, elect new officers for the ensuing year, tell a few stories, and adjourn to meet that night at the banquet table at some hotel. After the feast they would proceed to "make night hideous" with songs of mirth and side-splitting stories. But latterly these old fellows cannot stay out so late, so they banquet in the afternoon, sing few songs, and tell few stories.

The seal of this association represents a graveyard filled with tombstones and monuments, and in the midst thereof is one solitary old man leaning upon a cane. This is supposed to be the last one above the ground. At a recent meeting an old member referred to the sad fate of this lonely old man very feelingly, and endeavored to picture the sorrow and gloom by which he would be surrounded, whereupon Governor Ramsey, who does not grow old, remarked, "The association need give itself no uneasiness on that account; in a spirit of self-abnegation I will accept that place if it be the pleasure of the brethren." By law no new members can be taken in, so it is only a question of a few years when the association will expire by "constitutional limitation."

A rival association has been formed, known as the Ramsey County Pioneers. This association takes in all who were residents at the date of the admission of the State, May 11, 1858, and who were of age on December 15, 1871, the date upon which the association was organized. Among this number may be found the greater part of the prominent business men, as well as the leading men in all the professions.

As a general thing the early pioneers were poor in worldly goods, but rich in faith as to the future growth and prosperity of the great Northwest. In truth, they were men of foresight, energy, and enterprise. Some of them seem to have instinctively known where corner lots would be found in the future and secured many of them; and although panic after panic has rolled over and beat upon them, yet we find these same old pioneers holding on to their possessions with a degree of tenacity truly remarkable. Others have settled in this region,—men of capital and brains,—and they have used every persuasive possible to induce these pioneers to surrender their lands and tenements for glittering gold, but the words from their silver lips have fallen, as it were, upon deaf ears.

Many of the pioneers have fallen by the wayside; yet many remain who are numbered among the most enterprising citizens, who have contributed in a large degree to make one of the wealthiest and most prosperous States in the Union. With a wise administration of government, and the smiles of a gracious Providence, Minnesota will always be one of the cherished spots on the face of the earth consecrated as the home of religion and of liberty. Who can estimate the great work of these earnest pioneers in moulding the moral character and standing of the people of the State? They have encouraged the erection of churches and school-houses, and these will forever attest their foresight, intelligence, and moral worth.

These same men laid the foundation of our present railroad system. Others came in and improved upon their plans, and secured to us railroads radiating from our city like so many iron fingers to grasp and bring to our storehouses the vast surplus of the great empire, in extent, which lies to the West. Mr. James J. Hill and Mr. N. W. Kittson, and a few friends associated with them, did a great work in securing the St. Paul and Pacific, which they reorganized and extended until they control to-day one of the largest and best systems in the land. It was Mr. Hill's and Mr. Kittson's foresight that secured it, and it is Mr. Hill's intellect that guides and directs this mammoth enterprise to-day. Without railroad experience he at once entered upon the business as owner, manager, and leader, and the success which has attended his administration places him at the very head of the railroad men of this age.

By his own energy and business foresight he has become, without a doubt, the wealthiest man in the State, and this is more to his credit when it is remembered that he started life on a small salary, and without friends to push him forward.

It is to such men as George L. Becker, E. F. Drake, N. W. Kittson, James J. Hill, A. B. Stickney, General Herman Haupt, George A. Hamilton, Edmund Rice, H. H. Sibley, John L. Merriam, C. H. Prior, J. A. Chandler, and others equally prominent, that St. Paul is indebted for her grand system of railroads. Between St. Paul and Chicago there are now five trunk lines, a sixth soon to be completed, and a seventh under construction. The Rock Island, the Iowa and Minnesota division of the Milwaukee and St. Paul, the Omaha and the Minnesota Northwestern penetrate the fertile regions in the south and southwest; while over the track of the latter that grand and wealthy corporation, the Illinois Central, has access to this city. Railroad and river complete our transportation with the South. To the north and west the St. Paul, Minneapolis and Manitoba, and the North Pacific, with their branch lines and connections, afford the means of transportation to and from the far distant North and West. For all this vast western empire St. Paul and Minneapolis will remain the chief depot for distribution and supply. With these advantages the marvellous growth of the two cities named can be comprehended.

An evidence of the wonderful growth of St. Paul is found in the fact that last year more than nine millions of dollars were expended in buildings. The wholesale trade was something over eighty-one millions, and this enormous sum is only a trifle compared to what it will be when the rich prairies and valleys of Dakota, Montana, Wyoming, Idaho, and Washington Territories are densely settled with an industrious, thrifty population. New York is without doubt the chief commercial city of America, but gradually Chicago has been making inroads upon her trade, and in these latter days St. Paul draws heavily upon Chicago. The merchants of the latter recognize this fact and are striving by every means in their power to prevent it. But with an open lake to Duluth our merchants can sell on as small margins as Chicago, and country merchants save in the matter of rail transportation. That is, freights by water to Duluth are no higher than they are to Chicago, and the difference by rail is about two hundred and fifty miles in favor of St. Paul. In a few years merchants west of this city will not think of going east of St. Paul for the purpose of purchasing supplies, and then will be fulfilled the prophecy of the late Mr. Seward, who predicted such a wonderful future for the city situated in the geographical centre of the United States.

"It is impossible to touch upon all the items or to enumerate all the branches in which our city has achieved and is sure to win renown. As a direct importer of foreign commodities, its rank is rising rapidly, and St. Paul enterprise brings the choice teas of the Orient direct from the vessels that carried them across the ocean to this point for distribution. With each year outlets thought of little worth become densely-inhabited territory. Miles of new streets appear where months before there was only prairie, and costly public works are carried forward with the energy and foresight of a metropolis. The steady multiplication of postal business is a faithful and unbiased index of progress. Here, within a circle swayed by these cities, are laid the foundations of one grand metropolis. Here, by every argument of fact and experience, will rise the chief interior centre of a continent. And here, in the beginnings already made, is found no mean earnest and promise of that destiny whose dawn is now breaking upon our view."

CHAPTER XXXII.

Minnesota Admitted at a Critical Period in the Country's History—The Old Railroad Bonds—Democratic Party Declares in favor of their Payment—Both Candidates in favor of Settlement of the State's Liability—How the Question was Settled by Governor John S. Pillsbury—Lucius F. Hubbard his Successor—A Worthy and Well-qualified Executive—State Officers Associated with Him.

THE transformation of the Territory to the State of Minnesota, with all the rights, privileges, and responsibilities of a free and sovereign State, occurred at one of the most critical periods in our country. The great moneyed centres of the East were suffering from financial embarrassments, and the great stringency in the money market was seriously felt throughout the confines of the republic. Capital which the people hoped to secure for the upbuilding of our new State was required for the uses of eastern and northern enterprises. Such were the exigencies of the pioneer settlers that they were willing to adopt any measure calculated to relieve the pressing wants of a people absolutely and literally without money and without credit.

Congress, on the 5th day of March, 1857, granted to the Territory four million five hundred thousand acres of land to be used in the construction of railways. This afforded a field too fertile to remain long uncultivated by the shrewd and energetic men who had flocked hither in search of fortunes. An extra session of the legislature was called, and an act passed, May 22, 1857, giving the entire grant to certain chartered railroad companies.

But the people soon learned that the parties securing the lands had neither money nor credit to carry on these great improvements. During the winter of 1858 the legislature passed another act, submitting to the people an amendment to the constitution, providing for the loan of the public credit to the land grant railroad companies to the amount of five million dollars, upon condition that a certain amount of labor on the projected roads was performed. This amendment was opposed by some of the ablest men in the State, but it was carried by 25,023 in favor of it, with only 6733 against it.

The State, in other words, was to issue the bonds and turn them over to the railroad companies at the rate of ten thousand dollars for every mile graded, but the roads were to pay the interest and principal of all the bonds thus issued. Governor H. H. Sibley expressed his determination not to deliver any State bonds to the railway companies unless they would give first mortgage bonds, with priority of lien upon their lands, roads, and franchises in favor of the State. One of the companies applied for a mandamus from the Supreme Court of the State to compel the issue of the bonds without the restriction imposed by the governor. The court, Judge C. E. Flandrau dissenting, ordered the governor to issue State bonds as soon as the companies delivered their first mortgage bonds as provided by the constitution.

The bonds of a State without credit, placed on the

market under such peculiar circumstances, were not sought after as an investment. After the issue of about two million dollars of bonds not a rail was laid, and only a few hundred miles nominally graded. The roads failed, and all that was left to the State were the franchises and the limited work which had been done. These in time were transferred to other parties, and aided very materially in the building of roads over these same lines.

There is not much wonder why these bonds were repudiated so long. For a while they served as a basis for banking, and the money passed current in Minnesota, but was worthless elsewhere. In a short time the banks failed, and this did not elevate the bonds in the estimation of the people who held their worthless issue. I believe that the banking-house of Mr. E. S. Edgerton was the only one that survived, and that made good to the depositors and holders of this State money. I remember the bills. They were very handsome, and on one occasion I left St. Paul for New Orleans with my pocket-book well lined with "Glencoe" money. After passing Prescott, I could not pass it at any price. It was absolutely valueless, and I had to ship it back.

However disagreeable the task, Minnesota, having endorsed for a worthless creditor, was legally and morally bound to make these bonds good. Years passed and our population increased. The new-comers did not care to be taxed for indebtedness incurred before they came, and particularly as there seemed to be some doubt in regard to the validity of the bonds in the opinion of those who originally opposed their issue. Every year the opponents became more numerous, notwithstanding Governor Sibley never ceased to advocate the payment of every dollar due, and he was supported by many of the very best men in each party.

It could not be made a party issue, for both parties were divided on the subject. Advocates for and against the bonds were to be found in every political convention. The Republican party, which had given Garfield forty thousand majority, did not care to proclaim in their platform that it was in favor of an honest settlement of this liability, although a large number of the party favored it. The Democratic party, which had nothing to lose, boldly announced in favor of any settlement that could be made with the holders of the bonds, who in the mean time had expressed a willingness to accept fifty cents on the dollar. The Republican convention, which met in 1881 to place in nomination a candidate for governor, adopted a patriotic platform, but was silent upon the only living issue in our State. The Democratic convention soon followed, and, having no hope of success, could afford to adopt a platform, one plank of which was an outspoken resolution in favor of justice and fair dealing towards the bondholders.

Having boldly wrestled with this important subject, the next business was to select a candidate who was willing to go before the people as a leader of a "forlorn hope." However, the selection was finally made, and the nominee entered upon the hopeless task with all the energy possible. The Democratic Committee tried to get speakers to visit the various parts of the

State for the purpose of advocating the ticket; but all, with three honorable exceptions, knowing the hopelessness of the contest, declined to enter into the canvass. Colonel William Crooks, an old wheel-horse of the Democracy, Mr. John W. Willis, a prominent young lawyer of this city, and Mr. H. P. Hall did all in their power for the ticket; but, with these three exceptions, the labor of the campaign devolved upon the candidate himself. Of course the result was the defeat of the Democratic party. During that canvass it was made very clear to me that a legislature elected on that issue would never provide for the settlement of this vexed question, and I communicated my views to Governor John S. Pillsbury, who favored the payment of the bonds. I said that in my opinion the only way to secure the settlement was for him to call an extra session of the old legislature and submit the question to that body. I do not know that my recommendation influenced him at all, but the extra session was called, and the members met the question in a spirit of justice and fairness. By the provisions of the act the bondholders were to be paid in money or other bonds. Governor Pillsbury conceived the idea that the new bonds might be repudiated, and in order to avoid such an event he sold other bonds held by the State for the benefit of the schools, and with the money thus obtained purchased the new bonds and paid the old bondholders in money. This action on his part has forever settled the question, for no one in the State will ever dare to propose the repudiation of the bonds held in trust for the education of the rising and succeeding generations.

In the gubernatorial race before referred to, General Lucius F. Hubbard, a distinguished officer in the late war, was the Republican candidate, and it is but just to him to say that he was as much in favor of the payment of the bonds as the Democratic nominee, but as his party convention had ignored the question he did not feel called upon to proclaim his individual opinions. He has been the executive of the State for more than four years, and has proven himself worthy and well qualified for the office, and demonstrated very fully that the convention which placed him in nomination did not overestimate him as a man and as a faithful, laborious public servant. His admirable administration has met the approval of both parties, and when he lays aside his official cares men of all shades of political faith can truthfully say, " Well done, thou good and faithful servant."

Governor Hubbard has been fortunate in having around him men of ability in all the departments of the State government. His worthy private secretary, General S. P. Jennison, has discharged his duties faithfully and well, and the same may be said of Attorney-General Hahn, Auditor W. H. Braden, Secretary of State Fred. Von Baumbach, and Treasurer Charles Kittelson. Most of these, if not all, were in the army during the war, where they earned the reputation of being brave and gallant soldiers. The people of the State have honored themselves in honoring these noble defenders of our country.

The reference to the State officers would be incomplete without a notice of that grand old veteran, Captain Joseph Burger, who has charge of the arms and munitions of war appertaining to the State. In the late war he lost an arm and in addition received a half-dozen wounds, any one of which would have killed any ordinary man. With the disabilities resulting from these wounds he still manages to take most excellent care of the State arms, and to be on hand for any service required of him. He is well qualified for his office, and should hold it as long as he lives.

CHAPTER XXXIII.

Seasons in Minnesota—Comparison of Cold Weather North and South—Indian Summer—Squaw Winter—Labor for the People in all Seasons—Amusements in Winter—Ice-Palace—Reception of King Borealis—The King and Queen's Reception—Snow-Shoe Clubs—Toboggan Clubs—The Fire-King attacks the Ice-King—Desperate Assault with Roman Candles—The Armistice—March through the Streets—The Ice-Palace, a thing of Beauty—Minneapolis—Colonel Girart Hewitt.

SOME one has said that there are four seasons in Minnesota, viz., June, July, August, and winter. Another remarked that Minnesota was furnished with eight months of winter and four months of cold, raw, disagreeable fall weather. Either of these statements misrepresents the delightful climate of the State. The winters are truly cold, but then the houses are constructed with that in view and the wearing apparel is regulated accordingly. In the South the houses are frail and the clothing light, and when the mercury falls below the freezing point, the people suffer as much as the Minnesotians do when the thermometer marks thirty degrees below zero.

A lady of St. Paul, who passed a winter at Thomasville, Georgia, remarked that she would have perished from cold, had she not taken a seal-skin sack with her. This she used as a gown to wear at all hours, night and day. Recently, while on a visit to Atlanta, Georgia, the mercury passed below zero. I occupied a large room heated by a small grate which held possibly a peck of coal. Supposing that one-third of the heat passed up the chimney, one can readily calculate that two-thirds of the heating capacity of a peck of soft coal was hardly sufficient to keep the room warm. Water froze at my bedside. I tried to keep warm by getting close to the grate. My knees were burning while the temperature of my back was near the freezing point. Ice rarely ever enters the rooms of our people except in water-pitchers, and hence we know very little of cold in our houses. When we go upon the streets fur wraps are brought into requisition. Those who go out ill prepared for cold weather must of necessity suffer, and if out any great length of time are apt to have their ears and noses frozen, but an early application of snow prevents any serious consequences. The winter fairly begins by December 1, and continues until about April 1; then we are sure to have delightful spring weather, followed by several months during which the mercury often climbs up among the nineties. Then comes the fall, and with it frost, which changes the foliage into every imaginable hue, and transforms the forests into pictures of transcendent beauty. Before the setting in of winter we have several weeks of Indian summer, generally abruptly terminated by a fall of snow. This the old settlers call "squaw winter." After this we are likely to have a second edition of Indian summer. It is then that the thoughtful man looks to the coal-bin and the good wife brings out the furs and places them in position to be called into requisition on a moment's notice. Thus it is that in the bright rounds the seasons come and go in this land of blue skies, clear water, and pure, invigorating, health-giving atmosphere.

An acquaintance of mine awakening one morning at four o'clock, and desiring to know just how cold it was on the outside, scantily clad, went down-stairs and passed out on the porch, closing the door after him. The thermometer was hanging against one of the outer posts of the veranda. Striking a match he saw that the mercury stood at thirty-two degrees below zero. The wind was high and whistled around his unprotected limbs. Hastening to return he found the dead-latch down,—his night key,—but, alas! he had left his pocket in his bedroom. The bell that answered to the front door was in the kitchen, and the girls were up-stairs and sound asleep. What was he to do? Could it be possible that he was to freeze to death on his own porch and within a few feet of the warm bed he had just left? The coachman had a key to the outside cellar door, through which an entrance could be effected, but he was sleeping the sleep of innocence in his room in the stable at the rear end of the lot. However, the only escape from freezing to death was to push out to the stable and arouse him from his slumbers. The coachman insisted upon dressing, but my friend informed him that the necessity was too pressing to allow him to make his toilet. So out he came and back through the snow-drifts they went. The key to the cellar door was in his pocket, but, unfortunately, in his haste he had left it in his room, and so he had to return for it. At last the door was opened and my friend was rescued from a horrible death. He says he knows just how cold it is when the mercury indicates thirty-two degrees below zero, and that he learned a lesson on that cold and eventful morning which he will never forget. "Never leave your pocket behind you when you go out in midwinter to see how cold it is."

It may be asked, What do the laboring classes do for work during the long winter months? Builders make contracts for erecting houses, and always agree to have them finished by November 1, weather permitting; but it is a very rare circumstance that the weather is favorable enough to enable them to comply fully with the contract. The fact is, these far-seeing builders are looking ahead for something to do when the chilling blasts of winter render out-door work unpleasant, if not impossible. The houses, however, are closed in on time, the arrangements for heating placed in position, and when cold weather comes the furnace is "fired up," making the temperature on the inside warm, and work can be carried on as conveniently and pleasantly as in summer time. A few places of this character afford mechanics constant work throughout the entire winter season.

Here there is work, at remunerative wages, for all who desire it, and hence all classes of our people are contented, prosperous, and happy.

The winter amusements are of varied character, and participated in by all who have nothing else to demand their time and attention. Among these amusements I mention the opera, theatre, sleigh-riding, skating, dancing parties and parties without dancing, etc., etc.

A new form of amusement came into vogue last winter.

A number of enterprising citizens conceived the idea of erecting an ice-palace and inaugurating out-door exercises for the entertainment and amusement of the people. The plan was approved of by all classes, a company was formed, and George R. Finch was elected president; George Thompson, vice-president; A. S. Talmadge, secretary; Albert Scheffer, treasurer, and W. A. Van Slyke, manager. The erection of the palace began as soon the ice was thick enough, and the work was pushed rapidly forward. The picture of it gives a very inadequate idea of its beauty. Snowshoe clubs, toboggan clubs, and clubs of all kinds were formed, each with a different uniform.

The king of the carnival, Borealis, arrived and was hailed with delight by all. He was taken from the depot to the City Hall in a small boat secured to the running-gear of a sleigh and drawn by twelve white horses, where he was received by the mayor and presented with the keys of the city. On the same night he and the queen, surrounded by the members of the royal court, gave a reception in Carnival Hall, which was attended by at least ten thousand persons. On the night following, he and his soldiers were attacked in the palace by the Fire-King and his troops. Both armies were armed with Roman candles, and used rockets and other fireworks. During the battle the palace was kept in a blaze by red lights properly arranged on the inside. This light revealed the structure in all its parts, and, taken in connection with the magnificent display of fireworks without, formed a picture of indescribable beauty. Finally, an armistice was agreed upon and hostilities ceased. Both kings, followed by the contesting forces, marched through the streets of the city, amid the ringing of bells, the firing of guns, the explosion of rockets, and the shouts and yells of a delighted populace. In this procession, seated in gayly-attired sleighs, ladies, young and old, were to be seen, and all seemed to enjoy themselves to the fullest extent, yet the thermometer indicated twenty degrees below zero.

For the success of this day's work the people were indebted to Mr. D. A. Monfort and Mr. C. W. McIntyre, who arranged all the details with mathematical precision.

Throughout the carnival season some new phase was presented each day, and thus for several weeks not only our own people but thousands attracted to the city were amused and interested by the novelty of the entertainment.

The winter carnival is an institution which has come to stay. Already a corporation has been formed for the erection of an ice-palace every winter for the next thirty years, and I am sure that all who witness the annual carnival will be well repaid. It is a good way to enliven the cold winter months, and I simply voice the public sentiment when I extend thanks to the projectors of this delightful entertainment.

Our neighboring city, Minneapolis, has arranged to have every summer a "Northwestern Exposition," which will supplement our carnival season and furnish pleasant and agreeable entertainments for all seasons of the year.

Minneapolis has been built up by the same kind of people who settled in St. Paul. They have never faltered in any enterprise calculated to advance the interests of their city.

Such men as Franklin Steele, now dead, Isaac Atwater, Thomas Lowry, John B. Atwater, Eugene M. Wilson, Anthony Kelly, John H. Stevens, Richard Chute, R. P. Russell, S. H. Chute, Winthrop Young, W. S. King, John S. Pillsbury, Sidle Brothers, Charles A. Pillsbury, and others of equal prominence, are the men who have contributed towards the upbuilding of this beautiful city, and the growth of the place has been simply wonderful.

Thirty-seven years ago I encamped near the end of the present suspension-bridge, from which point there was not a house to be seen except an old saw-mill, owned and operated by the government. In fact, the Indian title to the land had not been extinguished. To-day they have a population considerably over one hundred thousand, with miles and miles of paved streets and massive buildings which would be a credit to any city in the land. The corporate limits join those of St. Paul, and, if the two cities make the same progress in the next decade as they have in the last, the stranger will not know when he passes from one city to the other. In other words, the two will be practically united, and then will come to pass the fulfilment of the prophecy made by the late Colonel Girart Hewitt, who could see farther into the future than any of those around him. Colonel Hewitt was born in the State of Pennsylvania in the year 1825, studied law and located in Alabama, but in 1856 came to Minnesota for his health. He was one of the most active and successful real estate dealers in St. Paul from the date of his arrival up to the day of his death. When I recall the many conversations we had on the future prospects of this city, and see how fully his predictions have been verified, I realize how thoroughly he had considered every aspect of the case, and how far he was in advance of many of those with whom he was daily associated. He had the confidence of the people of this city, by whom he was greatly admired, and in his death St. Paul lost one of her most valuable and highly-esteemed citizens.

CHAPTER XXXIV.

Henry Jackson. His Claim Shanty. His Hospitality. He marries a Couple by Bond—A. L. Larpenteur—Governor Sibley's Staff—Active Service of Colonel John S. Prince, A. C. Jones, W. H. Forbes—Mob Law in Wright County—Causes of Sioux Outbreak in 1862, and final Suppression—Execution of Thirty-eight of the Ringleaders.

AMONG the early settlers in this section of the country there were many men who deserve mention at this time. I recall first Henry Jackson, from whom Jackson Street receives its name. My first interview with him was under peculiar circumstances. It was currently reported that the military reservation at Fort Snelling was to be reduced,—that is, that part of it lying on the east side of the Mississippi River was to be thrown open for pre-emption by actual settlers. The final action of Congress was anticipated by a large number, who constructed rude shanties at various points on what is now known as Reserve Township, in Ramsey County. Among this number was Henry Jackson, who occupied a claim between St. Paul and Fort Snelling. It was generally understood that as soon as the commander at Fort Snelling heard of this wholesale invasion of his domain he would compel the temporary sojourners to remove their improvements without unnecessary delay. Jackson was bold in his declaration that he had located to stay, and that he would not tear down his shanty without a fight. In a short time the matter was brought to the notice of Colonel Loomis, who directed a lieutenant to proceed in charge of a detachment of twenty dragoons and destroy every claim shanty erected on the east side of the river. When the lieutenant reached Jackson's place he feared that he might meet with some opposition, but on letting him know his instructions from the post commander, he remarked, "Well, lieutenant, before you level my shebang come in and let us take a drink." It is not definitely known what the lieutenant did do then and there, but, when the habit which was so general in those days of never refusing a good thing is recalled, it is shrewdly suspected that he responded to his kind invitation in such a way as not to offend the aforesaid Jackson. On the conclusion of the ceremonies incident to the occasion the underpinning was knocked from under the house and down it came, and great was the fall thereof, for a large part of Jackson's worldly goods were buried beneath the ruins. Mr. J. Fletcher Williams, in his "History of St. Paul," refers to Henry Jackson as follows:

"During the year 1844, Jackson was appointed by the Governor of Wisconsin Territory a justice of the peace. There was some delay in getting his commission, etc., after his bonds had been sent to Madison, as the mails in winter were very slow. One day, a couple came to his house, very anxious to be married. Jackson informed them that he was not yet authorized to perform that ceremony legally, and they would have to defer their marriage a few days. This was a great disappointment to the loving hearts that were so anxious to beat as one, but they could not think of postponing the happy hour. Jackson was equal to the dilemma. He proposed to *marry them by bond,*—*i.e.*, that they should give a bond that, when his commission arrived, they would appear and be legally married by him, and in the mean time they could live together. They gladly consented to this. The bond was made out and signed, and the happy couple went on their way rejoicing. Any public officer who could bridge over little difficulties like this was a handy man to have around."

Jackson held at one and the same time several important offices. He was justice, postmaster, hotel-keeper, legislator, clerk of court, and possibly others. He was a valuable man in his day and generation,— kind, generous, liberal. He had many friends and few, if any, enemies.

A. L. Larpenteur, another old landmark, has passed through all the vicissitudes common to frontier life. In 1849 he had the largest dry-goods house in the Territory, and made money, but misfortune overtook him and he lost everything save his energy. Fickle fortune dallied with him time and again, but at last he is on a firm foundation, and has all the worldly goods he needs to make him in the evening of his life comfortable and happy.

When Governor Sibley was inaugurated he proceded at once to place the State on a war footing, at least he surrounded himself by a staff large enough for an army of one hundred thousand men, and all of these staff officers hungered and thirsted for information in the art of war. I happened to visit the city during his term of office, and was requested to drill the members of the staff in the sabre exercise, and also explain how to mount and dismount and go through some of the simple movements laid down in the school of the trooper mounted. The names of all those who took part in these drills cannot now be recalled, but

John Farrington, D. A. Robertson, Dr. A. G. Brisbine, W. H. Forbes, A. C. Jones, John S. Prince, N. W. Kittson, and L. C. Dayton were among them. Little did we dream that at that very time the fires of sectional strife were only smothered for a season, and that they were soon to burst forth and be seen and felt in the North and South, the East and the West, involving the country in a contest unequalled in the whole annals of civilized warfare for fierceness and tenacity. Three of the above named subsequently saw active service: Jones, unfortunately, on the wrong side, Forbes in the Subsistence Department, and Colonel John S. Prince in the Wright County war, where by good management he suppressed a rebellion against the peace and dignity of the good people of that county without the shedding of blood.

The nature and character of this rebellion was the taking of the law out of the courts and the administration thereof by a mob. The governor resolved to suppress such lawlessness, and sent three companies under command of Colonel Prince to arrest the leaders, which was promptly done, and this caused the disbandment of the law-breakers and the restoration of law and order.

Mob law can never be justified, and particularly in localities where the courts are open for the trial of misdemeanors; but the punishment prescribed by law for some offences is so inadequate that it is not strange aggrieved parties should disregard the courts and proceed to inflict suitable punishment without the forms of law. To prevent this the laws should be changed so that every crime and misdemeanor can be appropriately punished, and until such legislation is enacted, mob law will be occasionally resorted to, and the verdict of the people will be, "Served him right."

The Sioux outbreak in 1862 afforded an opportunity for all of these gentlemen to see, and take part in, active service on the frontier. The cause of the outbreak has never been definitely known. It does not seem to have been a deliberate and predetermined affair, but rather the result of various concurrent causes, such as long delay in the payment of the annuities after the Indians were assembled, and an insufficient supply of food; dissatisfaction with the traders; encroachment of settlers upon the reservations; dislike of the missionaries and their converts, and finally an insane idea that they could defeat and destroy the white people and ultimately have the entire control of the whole country. This the Indians thought possible from the fact that many of our young men were out of the State with the various armies operating against the rebels. The military posts were practically abandoned; in fact, it seemed to them that the time for action had arrived. A few young warriors, wearied with a life of idleness, started out on the war-path for the purpose of securing a few Chippewa scalps, but finally reached Acton, drank freely, and became intoxicated. They demanded more liquor and were refused, whereupon the infuriated savages fired upon and killed not only the bartender, but also four other persons. This seems to have been the beginning. At once a general gathering of the Sioux took place, and at a given signal they began the annihilation of the people on the frontier, and within thirty-six hours over eight hundred men, women, and children were brutally murdered. Some of the young women were carried off to suffer more than death. Governor Ramsey commissioned General Sibley to raise a force and start for the frontier. After a long and tedious march the Indians were overtaken and defeated, and by good management on the part of General Sibley, the captives were retaken and restored to their friends. Thirty-eight of the ringleaders were executed after trial and conviction. The summary punishment inflicted upon the tribe has proven a wholesome lesson, and from that time to the present the frontier of Minnesota has not been disturbed by Indian outbreaks.

CHAPTER XXXV.

Learn a Trade—The Labor Question—Antagonism between Capital and Labor—Each Dependent upon the Other—Troubles likely to arise from Inconsiderate Discussions of this Question—Strikes and Threats will not adjust the Difficulty—American Politicians—Retrogression—Political "Bummers."

SOME time since a young man, who had been for several months unsuccessful in securing employment as a clerk or salesman in some dry-goods house, complained to a friend of his ill-luck, whereupon the friend remarked, "Why do you not learn a trade?" The reply was, "A trade is not so respectable as mercantile occupation." Under this delusive idea the stores and business houses are crowded with young men who have no capacity for business, and who, because of the fancied respectability of doing nothing, waste their minority upon salaries which cannot possibly furnish them with the means necessary to meet their expenses. Too late in life they discover their error, and before they reach the age of thirty years many of them look with envy upon the thrifty mechanic, whom, in the days of their boyhood, they were accustomed to deride.

The false idea of respectability which prevails in the fashionable society of the present day has ruined thousands of young men, and will ruin thousands more. The cities and towns all over the land are filled with this class of persons in search of something to do,—just anything to keep body and soul together.

Philosopher Greeley was in the habit of saying to this class of persons, "Go West," but his advice would have been better had he said "Learn a trade, young man, and then the great workshops of the West will send for you."

Let every young man learn a trade. It may not be necessary for him to live by it, but it will be something that cannot be taken from him. The permanency of wealth is one of the most uncertain things in man's experience. A storm at sea, a fire that cannot be controlled, a destructive cyclone, a failure of a bank, and a thousand other causes may sweep it away in a moment, and the possessor, rich to-day, may be poor when the sun rises on the morrow. In such cases it may be a matter of some importance to have a trade upon which to fall back.

And then, too, the learning of a trade is very often the quickest passport to the very position of wealth and respectability which these short-sighted young men so ardently crave. Business tact, joined to skilled mechanical talent, is sure to reap a rich reward. The best business managers of great manufacturing or mercantile firms and corporations are the men who have risen from the ranks,—men trained in every process of the production of the articles manufactured, bought, and sold.

Parents should guide their sons in the direction of a thorough preparation for the possible adversities of the life before them, by the acquisition of a knowledge of some self-supporting mechanical trade, and as far as lies within their power they should strive to keep them away from the cities, unless the young men are financially prepared to engage in some business on their own account.

Every State has an agricultural college, but the sons of farmers who should take such a course decline to do so. They seem unwilling to become farmers, but drift to the cities to take positions as clerks or join some of the professions, for which they are often unfitted. Every city in the land has men in the profession who can never attain any position of prominence, but who as mechanics or farmers would take high rank and be men of mark and influence, and aid in the development of their respective localities. The sooner the young men of this country disabuse their minds of the false idea that labor is derogatory to the character of a gentleman, the better it will be for them and for the country at large. Labor is disgraceful only when disgracefully performed.

The country is at this time agitated over the labor question,—that is, the imaginary conflict between labor and capital. Unprincipled political "bummers" are endeavoring to antagonize these two classes for the purpose of riding into power. Every right-thinking man is willing to accord to labor everything within the limits of reason, but all must admit that capital has some rights which cannot be totally disregarded. In fact, labor and capital are so closely united that they go hand in hand, each one being essential to the interests of the other, and any man who attempts to engender strife between them is an open enemy of both. What would the workingman do without the aid of capital, and of what earthly use would capital be to any one without labor? Another cause of complaint now is the number of hours laborers are required to toil every day. In this country, where every man is free to do as he pleases, he can work just as many hours as he wishes, but then the man who employs him is not compelled to pay him as much for eight hours as for ten hours of labor. As many men are unable to meet their liabilities with the pay for ten hours, how can they better themselves by working a less number of hours daily and for less wages?

At all times, and under all circumstances, my sympathies are with those who are compelled to work for their daily bread; and in this class will be found men of good, sound, practical sense, who are abundantly able to adjust all differences existing between themselves and capital or employers, if allowed to do so in their own good way. But as this class is much larger than the one controlling capital, the "political bummer" must needs come in, not for the purpose of bettering the condition of the laborer, but to use him as a tool for political and selfish ends. Hence we see among the champions of this labor movement men who never did an honest day's work in their lives. Now if the sun-bronzed tiller of the soil, the horny-handed carpenter, the mason, and other laboring men leave their interests in the hands of these unprincipled political hacks they will be led into trouble. It is not the hard-working man who is stirring up the strife, but the shrewd, unprincipled politician, who expects political preferment through the votes of this large and intelligent body of men. It is readily seen that the country is on the verge of troublesome times, which it is hoped the sensible men engaged in these labor movements may see and avert. Strikes and threats will not settle this question, but it must be met in a spirit of fairness on the part of the labor classes, and they will find that capital will meet them upon terms satisfactory to all concerned. The politicians must be remanded to the background, and the sensible men of these labor organizations must act for themselves.

In America, politics is a profession, and many men become active politicians and discourse learnedly about the requirements of the Constitution who never read that instrument, and who could not comprehend it if they did read it. It does, in truth, seem that there has been a retrogression,—that politicians are not so able and so true as formerly. Where the statesman, whose rapturing eloquence can make the hearts of nations and of senates thrill and tremble to the magic of his master-touch, as did the immortal Henry Clay? Alas! his mantle descended upon no one, and in these degenerate days there are no great men whose lips are music and whose hearts are fire. Statesmanship belongs to the past and demagogy to the present. Has there not been retrogression in other departments as well? The lyre of Orpheus is unstrung, and the rust is gathering redly on the sword of Cœur de Lion. No living minstrel can wake the "tranced melodies" of the one,—no living warrior can uphold the ponderous weight of the other. No monarch like Charlemagne, no cavalier like Bayard, no bard like him of Stratford-on-Avon. Where is the man who could lead the conquering armies of a Gustavus or a Napoleon? The fact is, Liliput has been "riding a raid," and seems to have subjugated pretty much every portion of the habitable globe. The world no longer produces intellectual giants who are venerated and applauded for their genius and eloquence, because the young men are too anxious to begin the accumulation of wealth to remain in school or college long enough to acquire thorough educations.

Unfortunately, money, not moral or intellectual worth, seems now to be the measure of human ambition and of human greatness.

About the time I located in St. Paul, the State was ravaged by grasshoppers, and the ruin and desolation to be seen in their wake can scarcely be described. A farmer, while taking his frugal noon-day meal, could look out upon his waving grain, so full of promise of a bountiful harvest, when suddenly the heavens would be darkened as if by a heavy cloud, the grasshoppers would descend upon his wheat, and within a few hours the beautiful green field would be changed to one of blackness as if burnt by a passing fire,—his bright hopes of noon would be blasted and blighted before the sun went down behind the western hills. Scarcely a green thing could be seen after these pests had a few hours to carry on their work of destruction. Truly the condition of the poor farmer was pitiable. The State legislature made an appropriation for the purpose of buying seed-wheat for the destitute, and Dr. David Day, William Lindeke, and myself were appointed commissioners to purchase and distribute the grain. To do this intelligently and fairly it was necessary for us to visit the various sections which had been devastated. In order that the aid should reach the farmers in time for seeding, we started out on our trip early in March, before the snow had disappeared, and over wretched roads we passed from settlement to settlement. This trip gave me an insight into the wretchedness and misery entailed upon the poor farmers by the grasshopper scourge. Many of the frontier people we found living in caves, and in many instances they had not had any meat or bread for months, during which time they subsisted on milk and potatoes, and often we found families who had only one of these. In many instances these poor people were on the prairie far away from wood, and the only fuel they had was straw twisted compactly together, in which state it would burn for some time and give out heat enough to prevent suffering from intense cold. We were not long in learning that our own safety required that we should carry along with us a bountiful supply of creature comforts, so when we reached a town our lunch basket was always replenished. I recall the day we drove from Redwood Falls to Marshall. It was a very cold day and we suffered very much. Seeing a shanty some distance in our front we drove rapidly to reach it, hoping to find shelter and a fire. It was occupied by an old couple, both of whom were in bed and suffering from rheumatism. There was not a particle of heat in the shanty, but we soon got some hay and twisted it and started a fire, then drawing out our lunch basket we gave the old people something to eat, and when we were about leaving, Mr. Lindeke insisted that we should leave them something upon which to live for a few days. So dividing our stores we left them much better supplied than they had been for months. I never heard of them after this, although I fear they did not survive the winter. This was by no means an isolated case. There were hundreds of families in about the same condition, barring the rheumatism.

The following year the grasshoppers again appeared, and during the following winter we went over pretty much the same ground and distributed aid. Again, when the wheat was well up, the pests appeared. The Christian people prevailed upon Governor Pillsbury to appoint a day of fasting and prayer to God for deliverance from the scourge. He was ridiculed for his action, but meetings were held in all the cities of the State at the appointed time, and from that date to the present we have escaped their annual visitation. Had the grasshoppers risen and passed on to some other locality it might be said by some to have been simply a coincidence, but the fact is they left and no one knows to this day where they went. In truth, it looks as if they disappeared from the face of the earth.

And thus the story is told. I trust that the foregoing pages will have enabled the reader to pass a few hours pleasantly while hastily glancing at the recollections of one now approaching the sunset shore of a life prolonged beyond the average age of man.

APPENDIX.

THE information contained under this head will prove of interest to my army friends, who on the frontier have not access to libraries.

The cost of the war to the United States was over four thousand millions of dollars.

CASUALTIES DURING THE WAR.

The number of casualties in the volunteer and regular armies of the United States during the war of 1861–65 was reported by the provost-marshal-general in 1866:

Killed in battle, 61,362; died of wounds, 34,727; died of disease, 183,287; total died, 279,376; total deserted, 199,905.

Number of soldiers in the Confederate service who died of wounds or disease (partial statement), 133,821; deserted (partial statement), 104,428.

Number of United States troops captured during the war, 212,608; Confederate troops captured, 476,169.

Number of United States troops paroled on the field, 16,431; Confederate troops paroled on the field, 248,599.

Number of United States troops who died while prisoners, 29,725; Confederate troops who died while prisoners, 26,774.

TROOPS ENGAGED IN THE WAR.

Table exhibiting, by States, the Aggregate of Troops furnished to the Union Army, 1861–65.

[Compiled and condensed from the Official Reports of the War Department.]

STATES AND TERRITORIES.	Population in 1860.	Troops furnished, 1861–65.	Colored Troops furnished, 1861–65.
New England States.			
Connecticut	460,147	57,379	1,764
Maine	628,279	72,114	104
Massachusetts	1,231,066	152,048	3,966
New Hampshire	326,073	34,629	125
Rhode Island	174,620	23,699	1,837
Vermont	315,098	35,262	820
Total	3,135,283	375,131	7,916
Middle States.			
New Jersey	672,035	81,010	1,185
New York	3,880,735	467,047	4,125
Pennsylvania	2,906,215	366,107	8,612
Total	7,458,985	914,164	13,922
Western States and Territories.			
Colorado Territory	34,277	4,903	95
Dakota Territory	4,837	206	
Illinois	1,711,951	259,147	1,811
Indiana	1,350,428	197,147	1,537
Iowa	674,913	76,309	440
Kansas	107,206	20,151	2,080
Michigan	749,113	89,372	1,387
Minnesota	172,023	25,052	104
Nebraska Territory	28,841	3,157	
New Mexico Territory	93,516	6,561	
Ohio	2,339,511	319,659	5,092
Wisconsin	775,881	96,424	165
Total	8,042,497	1,098,088	12,711

APPENDIX.

TROOPS ENGAGED IN THE WAR—*Continued.*

States and Territories.	Population in 1860.	Troops furnished, 1861-65.	Colored Troops furnished, 1861-65.
Pacific States.			
California	379,994	15,725	
Nevada	6,857	1,080	
Oregon	52,465	1,810	
Washington Territory	11,594	964	
Total	450,910	19,579	
Border States.			
Delaware	112,216	13,670	954
District of Columbia	75,080	16,872	3,269
Kentucky	1,155,684	79,025	23,703
Maryland	687,049	50,316	8,718
Missouri	1,182,012	109,111	8,344
West Virginia[1]	393,234	32,068	196
Total	3,605,275	301,062	45,184
Southern States.			
Alabama	964,201	2,576	4,969
Arkansas	435,450	8,289	5,526
Florida	140,424	1,290	1,044
Georgia	1,057,286		
Louisiana	708,002	5,224	3,486
Mississippi	791,305	545	17,869
North Carolina	992,622	3,156	5,035
South Carolina	703,708	....	5,462
Tennessee	1,109,801	31,092	20,133
Texas	604,215	1,965	47
Virginia[1]	1,203,084	....	
Total	8,710,098	54,137	63,571
Indian Nation		3,530	
Colored troops[2]		93,441	
Grand total		³2,859,132	173,079
At large			733
Not accounted for			5,083
Officers			7,122
			186,017

[1] Virginia and West Virginia populations by census of 1860, as divided by counties in 1863.
[2] This gives colored troops enlisted in the States in rebellion; besides this, there were 92,576 colored troops included (with the white soldiers) in the quotas of the several States. The third column gives the aggregate of colored, but many enlisted South were credited to Northern States.
[3] This is the aggregate of troops furnished for all periods of service, from three months to three years' time. Reduced to a uniform three-years' standard, the whole number of troops enlisted amounted to 2,320,272.

APPENDIX.

BATTLES OF THE REBELLION.

Date.	Where Fought.	Commanding Generals.	
		Union.	Confederate.
1861.			
July 21	Bull Run, Va.	McDowell	Beauregard.
Aug. 10	Wilson's Creek, Mo.	Lyon	McCulloch.
Oct. 21	Ball's Bluff, Va.	Col. C. P. Stone	Evans.
1862.			
Feb. 8	Roanoke Island, N. C.	Burnside	Wise.
Feb. 14, 15, 16	Fort Donelson, Tenn.	Grant	Pillow.
March 6-8	Pea Ridge, Ark.	Curtis	Van Dorn.
April 6, 7	Shiloh, Tenn.	Grant	{ A. S. Johnston. Beauregard.
May 7	Williamsburg, Va.	McClellan	{ J. E. Johnston.
May 31	Fair Oaks, Va.	McClellan	{ J. E. Johnston.
June 26	Wilderness	McClellan	Lee.
Aug. 9	Cedar Mountain, Va.	Banks	Jackson.
Aug. 30	Second Bull Run, Va.	Pope	Lee.
Sept. 14	South Mountain, Md.	McClellan	Lee.
Sept. 17	Antietam, Md.	McClellan	Lee.
Oct. 3	Corinth, Miss.	Rosecrans	{ Price and Van Dorn.
Oct. 8	Perryville, Ky.	Buell	Bragg.
Dec. 13	Fredericksburg, Va.	Burnside	Lee.
Dec. 28	Vicksburg, Miss.	Sherman	Pemberton.
Dec. 31	Stone River	Rosecrans	Bragg.
1863.			
May 1	Port Gibson, Miss.	Grant	Pemberton.
May 1-4	Chancellorsville, Va.	Hooker	Lee.
May 16	Champion Hills, Miss.	Grant	Pemberton.
May 17	Big Black River, Miss.	Grant	Pemberton.
May 18 to July 4	Vicksburg, Miss.	Grant	Pemberton.
May 27 to July 9	Port Hudson, La.	Banks	Gardner.
June 23-30	Murfreesboro' to Tullahoma, Tenn.	Rosecrans	Bragg.
July 1-3	Gettysburg, Pa.	Meade	Lee.
July 1-26	Morgan's raid	Hobson	Morgan.
July 4	Helena, Ark.	Prentiss	Holmes.

BATTLES OF THE REBELLION—*Continued.*

Date.	Where Fought.	Commanding Generals. Union.	Commanding Generals. Confederate.
1863.			
July 9–16	Jackson, Miss.	Sherman	Johnston.
Sept. 19, 20	Chickamauga, Ga.	Rosecrans	Bragg.
Oct. 27	Wauhatchie, Tenn.	Thomas	Bragg.
Nov. 7	Rappahannock, Va.	Meade	Lee.
Nov. 23–25	Chattanooga, Tenn.	Grant	Bragg.
1864.			
Feb. 20	Olustee, Fla.	Seymour	Finnegan.
April 8	Sabine Cross Roads, La.	Banks	Mouton.
April 9	Pleasant Hills, La.	Banks	Mouton.
May 5–7	Wilderness, Va.	Grant	Lee.
May 8–18	Spottsylvania Court-House, Va.	Grant	Lee.
May 12–16	Fort Darling, Va.	Grant	Lee.
May 13–16	Resaca, Ga.	Sherman	Johnston.
May 16–30	Bermuda Hundred, Va.	Grant	Lee.
May 23–27	North Anna River, Va.	Grant	Lee.
May 25 to June 4	Dallas, Ga.	Sherman	Johnston.
June 1–12	Cold Harbor, Va.	Grant	Lee.
June 9–30	Kenesaw Mountain, Ga.	Sherman	Johnston.
June 10	Brice's Cross Roads, Miss.	Sturgis	Forrest.
June 15–19	Petersburg	Grant	Lee.
June 20–30	Petersburg	Grant	Lee.
June 22–23	Weldon R. R., Va.	Grant	Lee.
June 27	Kenesaw Mountain, Ga.	Sherman	J. E. Johnston.
July 1 to 31	Petersburg, Va.	Grant	Lee.
July 9	Monocacy, Md.	Wallace	Early.
July 20	Peach Tree Creek, Ga.	Sherman	Hood.
July 22	Atlanta, Ga.	Sherman	Hood.
July 24	Winchester, Va.	Crook	Early.
July 28	Atlanta, Ga.	Sherman	Hood.
Aug. 5–23	Mobile Harbor, Ala.	Granger Ad. Farragut	Buchanan.
Aug. 14–18	Strawberry Plains, Va.	Grant	Lee.
Aug. 18–21	Six Mile House, Va.	Grant	Lee.
Aug. 25	Reams's Station, Va.	Grant	Lee.
Aug. 31	Jonesboro', Ga.	Sherman	Hood.
May 5 to Sept. 8	Chattanooga to Atlanta, Ga.	Sherman	J. E. Johnston. Hood.
Sept. 1 to Oct. 30	Petersburg, Va.	Grant	Lee.

APPENDIX

BATTLES OF THE REBELLION—*Continued.*

Date.	Where Fought.	Commanding Generals.	
		Union.	Confederate.
1864.			
Sept. 19.........	Opequan, or Winchester, Va.	Sheridan.........	Early.
Sept. 22.........	Fisher's Hill, Va...............	Sheridan.........	Early.
Sept. 23.........	Athens, Ala.......................	Thomas...........	Forrest.
Sept. 26, 27.....	Pilot Knob, Mo................	Ewing.............	Price.
Sept. 28–30	New Market Heights, Va....	Grant	Lee.
Sept. 30.........	Preble's Farm, Va.............	Grant	Lee.
Oct. 5..............	Allatoona, Ga...................	Sherman..........	Hood.
Oct. 7..............	Darbytown Roads, Va........	Grant	Lee.
Oct. 19...........	Cedar Creek, Va...............	Sheridan.........	Early.
Oct. 27...........	Hatcher's Run, Va.............	Grant	Lee.
Oct. 27, 28......	Fair Oaks, Va....................	Grant	Lee.
Nov. 30..........	Franklin, Tenn...................	Schofield.	Hood.
Dec. 10–21.....	Savannah, Ga....................	Sherman..........	Hood.
Dec. 15, 16.....	Nashville, Tenn.................	Thomas..........	Hood.
1865.			
Jan. 13–15.......	Fort Fisher, N. C...............	Terry..............	Whiting.
Feb. 5–7.........	Hatcher's Run, Va....	Grant	Lee.
March 8–10....	Wilcox Bridge, N. C...........	Schofield	{ J. E. Johnston.
March 19–21...	Bentonville, N. C................	Sherman..........	{ J. E. Johnston.
March 25.......	Fort Steadman, Va.............	Grant	Lee.
March 22 to April 24......	Wilson's raid, Chickasaw to Macon, Ga...............	Wilson.............	Forrest.
March 31........	{ Boydton and White Oak Roads, Va..............	Grant	Lee.
April 1	Five Forks, Va...................	Sheridan.........	Lee.
April 2	Selma, Ala........................	Wilson.............	Forrest.
April 2	Petersburg, Va....................	Grant	Lee.
April 3	Richmond, Va....................	Grant	Lee.
April 6	Sailor's Creek, Va..............	Sheridan.........	Ewell.
April 6	High Bridge, Va.................	Read..............	Lee.
April 9	Fort Blakely, Ala................	Canby............	Taylor.
April 9	Appomattox, Va.................	Grant	Lee.
April 16.........	Columbus, Ga....................	Wilson............	Forrest.
April 20.........	Macon, Ga........................	Wilson............	Forrest.
April 26.........	Raleigh, S. C.....................	Sherman..........	{ J. E. Johnston.
May 4............	Citronelle, Ala...................	Canby............	Taylor.
May 10..........	Tallahassee, Fla..................	McCook..........	Jones.
May 11..........	Chalk Bluff, Ark.................	Thompson	Dodge.
May 26..........	New Orleans, La................	Canby............	Smith.

In addition to the foregoing, there were many combats in which only a part of the army was engaged, and which are not reported as among the battles.

GENERAL U. S. GRANT.

Born April 27, 1822, at Mount Pleasant, Ohio.
Cadet from July 1, 1839, to July 1, 1843.
Brevet Second Lieutenant Fourth Infantry, July 1, 1843.
    Second Lieutenant Fourth Infantry, September 30, 1845.
    First Lieutenant Fourth Infantry, September 16, 1847.
    Captain Fourth Infantry, August 5, 1853.
Resigned July 31, 1854.
Colonel Twenty-first Illinois Volunteers, June 17, 1861.
Brigadier-General of Volunteers, to date May 17, 1861.
Major-General of Volunteers, February 16, 1862.
Major-General United States Army, July 4, 1863.
Lieutenant-General United States Army, March 2, 1864.
General United States Army, July 25, 1866.
Secretary of War *ad interim*, Aug. 12, 1867, to Jan. 14, 1868.
President of the United States, March 4, 1869, to March 4, 1877.
Died at Mount McGregor, New York, July 23, 1885.

This is, in brief, the history of one of the most illustrious men of this or any other age. He was irresistible alike in war and in peace, yet he went down into the valley of the shadow of death, and surrendered calmly to the Greater than he. Measuring him by his success, he was too great to eulogize. Peace was enthroned in his heart while he waged war; and great as were his battle-victories, greater far, and grander for himself and country, the achievements of his last days of heroic endurance, in which he spoke such words of reconciliation and won heart-victories. He lived to realize the full fruition of his own immortal prayer, "Let us have peace." And now, although removed from the scenes of his labors on earth, yet he is not dead, but lives,—lives in the nation's grandest history,—lives in the hearts and in the affections of the American people.

    Live on, then, brave soldier,
    In the nation's proudest annals,
    In the people's warmest hearts!
    Great in courage, noble in truth,
    Pure as the sunlight in soul;
    Dead, but imperishable!

SECRETARIES OF WAR FROM THE FOUNDATION OF THE GOVERNMENT TO THE PRESENT TIME.

1. Henry Knox..Sept. 12, 1789.
   Henry Knox..March 4, 1793.
2. Timothy Pickering......................................Jan. 2, 1795.
3. James McHenry..Jan. 27, 1796.
   James McHenry..March 4, 1797.
4. Samuel Dexter..May 13, 1800.
5. Roger Griswold..Feb. 3, 1801.
6. Henry Dearborn...March 5, 1801.
   Henry Dearborn...March 5, 1805.
7. William Eustis..March 7, 1809.
8. John Armstrong...Jan. 13, 1813.
   John Armstrong...March 4, 1813.
9. James Monroe..Sept. 27, 1814.
10. William H. Crawford..................................Aug. 1, 1815.
11. George Graham..*Ad interim.*
12. John C. Calhoun.......................................Oct. 8, 1817.
    John C. Calhoun.......................................March 5, 1821.
13. James Barbour..March 7, 1825.
14. Peter B. Porter..May 26, 1828.
15. John H. Eaton...March 9, 1829.
16. Lewis Cass..Aug. 1, 1831.
    Lewis Cass..March 4, 1833.
17. Joel R. Poinsett...March 7, 1837.
18. John Bell..March 5, 1841.
    John Bell..April 6, 1841.
19. John C. Spencer..Oct. 12, 1841.
20. James M. Porter.......................................March 8, 1843.
21. William Wilkins..Feb. 15, 1844.
22. William L. Marcy......................................March 6, 1845.
23. George W. Crawford.................................March 8, 1849.
24. Charles M. Conrad....................................Aug. 15, 1850.
25. Jefferson Davis..March 5, 1853.
26. John B. Floyd..March 6, 1857.
27. Joseph Holt...Jan. 18, 1861.
28. Simon Cameron..March 5, 1861.
29. Edwin M. Stanton.....................................Jan. 15, 1862.
    Edwin M. Stanton.....................................March 4, 1865.
    Edwin M. Stanton.....................................April 15, 1865.
    Ulysses S. Grant, *ad interim*....................Aug. 12, 1867.
    Lorenzo Thomas, *ad interim*....................Feb. 21, 1868.
30. John M. Schofield......................................May 28, 1868.
31. John A. Rawlins..March 11, 1869.
32. William W. Belknap..................................Oct. 25, 1869.
    William W. Belknap..................................March 4, 1873.
33. Alphonso Taft...March 8, 1876.
34. James D. Cameron....................................May 22, 1876.
35. George W. McCrary.................................March 12, 1877.
36. Alexander Ramsey....................................Dec. 10, 1879.
37. Robert T. Lincoln......................................March 5, 1881.
38. W. C. Endicott..March 4, 1885.

PRESIDENTS OF THE UNITED STATES.

No.	Name.	Qualified.
1.	George Washington	April 30, 1789.
2.	George Washington	March 4, 1793.
	John Adams	March 4, 1797.
3.	Thomas Jefferson	March 4, 1801.
	Thomas Jefferson	March 4, 1805.
4.	James Madison	March 4, 1809.
	James Madison	March 4, 1813.
5.	James Monroe	March 4, 1817.
	James Monroe	March 5, 1821.
6.	John Quincy Adams	March 4, 1825.
7.	Andrew Jackson	March 4, 1829.
	Andrew Jackson	March 4, 1833.
8.	Martin Van Buren	March 4, 1837.
9.	William H. Harrison*	March 4, 1841.
10.	John Tyler	April 6, 1841.
11.	James K. Polk	March 4, 1845.
12.	Zachary Taylor*	March 5, 1849.
13.	Millard Fillmore	July 9, 1850.
14.	Franklin Pierce	March 4, 1853.
15.	James Buchanan	March 4, 1857.
16.	Abraham Lincoln	March 4, 1861.
	Abraham Lincoln*	March 4, 1865.
17.	Andrew Johnson	April 15, 1865.
18.	Ulysses S. Grant	March 4, 1869.
	Ulysses S. Grant	March 4, 1873.
19.	Rutherford B. Hayes	March 5, 1877.
20.	James A. Garfield*	March 4, 1881.
21.	Chester A. Arthur	Sept. 20, 1881.
22.	Grover Cleveland	March 4, 1885.

* Died in office.

LIST OF THE UNITED STATES AND TERRITORIES, SHOWING THE AREA OF EACH IN SQUARE MILES AND IN ACRES; DATE OF ADMISSION OF NEW STATES INTO THE UNION.

The Thirteen Original States.	Ratified the Constitution.	Area of the Original States.	
		In Square Miles.	In Acres.
New Hampshire	June 21, 1788	9,305	5,955,200
Massachusetts	Feb. 6, 1788	8,315	5,321,600
Rhode Island	May 29, 1790	1,250	800,000
Connecticut	Jan. 9, 1788	4,990	3,193,600
New York	July 26, 1788	49,170	31,468,800
New Jersey	Dec. 18, 1787	7,815	5,001,600
Pennsylvania	Dec. 12, 1787	45,215	28,937,600
Delaware	Dec. 7, 1787	2,050	1,312,000
Maryland	April 28, 1788	12,210	7,814,400
Virginia	June 25, 1788	42,450	27,168,000
North Carolina	Nov. 21, 1789	52,250	33,440,000
South Carolina	May 23, 1788	30,570	19,564,800
Georgia	Jan. 2, 1788	59,475	38,064,000

STATES ADMITTED.

Name.	Act Admitting State.	Admission Took Effect.	Area of Admitted States and Territories.	
			In Square Miles.	In Acres.
Kentucky	Feb. 4, 1791	June 1, 1792	40,400	25,856,000
Vermont	Feb. 18, 1791	Mar. 4, 1791	9,565	6,121,600
Tennessee	June 1, 1796	June 1, 1796	42,050	26,912,000
Ohio	April 30, 1802	Nov. 29, 1802	41,060	26,278,400
Louisiana	April 8, 1812	April 30, 1812	48,720	31,180,800
Indiana	Dec. 11, 1816	Dec. 11, 1816	36,350	23,264,000
Mississippi	Dec. 10, 1817	Dec. 10, 1817	46,810	29,958,400
Illinois	Dec. 3, 1818	Dec. 3, 1818	56,650	36,256,000
Alabama	Dec. 14, 1819	Dec. 14, 1819	52,250	33,440,000
Maine	Mar. 3, 1820	Mar. 15, 1820	33,040	21,145,600
Missouri	Mar. 2, 1821	Aug. 10, 1821	69,415	44,425,600
Arkansas	June 15, 1836	June 15, 1836	53,850	34,464,000
Michigan	Jan. 26, 1837	Jan. 26, 1837	58,915	37,705,600
Florida	Mar. 3, 1845	Mar. 3, 1845	58,680	37,555,200
Iowa	Mar. 3, 1845	Dec. 28, 1846	56,025	35,856,000
Texas	Mar. 1, 1845	Dec. 29, 1845	265,780	170,099,200
Wisconsin	Mar. 3, 1847	May 29, 1848	56,040	35,865,000
California	Sept. 9, 1850	Sept. 9, 1850	158,360	101,350,400
Minnesota	May 4, 1858	May 11, 1858	83,365	53,353,600
Oregon	Feb. 14, 1859	Feb. 14, 1859	96,030	61,459,200
Kansas	Jan. 29, 1861	Jan. 29, 1861	82,080	52,531,200
West Virginia	Dec. 31, 1862	June 19, 1863	24,780	15,859,200
Nevada	Mar. 21, 1864	Oct. 31, 1864	110,700	70,848,000
Nebraska	Feb. 9, 1867	Mar. 1, 1867	76,855	49,187,200
Colorado	Mar. 3, 1875	Aug. 1, 1876	103,925	66,512,000

ORGANIZED TERRITORIES.

Territories.	Act Organizing Territory.	Area of the Territories.	
		In Square Miles.	In Acres.
New Mexico	Sept. 9, 1850	122,580	78,451,200
Utah	Sept. 9, 1850	84,970	54,380,800
Washington	March 2, 1853	69,180	44,275,200
Dakota	March 2, 1861	149,100	95,424,000
Arizona	Feb. 24, 1863	113,020	72,332,800
Idaho	March 3, 1863	84,800	54,272,000
Montana	May 26, 1864	146,080	93,491,200
Wyoming	July 25, 1868	97,890	62,649,600
Indian[1]	June 30, 1834	64,690	41,401,600
District of Columbia[1]	July 16, 1790 / March 3, 1791	[2]70	44,800
Alaska	July 27, 1868	577,390	365,529,600
		1,509,770	

[1] No Territorial government.
[2] Reduced from 100 to 70 square miles by recession of part to Virginia in 1846.

The whole area of the States and Territories, including water-surface of lakes and rivers, is nearly equal to four million square miles.

APPENDIX.

ALASKA ceded by Russia to the United States, June 20, 1867.
BLACK HAWK WAR with the Winnebagoes, 1832.
BRADDOCK'S defeat at Monongahela, July 9, 1755.
BROWN, JOHN, executed at Charlestown, Va., December 2, 1859.
CANBY, Brig.-Gen. Edward R. S., born 1819, murdered by Modoc Indians April 11, 1873, while holding conference.
CITY OF MEXICO captured by General Scott, September 14, 1847.
CREEK WAR in Georgia, 1836.
CROOK, Brevet Maj.-Gen. George, born September 8, 1828.
CUSTER, Gen. George A., massacred with three hundred and sixty-five men of the Seventh Cavalry, July 25, 1876.
DONELSON, Fort, Tenn., surrendered to General U. S. Grant, February 16, 1862.
EMANCIPATION Proclamation, January 1, 1863.
ERIE, battle of Lake, Com. Perry's victory, September 10, 1813.
FENIAN raids into Canada, May 31, 1866, and resumed February 3, 1870.
FLAG, American, first used by Washington at Cambridge, January 1, 1776, and legally established by Congress, June 14, 1777.
FLORIDA acquired from Spain, February 22, 1819.
FLORIDA, war with Seminoles, 1835–1842.
FUGITIVE-SLAVE law passed Congress, September 12, 1850.
GIBBON, Brevet Maj.-Gen. John, born 1826.
GOLD discovered in California, 1848.
HANCOCK, Maj.-Gen. W. S., born February 14, 1824, died February 9, 1886.
HARPER'S FERRY, John Brown's insurrection, October 16, 1859.
HOWARD, Maj.-Gen. O. O., born November 8, 1830.
JOHNSON, Andrew, born December 29, 1808, died July 31, 1875.
LEE'S surrender to General Grant at Appomattox, April 12, 1865.
LINCOLN, President Abraham, born February 12, 1809, assassinated April 15, 1865.
LOUISIANA acquired from France, April 30, 1803.
MEXICO, war with declared by Congress, May 13, 1846, closed February 2, 1848.
MILITARY ACADEMY, West Point, founded by Congress, March 16, 1802.

MILES, Brevet Maj.-Gen. N. A., born August 8, 1839.
MISSOURI COMPROMISE, restricting slavery to south of 36° 30′, passed March 3, 1820, and repealed May 24, 1854.
MODOC WAR in California begun November 29, 1872.
MORMONS arrive at Salt Lake Valley, Utah, July 24, 1847, having been driven from Nauvoo, Ill.
NAPOLEON I. proclaimed emperor May 18, 1804. Abdicated after Waterloo, June 22, 1815.
NAPOLEON III. elected President French Republic, December 10, 1848. Proclaimed emperor December 2, 1852. Deposed and Republic proclaimed September 4, 1870.
NAVAL ACADEMY at Annapolis, October 10, 1845.
NEW ORLEANS, battle of, Jackson defeated British, January 15, 1815; captured by Farragut, April 26, 1862.
NULLIFICATION ORDINANCE passed by South Carolina, November 19, 1832.
PHILADELPHIA founded by William Penn, 1682.
PILGRIMS landed at Plymouth, Mass., December 21, 1620.
POPE, Maj.-Gen. John, born March 16, 1823.
POTTER, Brig.-Gen. J. H., born October, 1822.
REPUBLICAN PARTY, first convention, Pittsburg, Pa., February 22, 1856.
RESUMPTION of specie payments in United States, act approved January 14, 1875, and took effect January 1, 1879.
REVOLUTIONARY WAR beginning with battle of Lexington, April 19, 1775. Last battle, Combahee, August 27, 1782. Preliminary treaty of peace, November 30, 1782.
RICHMOND, VA., evacuated by the Confederates, April 3, 1865.
RUGER, Brig.-Gen. Thomas H., born April 2, 1833.
SAVANNAH—First steamer crossed the Atlantic, twenty-five days from Savannah to Liverpool, May 24, 1819.
SCHOFIELD, Maj.-Gen. J. M., born September 29, 1831.
SCOTT, Brevet Lieut.-Gen. Winfield, born June 13, 1786, died May 29, 1866.
SEMINOLE WAR, first in Georgia, 1817–1818; then in Florida, 1835–1842.
SHERIDAN, Lieut.-Gen. Philip H., born March 6, 1831.
SHERMAN, General W. T., born February 8, 1820.

APPENDIX. 413

SIOUX WAR in Minnesota, 1862-1863.
SMITH, JOSEPH, Mormon leader, killed at Carthage, Ill., June 27, 1844.
STANLEY, Brevet Maj.-Gen. D. S., born June 1, 1828.
SUMTER, Fort, captured by Confederates, April 14, 1861.
TERRY, Maj.-Gen. Alfred H., born November 10, 1827.
TEXAS annexed as State by act of Congress, March 1, 1845.
THOMAS, Maj.-Gen. George H., born July 31, 1816, died March 28, 1870.
TRIPOLI WAR with United States, 1803-1805.
UNION of England and Scotland, 1707; of Great Britain and Ireland, 1800.
VICKSBURG surrendered July 4, 1863.
WAR WITH GREAT BRITAIN declared June 19, 1812; ended by treaty of Ghent, February 18, 1815.
WASHINGTON inaugurated first President, April 30, 1789.
WATERLOO, battle of, June 18, 1815.
YORKTOWN, surrender of Cornwallis to Washington, October 19, 1781.

CASUALTIES AMONG GENERALS IN THE ARMY OF THE REPUBLIC AND IN THE REBEL CONFEDERACY.

Federals.

Bayard, G. D., brigadier-general, killed at Fredericksburg.
Berry, H. G., major-general, killed at Chancellorsville.
Boomer, George, brigadier-general, killed at Vicksburg.
Bidwell, D. D., brigadier-general, killed at Cedar Creek.
Bohlen, H., brigadier-general, killed at Rappahannock Ford.
Burnham, Hiram, brigadier-general, killed at Chapin's Farm.
Cochran, Michael, brigadier-general, killed at Fairfax Court-House.
Farnsworth, E. J., brigadier-general, killed at Gettysburg.
Hackelman, P. A., brigadier-general, killed at Corinth.
Harker, Charles G., brigadier-general, killed at Kenesaw Mountain.
Howell, J. B., brigadier-general, killed at Petersburg.
Jackson, C. F., brigadier-general, killed at Fredericksburg.
Jackson, James F., brigadier-general, killed at Perryville.

APPENDIX.

Kearney, Phil., major-general, killed at Chantilly.
Kirby, E., brigadier-general, killed at Chancellorsville.
Kirk, E. N., brigadier-general, killed at Stone River.
Lander, F. W., brigadier-general, killed at Edward's Ferry.
Lyon, Nathaniel, brigadier-general, killed at Wilson's Creek.
Lytle, William H., brigadier-general, killed at Chickamauga.
Mansfield, J. K. T., major-general, killed at Antietam.
McCook, Daniel, brigadier-general, killed at Kenesaw Mountain.
McCook, Robert L., brigadier-general, murdered by guerillas.
McPherson, J. B., major-general, killed at Atlanta.
Nelson, William, major-general, killed by General Davis, September 29, 1862.
Patterson, F. E., brigadier-general, accidentally killed November, 1862.
Reno, J. L., brigadier-general, killed at South Mountain.
Reynolds, J. F., brigadier-general, killed at Gettysburg.
Rodman, Isaac P., brigadier-general, killed at Antietam.
Sedgwick, John, major-general, killed at Spottsylvania.
Sill, Joshua W., brigadier-general, killed at Stone River.
Smyth, Thomas A., brigadier-general, killed at Farmville, Virginia.
Stevens, Isaac I., major-general, killed at Chantilly.
Strong, G. C., brigadier-general, killed at Morris Island.
Taylor, G. W., brigadier-general, killed at Manassas.
Terrill, W. K., brigadier-general, killed at Perryville, Kentucky.
Wallace, W. H. L., brigadier-general, killed at Shiloh.
Weed, S. H., brigadier-general, killed at Gettysburg.
Whipple, A. W., major-general, killed at Chancellorsville.
Williams, Thomas, brigadier-general, killed at Baton Rouge.
Zook, S. K., brigadier-general, killed at Gettysburg.

The following died during the war, but not of wounds:

Buford, John, major-general, died December, 1863.
Cooper, James, brigadier-general, died March 28, 1863.
Jameson, C. D., brigadier-general, died November, 1862.
Jennesen, O. C., brigadier-general, died ——
Keim, W. H., brigadier-general, died May 18, 1862.
Mitchell, O. M., major-general, died October 30, 1862.
Plummer, Joseph B., brigadier-general, died August 9, 1862.

APPENDIX.

Smith, C. F., major-general, died April 25, 1862.
Sumner, E. V., major-general, died March 21, 1863.
Walsh, Thomas, brigadier-general, died ——

The above list is necessarily imperfect, as I have been compelled to rely solely upon memory or such newspaper slips as I preserved during the war. But the list of the rebel generals is complete, and for which I am indebted to the kindness and courtesy of Colonel Robert N. Scott, United States army, in charge of the rebellion records.

Rebel General Officers.

Adams, John, brigadier-general, killed November 30, 1864, at Franklin, Tennessee.
Anderson, George T., brigadier-general, died October 16, 1862, of wounds received at Sharpsburg.
Archer, James J., brigadier-general, died October 24, 1864.
Armistead, Louis A., brigadier-general, killed July 2, 1863, at Gettysburg.
Ashby, Turner, brigadier-general, killed June 6, 1862.
Baldwin, William E., brigadier-general, died February 19, 1864.
Barksdale, William, brigadier-general, killed July 1, 1863, at Gettysburg.
Bartow, F. S., brigadier-general, killed July 21, 1861, at Bull Run.
Bee, Barnard E., brigadier-general, killed July 21, 1861, at Bull Run.
Bowen, John S., major-general, died July 16, 1863.
Branch, L. O'B., brigadier-general, killed September 17, 1862, at Sharpsburg.
Carter, John C., brigadier-general, killed November 30, 1864, at Franklin.
Chambliss, J. R., Jr., brigadier-general, killed August 16, 1864.
Cleburne, P. R., major-general, killed November 30, 1864, at Franklin.
Cobb, T. R. R., brigadier-general, killed December 13, 1862, at Fredericksburg.
Daniel, Junius, brigadier-general, died May 12, 1864, of wounds.
Dearing, James, brigadier-general, killed April 6, 1865, at High Bridge, Virginia.

APPENDIX.

Deshler, James, brigadier-general, killed September 20, 1863, at Chickamauga.
Doles, George, brigadier-general, killed May 30, 1864, at Bethesda Church.
Donelson, D. S., major-general, died April 17, 1863.
Duncan, J. K., brigadier-general, died December 18, 1862.
Dunovant, John, brigadier-general, killed October 1, 1864.
Garland, S., Jr., brigadier-general, killed September 14, 1862, at South Mountain.
Garnett, Richard B., brigadier-general, killed July 2, 1863, at Gettysburg.
Garnett, Robert S., brigadier-general, killed July 13, 1861, at Rich Mountain.
Garrott, I. W., brigadier-general, killed June 17, 1863, at Vicksburg.
Girardy, V. J. B., brigadier-general, killed August 16, 1864, at Petersburg.
Gist, S. R., brigadier-general, killed November 30, 1864, at Franklin.
Gladden, A. H., brigadier-general, killed April 6, 1862, at Shiloh.
Godwin, A. C., brigadier-general, killed September 19, 1864, at Winchester.
Gordon, James B., brigadier-general, killed May 11, 1864, at Yellow Tavern.
Gracie, A., Jr., brigadier-general, killed December 2, 1864, at Petersburg.
Granbury, H. B., brigadier-general, killed November 30, 1864, at Franklin.
Grayson, J. B., brigadier-general, died October 21, 1861.
Green, M. E., brigadier-general, killed June 27, 1863, at Vicksburg.
Green, Thomas, brigadier-general, killed April 12, 1864, at Bayou Prerie.
Gregg, John, brigadier-general, killed October 7, 1864, at Petersburg.
Gregg, Maxey, brigadier-general, killed December —, 1862, at Fredericksburg.

APPENDIX.

Griffith, Richard, brigadier-general, killed June 29, 1862, at Savage Station.
Hanson, R. W., brigadier-general, killed December 31, 1862, at Murfreesboro'.
Hatton, Robert, brigadier-general, killed June 1, 1862, at Edward's Farm.
Helm, B. H., brigadier-general, killed September 19, 1863, at Chickamauga.
Hill, A. P., lieutenant-general, killed April 2, 1865.
Hogg, J. L., brigadier-general, died May 16, 1862.
Jackson, T. J., lieutenant-general, died May 10, 1863, of wounds received at Chancellorsville.
Jenkins, M., brigadier-general, killed May 6, 1864, in the Wilderness.
Johnston, A. S., general, killed April 6, 1862, at Shiloh.
Jones, D. R., major-general, died January 11, 1863.
Jones, J. M., brigadier-general, killed May 10, 1864, near Spottsylvania.
Jones, W. E., brigadier-general, killed June 5, 1864, at Mount Crawford.
Kelly, J. H., brigadier-general, killed September 2, 1864, near Franklin, Tennessee.
Little, Henry, brigadier-general, killed September 19, 1862, at Iuka.
McCulloch, Ben., brigadier-general, killed March 7, 1862, at Elk Horn.
McIntosh, James, brigadier-general, killed May 7, 1862, at Pea Ridge.
Morgan, J. H., brigadier-general, killed September 3, 1864, at Greenville, Tennessee.
Mouton, Alfred, brigadier-general, killed April 9, 1864, near Mansfield, Louisiana.
Paxton, E. F., brigadier-general, killed May 3, 1863, at Chancellorsville.
Pegram, John, major-general, died February 6, 1865, of wounds received at Hatcher's Run.
Pender, W. D., major-general, died July 18, 1863, of wounds received at Gettysburg.

Perrin, Abner, brigadier-general, killed May 12, 1864, at Spottsylvania.

Pettigrew, J. J., brigadier-general, died July 18, 1863, of wounds received at Falling Waters.

Polk, Leonidas, lieutenant-general, killed June 14, 1864, at Pine Mountain.

Posey, Carnot, brigadier-general, died November 15, 1863, of wounds received at Bristoe Station.

Rains, J. E., brigadier-general, killed December 31, 1862, at Murfreesboro'.

Ramseur, S. D., major-general, killed October 19, 1864, at Cedar Creek.

Rodes, R. E., major-general, killed September 19, 1864, at Winchester.

Scurry, W. R., brigadier-general, killed April 30, 1864, at Jenkins Ferry.

Semmes, P. J., brigadier-general, died ——, of wounds received at Gettysburg.

Slack, W. Y., brigadier-general, killed March 6, 1862, at Pea Ridge.

Smith, Preston, brigadier-general, killed September 20, 1863, at Chickamauga.

Smith, W. D., brigadier-general, died October 4, 1862.

Stafford, L. A, brigadier-general, died May 8, 1864, of wounds received at Wilderness.

Starke, W. E., brigadier-general, killed September 17, 1862, at Sharpsburg.

Stevens, C. H., brigadier-general, killed July 20, 1864, at Peach Tree Creek.

Strahl, O. F., brigadier-general, killed November 30, 1864, at Franklin.

Stuart, J. E. B., major-general, died May 12, 1864, of wounds received at Yellow Tavern.

Terrill, J. B., brigadier-general, killed May 30, 1864.

Terry, William R., brigadier-general, killed March 25, 1865, at Fort Stedman.

Tilghman, L., brigadier-general, killed May 16, 1863, at Baker's Creek.

APPENDIX. 419

Tracy, E. D., brigadier-general, killed May 1, 1863, at Port Gibson.

Twiggs, D. E., major-general, died July 15, 1862.

Tyler, Charles H., brigadier-general, killed April 16, 1865, at West Point, Georgia.

Van Dorn, Earl, major-general, killed May 8, 1863.

Villepique, J. B., brigadier-general, died November 9, 1862.

Walker, L. M., brigadier-general, killed in duel.

Walker, W. H. T., major-general, killed July 22, 1864, near Atlanta.

Whiting, W. H. C., major-general, died March 10, 1865, of wounds received at Fort Fisher.

Wilson, C. C., brigadier-general, died November 24, 1863.

Winder, C. S., brigadier-general, killed August 9, 1862, at Cedar Mountain.

Winder, John H., brigadier-general, died February 7, 1865.

Zollicoffer, F. K., brigadier-general, killed January 19, 1862, at Fishing Creek.

HASTINGS, July 6, 1886.

MY DEAR GENERAL JOHNSON:

The proof-sheet received and read. Please accept my thanks for your kindly mention, but you give me credit overmuch. If not beyond your control, could you not have the text changed, so as to express the exact truth, which was that I found a scow in process of construction on the banks of the Tennessee River when I arrived there with General Hooker's command, which, as you of course know, was sent from the Army of the Potomac to the assistance of Rosecrans? Our first duty being to secure the long line of communication between Nashville and Chattanooga, and to do whatever might be done to forward supplies to the famishing army at Chattanooga, Rosecrans, with prudent forethought, had ordered the construction of five steamers on the Tennessee, and the repair of the railroad, two very important bridges of which had been destroyed by the rebels, one across the Tennessee and one over the Rolling Stone, half-way between Bridgeport and Chattanooga. One of these flat-bottomed steam scows had been put on some posts and blocking near the bank of the river, and the work was prosecuted by a very competent ship-carpenter by the name of Turner, who was employed by Captain Edwards, A.Q.M. The timbers and lumber for the boats had to be made from the stump, and it was with difficulty that the machinery was shipped over the railroad from Nashville, as every engine and car was needed to transport rations. When the rains and rebel cavalry had made the wagon-road on the north side of the river impassable, rapid building of the steamboat became of the highest importance. I took personal supervision of the work, and crowded it forward night as well as day, saving the hull from destruction by floating it upon pontoons, and navigated it, as you describe, to Kelly's Ferry, with the first cargo of rations to reach the starving army. But for my action it is quite safe to say this boat would not have been launched for some weeks after it was, if at all, and certainly could not have contributed, as it did materially, to the success of our efforts to secure possession of that very important strategic position, Chattanooga.

General Rosecrans has not received the credit due him for his skilful conduct of the campaign. He foresaw the probable need of river transportation, and, so far as giving orders, provided for the emergency. Had those intrusted with the execution of these orders pushed through their work more energetically, and had the boats ready for use when needed, great loss of animals and distress of men would have been saved, and Rosecrans would have retained his position as commander of the Army of the Cumberland. The unfriendliness of Assistant Secretary Dana and the impatience of Secretary Stanton secured his downfall.

Respectfully, etc.,
Wm. G. Le Duc.

INDEX.

A.

Absent from tattoo, 27.
Adams, Gen. John, 286.
Alden, Capt. B. R., 30.
Allen, Moon & Co., 357.
Alvord, Cadet C. B., 30, 38.
American politics, 397.
Anderson, Gen. Robert, 170.
Anderson, Col. Chas, 205, 207.
Andrews, Gen. C. C., 348.
Appointed adjutant, 80.
Appointed brigadier-general of volunteers, 179.
Appointment to West Point, 18.
Arnold, Lieut. A. K., 151.
Arrival at Carlisle Barracks, 158.
Arrival at home, 34.
Arrival at Louisville, 175.
Arrival at Fort Snelling, 38.
Arrival at West Point, 19.
Arrival in Havana, 151.
Arrival in New York, 156.
Arrival of King Borealis, 383.
Assassination of President Lincoln, 323.
Atkins, Com. J. D. C., 145, 147.
Attachments between classmates, 25.
Atwater, Isaac, 385.
Atwater, John B., 385.
Auerbach, Finch & Van Slyke, 357.
Averill, Gen. J. T., 349.
Ayers, Cadet R. B., 20.
Ayers, Lieut., 263.

B.

Backus, Lieut.-Col., 66.
Bailey, Prof. J. W., 31.
Bainbridge, Lieut.-Col. II., 76, 78, 79, 80, 91.
Baird, A., 30, 37, 229, 230, 311.
Baker, Gen. J. H., 349.
Baker, Lieut. Chas. T., 30.
Banning, Hon. W. L., 358.
Bartlett, Prof. W. H. C., 31.
Barton, S. M., 30, 38, 59, 80, 90.
Battle of Chickamauga, 227, 228.
Beale, Lieut., 129.
Beatty, Gen. S., 229, 230.
Beaupre & Keogh, 357.
Beauregard, P. G. T., 168, 169.
Becker, Gen. Geo. L., 369.
Bell, Robert, 272.
Benny Havens, 263.
Berkey, Peter, 357.
Berry, Col. W. W., 205, 207, 318.
Benét, S. V., 30, 37.
Bigelow, Horace R., 357.
Birth, date and place, 10.
Bishop, Gen. J. W., 347.
Blakely, Hon. R., 358.
Bohan, Lieut. John, 259.
Borgesrode, Col. R., 348.
Boussey, Drum-Major, 20.
Brackett, Col. A. B., 350.
Braden, W. H., 377.
Bradfute, Capt. W. R., 102.

Bragg, Gen. Braxton, 194, 195, 203.
Brewerton, Capt. H., 31.
Brisbin, John B., 357.
Brisbine, Dr. A. G., 390.
Bryan, Cadet E. B., 28.
Buckner, Gen. S. B., 175, 184.
Buell, D. C., 184, 185, 188.
Buffalo, extinction of, 122.
Buffalo, harnessed, 127.
Bull-fighting, 68.
Bull Run, battle of, 170.
Bullitt, Joshua F., 268.
Burger, Capt. J., 377.

C.

Caldwell, Capt. J. N., 79.
Camels introduced in United States, 130.
Cameron, Simon, Secretary of War, 160.
Camp, 78.
Camp-stove, 105.
Captain-General's garden, visit to, 154.
Capture of Corinth, 193.
Carlin, Gen. W. P., 225, 240, 241, 242, 245, 310.
Carpenter, Capt. S. D., 79.
Carr, Lieut. E. A., 84.
Castor, Lieut. T. F., 41.
Cathcart, A. H., 357.
Cause of the Mexican war, 61.
Chambliss, Lieut. W. P., 97, 98.
Chandler, J. A., 369.
Changes in style, 92.
Cheatham, Gen. B. F., 211.
Cholera in Nashville, 305.
Church, Prof. A. E., 31.
Chute, Col. Richard, 385.
Chute, Dr. S. H., 385.
Cigar-making, 155.
Circus in Owensboro', 35.
Clark, D. D., 30, 38.
Clark, Hon. Greenleaf, 359.
Clarke, Lieut. H. F., 32.
Clarke, Lieut. F. N., 21.

Climate of Minnesota, 379.
Cogswell, Milton, 30, 38.
Columbia, 342.
Colville, Col. William, 347.
Conch-shell, 15.
Conkling, Roscoe, 191.
Coon- and possum-hunting, 17.
Cooper, Hon. D., 365.
Cooper, Surg. G. E., 85.
Corn-husking, 17.
Corn-songs, 17.
Court of Inquiry, 197.
Crafton, Col. R. E. A., 304.
Crittenden, Cadet Lieut. W. L., 23.
Crittenden, Gen. T. L., 203, 204, 228, 247, 319.
Crooks, Col. William, 348, 376.
Cumming, A., 38.
Custer, Gen. G. A., 334.

D.

Dana, Gen. N. J. T., 347.
Davant, Lieut. W. M., 84.
Davidson, W. F., 358.
Davis, Gen. J. C., 206, 209, 257, 283, 314.
Davis, Lieut. Edward, 235.
Davis, Mrs. B. O., 235.
Davis, Jeff., Sec. of War, 129.
Dawson, Smith & Scheffer, 357.
Day, Dr. David, 398.
Dayton, Lyman C., 390.
Death of parents, 17.
Deaton, Capt. E. F., 258.
De Lano, H. F., 30, 37.
Delay in Pittsburg, 33.
Denman, Lieut., F. J., 79, 80.
Dickey, Col. M. R., 180
Disloyalty in Nashville, 185.
Dodge, Col. J. B., 213, 226.
Donan, Col. Pat., 344.
Donnelly, Lieut.-Gov. I., 351.
Drake, Hon. E. F., 356, 369.

INDEX.

Drake, Maj. Lewis, 180.
Drury, Capt. L. H., 258.
Du Barry, Beckman, 30, 37.
Dudley, Capt. Ethalbert, 268.
Duncan, J. K., 38.
Dunkers of Pennsylvania, 159.

E.

Early memory, 9.
Edgerton, E. S., 357, 374.
Edwards, Capt. J. E., 259.
Elliott, Gen. W. L., 335.
Ellis, Capt. E. C., 230.
Emory, Maj. W. H., 96.
English, T. C., 30, 38.
Erwin, W. W., 359.
Evans, Lieut. N. G., 101, 102, 103.
Evans, Maj. J. D., 181.
Execution of spies, 222, 223.

F.

Family visits Kentucky, 162.
Farrington, John, 390.
Feed your enemies, 260.
Felix the dog, 43.
Field, C. W., 30, 33, 34, 37, 100.
Finch, George R., 383.
Finnell, Gen. J. W., 234.
First encampment, 21.
First legislature, 365.
First lesson in writing, 13.
Flandrau, Hon. C. E., 357, 373.
Flirtation Walk, 25.
Floyd, Gen. J. B., 184, 185.
Forbes, W. H., 390.
Forepaugh, J. L., 357.
Forrest, Gen. N. B., 335.
Fort Duncan, how situated, 61.
Fourth great-grandfather, 10.
Fraser, J. W., 38.
From West Point to New York, 33.
Fry, Gen. J. B., 247.

G.

Gambling in Mexico, 67.
Game around Fort Terrett, 81.
Gardener, J. W. L., 41.
Garlington, Lieut. E. A., 315, 316.
Garrard, General K., 335.
Gear, Chap. E. G., 41.
George, Gen. James, 347.
Gibson, Col. W. H., 180, 188, 213, 215, 316.
Gilfillan, Col. James, 349.
Gillmore, Cadet Q. A., 30, 37.
Goodrich, Hon. A., 357, 365.
Gorman, Gen. W. A., 347.
Granger, Capt. R. S., 79, 149.
Granger, Maj.-Gen. Gordon, 239.
Grant, Gen. U. S., 184, 190, 191, 246, 309.
Greeley, Horace, 394.
Greely, Lieut. A. W., 316.
Green, Hon. Willis, 19.
Green, D. C., 30, 38.
Greene, Lieut. O. D., 103, 104.
Grierson, Gen. B. H., 335.
Grigg & Co., 357.
Griggs, Col. C. W., 348.
Growth of St. Paul, 370.

H.

Hahn, W. J., 377.
Haines, T. J., 30, 37.
Haley, my first teacher, 12.
Hall, Harlan P., 376.
Hall & Paar, 357.
Halleck, Gen. W. H., 189, 192.
Hambright, Gen. H. A., 263.
Hamilton, G. A., 369.
Hancock, Gen. W. S., 352.
Hardee, Bvt. Col. W. J., 58, 98.
Hardships endured by Federal soldiers, 187.
Harlan, Hon. James, 267.
Harlan, Gen. J. M., 268, 269, 270, 320.
Harris, V. H., 293.

INDEX

Harrison, Col. T. J., 181, 262.
Hatch, J. P., 171.
Hatch, Col. E. A. C., 350.
Haupt, Gen. H., 369.
Hazen, Gen. W. B., 227, 243, 302, 315.
Heard, I. V. D., 359.
Heavy rain-storm, 83.
Hewitt, Girart, 385.
Hickman, Beau, 173.
Hill, Mr. A. W., 279.
Hill, James J., 368, 369.
Holabird, S. B., 30, 38, 65, 77, 79.
Home religion, 13.
Hood, Gen. J. B., 335.
Hooker, Gen. Joe, 243.
Horn, H. J., 357.
Horse-race, Bumble-Bee, 103.
Hotchkiss, Maj. W. A., 263, 350.
Houston, Gov. Sam, 136.
Hubbard, Gov. L. F., 348, 377.
Hudson, E. McK., 30, 37.
Huston, Lieut. D., 80.

I.

Ice-palace, 383.
In the guard-house, 22.
Incompetent officers, 182, 183.
Indian conflict, 125.
Indian nomenclature, 143.
Indian policy, 137.
Indian ring, 47.
Indian story-tellers, 52, 53.
Ingersoll, D. W., 357.
Iron and nails, 77.

J.

Jackson, Henry, 387.
Jackson, Stonewall, 169, 194.
Jackson, James S., 171, 257.
Jennison, Gen. S. P., 377.
Johnson, Andrew, 300, 301.
Johnson, Dr. J. M., 18, 163, 261.
Johnson, R. W., 30, 38, 90.

Johnston, Gen. A. S., 63, 92, 99, 100, 106, 107, 117, 118.
Johnston, Gen. J. E., 164, 168, 169, 274.
Jones, Lieut. Saml., 32.
Jones, Lieut. John M., 32.
Jones, Adjt.-Gen., 38.
Jones, Lieut.-Col. F. A., 181, 212.
Jones, Thos., 301.
Jones, Gen. A. C., 390.
Jones, Capt. John, 350.

K.

Kellogg, John, 30, 37.
Kelly, Anthony, 385.
Kendrick, Prof. H. L., 31.
Kentucky Legislature asks for Anderson, 170.
Kettleson, Charles, 377.
Killing domestic animals, 264.
King, Gen. J. H., 79, 240, 261, 278.
King, Gen. J. R., 351.
King, Hon. W. S., 385.
Kirkham, Capt. R. W., 41.
Kirk, Gen. E. N., 213, 215.
Kittson, N. W., 50, 51, 355, 368, 369, 390.

L.

Labor question, 395.
Ladies in garrison, 27.
Lane, Capt. W. B., 86.
Larkin, Patrick, bugler, 121, 150.
Larpenteur, A. L., 357, 389.
Lawlessness in Texas, 62.
Learning a trade, 393.
Leather Breeches, 281.
Leavenworth, Lieut.-Col. H., 39.
Lecture at St. Anthony, 57.
Le Duc, Gen. W. G., 339.
Lee, Lieut.-Col. R. E., 132, 133.
Lee, Gen. Fitzhugh, 33.
Lee, William, 357.
Lester, Col. H. C., 348.

INDEX.

425

Lewis, W. H., 30, 38.
Library Association, 54.
Lincoln, President, 167, 172, 269, 299, 300, 322.
Lindeke Bros., 357.
Lindeke, William, 398, 399.
Location of family, 162.
Logan, Gen. J. A., 276, 282, 314.
Long, Gen. Eli, 355.
Loomis, Lieut.-Col. G., 36, 39, 41, 388.
Love-making at West Point, 25.
Lowe, Lieut. W. R., 259.
Lowry, Thos., 385.
Loyalty of officers, 161.

M.

Mahan, Prof. D. H., 29, 31.
Maize, Lieut. W. R., 259.
Mann, Walter, 357.
Mannheimer Bros., 357.
Manual labor not degrading, 24.
Marksmanship, Indian boys', 143.
Marks, Surgeon Solon, 259.
Married and off for Texas, 59.
Marshall, Gen. W. R., 349.
Marshall, L. H., 30, 38.
Mattson, Col. Hans, 348.
Maynadier, Lieut. H. E., 84.
McArthur, J. H., 30, 38, 97, 99.
McClure, David, 30, 37.
McCook, Gen. A. G., 242, 243, 280.
McCook, Gen. A. McD., 180, 182, 194, 204, 206, 210, 228, 307.
McCulloch, Maj. Ben., 96.
McDowell, Gen. Irwin, 168, 169.
McIntosh, James, 30, 38, 59.
McIntyre, Mr. C. W., 384.
McKeever, Chauncey, 30, 37.
McLaren, Surg. A. N., 41, 44.
McLaren, Gen. R. N., 349.
McLaughlin, John, 112.
McPhail, Col. Samuel, 350.
Measles at Camp Neven, 181.

Menial service, 23.
Merriam, W. R., 352.
Merriam, Hon. J. L., 369.
Merritt, Gen. Wesley, 334.
Metzner, Capt. A., 259, 263.
Mexican campaign, 41.
Mill Springs, battle of, 183.
Miller, Col. Steven, 349.
Miller, Gen. John F., 225.
Mills, Sergt. John, 80.
Milroy, Gen. R. H., 198.
Monfort, Mr. D. A., 384.
Monotony of cadet life, 21.
Monroe, Capt. James, 41.
Moore, J. C., 30, 37.
Moore, Col. B. F., 242.
Morgan, Col. George N., 347.
Morris, Lieut.-Col. T., 59.
Morris, Lieut. L. T., 259.
Morton, Gov. O. P., 256.
Moss, H. L., 365.
Mounted regiments consolidated, 170.
Moving Indians by contract, 48.
Murray, Hon. W. P., 357.

N.

Narrow escape, 82.
Nashville, battle of, 285.
Nelson, Gen. William, 247, 267.
Nelson, A. D., 41.
Nicols & Dean, 357.
Nimmo, W. A., 30, 37.
Northers in Texas, 66.
Northwestern Exposition, 384.
Norton, Lieut. W. A., 32.

O.

Oakes, Capt. James, 100.
Oath of allegiance, 161, 193.
Occupation of Nashville, 185.
Officers call on captain-general, Cuba, 153.
"Old Massa Johnson," 73.
Old Settlers' Association, 366.

O'Maher, Timothy, 19.
Opinion of President of United States, 22.
Orton, Lawrence W., 223.
Otis, Lieut. E. A., 236, 237.
Otis, Col. Elmer, 335.
Otis, Geo. L., 357.

P.

Palmer, Capt. I. N., 100.
Palmer, Gen. J. N., 229, 261, 264, 265, 274, 281, 310.
Parke, J. G., 30, 37.
Parkhurst, Gen. J. G., 302.
Patterson, Gen. Robt., 165, 168, 169.
Payment of bonds, 375.
Perkins, D. D., 30, 37.
Perryville, battle of, 195.
Peter, W. G., 221.
Pfaender, Col. Wm., 350.
Phifer, Lieut. C. W., 117.
Philadelphia City Troop, 165.
Pillow, Gen. G. J., 184.
Pillsbury, Gov. John S., 376, 385.
Pillsbury, C. A., 385.
Pitcher, Gen. T. G., 58.
Plebes distributed to companies, 21.
Plympton, Maj. Jos., 50.
Pope, Capt. Jno., 129.
Porter, Lieut. A. P., 110.
Porter, Lieut. Fitz-John, 32, 149.
Potatoes raised on board of steamer "Fashion," 75.
Powers Bros., 357.
Powers, Durkee & Co., 357.
Prince, Col. John S., 390.
Prior, C. H., 369.
Promoted to sergeant, lieutenant, and captain, 28.
Prophecy of Mr. Seward, 370.
Purchase of horses, 95, 160.

R.

Railroad, 369.

Ramsey, Gov. Alex., 47, 351, 353, 359, 365, 367, 392.
Randall, Hon. S. J., 166.
Rattlesnakes, 76, 115.
Rebel spies, 219.
Recruiting at Owensboro', 178.
Reeve, Col. I. V. D., 58.
Regiment ordered to Texas, 98.
Reno, Gen. J. L., 339.
Resignation of officers, 156.
Restoration of law and order at Pulaski, Tenn., 299.
Reynolds, Lieut. J. J., 21.
Reynolds, S. H., 30, 38, 55, 80.
Robert, Antoine, 52, 53.
Robertson, B. H., 30, 37.
Robertson, D. A., 390.
Rogers, E. G., 357.
Rollins, Hon. J. H., 344.
Rose, Capt. Thos. E., promoted colonel, 217.
Rosecrans, Gen. W. S., 194, 203, 210, 215, 218, 220.
Roster of Second Cavalry, 89.
Roy, J. P., 30, 38.
Royall, Col. W. B., 97, 344.
Russell, R. P., 356, 385.

S.

Sanborn, Gen. J. B., 348, 357.
Saxton, Rufus, 30, 37.
Scheffer, Albert, 383.
Schofield, Gen. J. M., 285, 286, 293, 342.
Schuyler, Lieut. H. P., 258.
Scott, Gen. Winfield, 20, 166, 169.
Scott, Col. Robert N., 415.
Scribner, Gen. B. F., 242.
Sea-sickness, 152.
Sheets, Lieut. Frank N., 234.
Shepherd, Col. O. T., 151.
Sheridan, Gen. P. H., 62, 85, 140.
Sherman, Gen. W. T., 170, 180, 184, 244, 257, 307.

INDEX.

Shiloh, battle of, 189.
Sibley, H. H., 41, 353, 355, 359, 369, 373, 389, 392.
Sidle Bros., 385.
Silvey, Wm., 30, 37.
Simon, the nurse, 71.
Sioux outbreak, 390.
Slavery in Kentucky, 74.
Smith, Gen. P. F., 76.
Smith, Gen. W. F., 243.
Smith, Brevet Maj. F. G., 289, 290.
Smith, Gen. A. J., 293.
Smith, Pascal, 357.
Snelling, Col. Josiah, 39.
Sprole, Prof. W. T., 31.
Staff department, 336.
Stafford, Maj. J. A., 207.
Stanley, Gen. D. S., 285, 303, 335.
Starkweather, Gen. J. C., 240.
Steedman, Gen. James, 320.
Steele, Franklin, 41, 50, 51, 385.
Stevens, Col. J. H., 56, 385.
Stickney, A. B., 369.
Stinson, Capt. H. A., 277.
Stockton, E. D., 30, 38.
Stoneman, Gen. Geo., 335.
Storming of Ice-Palace, 383.
Stuart, Gen. J. E. B., 335.
Sully, Gen. Alfred, 347.
Switzler, Hon. W. F., 344.
Sykes, Capt. Geo., 151.

T.

Talmadge, A. S., 383.
Taylor, Lieut. O. H. P., 93.
Terry, Maj.-Gen. A. H., 312.
Tevis, W. C., 30, 37.
Theatre visited, 174.
The building at Fort Duncan, 64.
Thomas, Capt. J. A., 27.
Thomas, Gen. G. H., 96, 97, 158, 161, 165, 171, 183, 204, 205, 233, 238, 246, 263, 285, 287, 292, 296, 302, 304, 305, 308.

Thomas, Adjt.-Gen. L., 171, 172.
Thomas, O. W., 272.
Thomas, Col. M. T., 349.
Thompson Bros., 357.
Thompson, Geo., 383.
Tidball, J. L., 30, 38.
Todd, Hon. R. L., 344.
Tourtelotte, Col. J. E., 348.
Tower, Z. B., 339.
Trowbridge, Capt. C. F., 258.
Twiggs, Gen. D. E., 94, 95, 118.
Tyler, John, Vice-President, 22.
Tyler, Lieut. C. H., 93.

U.

Uniform seized, 177.
Upham, H. P., 357.

V.

Van Camp, Lieut. C., 119.
Van Cleve, Mrs. C. O., 40.
Van Cleve, Gen. H. P., 347.
Vanderbilt's son, 173, 174.
Van Dorn, Maj., 109, 110, 118, 119, 120.
Van Slyke, W. A., 383.
Von Baumbach, F., 377.
Von Trebra, Lieut. Col. H., 181.

W.

Waite, Col. C. A., 134.
Walker, Capt. J. G., 84.
Wallace, Capt. G. W., 65.
Wallace, Thos. K., 65, 69.
Wallace, E. W., 65.
Washington, T. A., 30, 38, 59.
Water, scarcity of, 128.
Watkins, Col. L. D., 220.
Weir, Prof. R. W., 32.
Weitzel, Gen. Godfrey, 339.
Wells, Capt. E. T., 236, 258, 263.
Wetmore, Lieut. L., 41.

INDEX.

Wheeler, Gen. Joe, 335.
Whipple, Gen. W. D., 304.
Whiting, Capt. C. J., 105, 151.
Wild-cat money, 374.
Wild horses, 121.
Wilkin, Hon. Wescott, 359.
Wilkin, Col. A., 349.
Wilkinson, Hon. M. S., 353.
Williams, H. L., 357.
Williams, J. F., 388.
Williams, T. G., 30, 38.
Willich, Col. A., 181.
Willis, John W., 376.

Willius Bros., 357.
Wilson, Hon. E. M., 385.
Wilson, Gen. J. H., 286, 299.
Withers, John, 30, 38.
Wood, Gen. T. J., 182.
Woods, Maj. S., 41, 51, 56.
Wright, Gen. H. G., 339.

Y.

Young, Hon. Winthrop, 385.

Z.

Zollicoffer, Gen. F. A., 183.

THE END.

www.ingramcontent.com/pod-product-compliance
Lightning Source LLC
Chambersburg PA
CBHW051735300426
44115CB00007B/574